Praise for *3-D Negotiation* from corporate leaders:

"For many years, we searched for just the right firm and individual to find the best approach to enhance our senior executives' negotiating skills, and after endless presentations of tired win-win and win-lose clichés, we began working closely with Dr. Jim Sebenius. His 3-D approach is in use at many levels of the Estée Lauder Companies with excellent results. This down-to-earth book is packed with striking examples which help us to put his methods into practice."

—*William Lauder, President and CEO, the Estée Lauder Companies*

"Following the clear and innovative concept of *3-D Negotiation* has contributed invaluably . . . to many agreements that are critical to Novartis. These deals must sometimes accomplish conflicting objectives, be sustainable, and enhance relationships."

—*Daniel Vasella, MD, Chairman and CEO, Novartis AG*

"Lax and Sebenius understand better than anyone that the key to successful and sustainable agreements is to focus on those activities that take place away from the negotiating table, well before face-to-face tactics come into play. *3-D Negotiation* is a brilliant and rigorous exposition of key bargaining strategy techniques from two masters of negotiation. Building on their previous reputation, the authors analyze recent corporate and diplomatic experience to provide new insights into the field. I have used their advice to great success in the complex health care environment."

—*Paul F. Levy, President and CEO, Beth Israel Deaconess Medical Center*

"*3-D Negotiation* is simply the most sophisticated and practical guide to negotiation ever written. Its many fascinating case studies show you exactly how to apply its powerful method."

—*Mathias Doepfner, CEO, Axel Springer AG (one of Europe's top media companies)*

Praise for *3-D Negotiation* from the financial elite:

"Lax and Sebenius capture what I've seen great deal makers take years to perfect. Silver tongues and tactics can be a sideshow. As chess masters know, success at the table flows from advance preparation and strategically positioning your pieces to maximize leverage."

—*Stephen Friedman, former Chairman and Senior Partner,*
Goldman Sachs & Co.; Chair, President's Foreign Intelligence Advisory Board;
former Special Assistant to the President of the United States for Economic Affairs;
and Director, White House National Economic Council

"We faced some of the firm's most challenging and delicate negotiations during its start-up period. Over those early years, we worked daily with Jim Sebenius, who was often very helpful with critical deals at key moments. He later returned to Harvard, armed with this intensive experience, to make the theory and practice of effective negotiation his life work. He and his colleague, David Lax, have now blended messy reality with elegant analysis to produce a first-rate piece of work. Readers facing tough deals, along with generations of Harvard MBAs and executives, will benefit greatly from this lucid book and its highly relevant case studies. I recommend it highly."

—*Peter G. Peterson, Senior Chairman and Cofounder, The Blackstone Group (one of the world's largest private equity firms)*

"I have worked directly with the authors on some of the most challenging negotiations of my career. Their 3-D approach was important in helping to deliver hundreds of millions of pounds of value for shareholders."

—*Philip Yea, CEO, 3i Group plc (an FTSE 100 venture capital and private equity company that has invested more than £26 billion in more than fourteen thousand businesses)*

Praise for *3-D Negotiation* from thought leaders on negotiation:

"In negotiation, the moves you make away from the table are as important as any moves you can make at the table. Nowhere has this insight been more brilliantly and practically presented than in the 3-D negotiation method developed here by David Lax and James Sebenius. This is a landmark contribution, valuable for any negotiator. My hat is off to them!"

—*William Ury, coauthor of* Getting to Yes, *author of* Getting Past No

"At last, practical advice on how to overcome obstacles that prevent us from getting to yes."

—*Roger Fisher, coauthor of* Getting to Yes

"Every so often, a book comes along that sheds entirely new light on an old subject. Most negotiation books, my own included, focus too much on tactics at the table. Lax and Sebenius certainly draw on their extensive deal experience to offer plenty of battle-tested advice on tactics. Yet their striking new book opens up two new dimensions. Their chapters on the art and science of deal design go well beyond anything yet written on just how to create value on a lasting basis, including both the letter and spirit of the deal. And there is simply nothing like their systematic development of the art and science of moves away from table to set up the most promising possible situation for face-to-face tactics. Twenty years ago, Lax and Sebenius coined the phrase "creating and claiming value" and changed the negotiation field by making its implications the cornerstone of their first book. I predict that *3-D Negotiation* will do it again."

—*Howard Raiffa, Frank P. Ramsey Professor (Emeritus) of Managerial Economics, Harvard Business School and John F. Kennedy School of Government, author of* The Art and Science of Negotiation *and* Negotiation Analysis, *and coauthor of* Smart Choices

"Lax and Sebenius provide scholars and frontline negotiators with new and important insight in *3-D Negotiation*. The authors, influenced by their extensive deal experience and strong analytic backgrounds, provide a clever new organization of issues that negotiators need to consider in important, complex negotiations. Lax and Sebenius highlight aspects on the negotiation process too often ignored or given insufficient attention by other authors—moves away from the table to set up and reset the negotiation most favorably. The result is both original and powerful."

—*Max H. Bazerman, Jesse Isidor Straus Professor of Business Administration, Harvard Business School, and coauthor of* Negotiating Rationally

"Twenty years ago, *The Manager as Negotiator* by Lax and Sebenius raised the bar for negotiation theory and practice. With *3-D Negotiation*, they've done it again. With its highly original focus on away-from-the-table 'setup' moves and sophisticated prescriptions on value-creating deal designs, *3-D Negotiation* provides an innovative analytical framework that will prove indispensable for those seeking practical negotiation advice."

—*Robert H. Mnookin, Williston Professor of Law, Chair, Program on Negotiation, Harvard Law School, and coauthor of* Beyond Winning *and* Barriers to Conflict Resolution

"Finally, the negotiation book we've been waiting for—sophisticated, practical, multidimensional, and effective in the real world of commercial deals and disputes. Lax and Sebenius avoid the one-dimensional approach of the chest-thumpers, game-theorists, and idealists and demonstrate how the best negotiation results can be achieved by any serious bargainer who takes the time think through the problem, prepare, and apply a complete set of strategies and tactics. This is a giant step forward in the negotiation field, but also a magnificent contribution to those of us who work in the middle between negotiators who too often fail to find the deal or the best deal."

—*Eric D. Green, Professor of Law, Boston University; successful mediator in the* United States v. Microsoft *antitrust case and many other complex disputes; and Cofounder and Principal, Resolutions, LLC and EnDispute, Inc. (now JAMS)*

3-D
Negotiation

3-D
Negotiation

*Powerful Tools to Change the Game
in Your Most Important Deals*

David A. Lax and
James K. Sebenius

HARVARD BUSINESS SCHOOL PRESS
Boston, Massachusetts

Printed in the United States of America

10 09 08 07 06   5 4 3 2 1

Library of Congress Cataloging-in-Publication Data

Lax, David A.

  3-D negotiation : powerful tools to change the game in your most important deals / by David A. Lax and James K. Sebenius.

    p. cm.

  ISBN 1-59139-799-5 (alk. paper)

  1. Negotiation in business. I. Title: Three-D negotiation. II. Sebenius, James K., 1953- III. Title.

  HD58.6.L388 2006

    658.4'052—dc22

                              2006007901

The paper used in this publication meets the minimum requirements of the American National Standard for Information Sciences—Permanence of Paper for Printed Library Materials, ANSI Z39.48-1992.

Contents

Part Four: Stress Problem-Solving Tactics
"At the Table"

Part Five: 3-D Strategies in Practice
"Let Them Have Your Way"

3-D
Negotiation

Introduction

You've picked up a book on negotiation. Why? Chances are that you have found yourself—or expect to find yourself—involved in some sort of bargaining process. Maybe you've just been through a tough negotiation, and you have a sense that you could have done better. Maybe you are looking down the road in your professional or personal life and you see important negotiations looming ahead. Most likely, you're someone who's involved in negotiations on a fairly regular basis, and you are simply on the lookout for new and better ideas.

This book can help.

We've spent years doing deals. We advise companies and governments on their most challenging negotiations. We systematically analyze negotiations and teach what we've learned to senior executives, top government officials, and MBAs at Harvard and around the world. This long-term engagement with deals and dealmakers has left us increasingly dissatisfied with the model that dominates most of the negotiations—and the thinking about negotiations—that go on today.

What's the problem? Most negotiators focus on a single dimension of the bargaining process. They are "one-dimensional," in our terminology, and the single dimension that they embrace is *tactics*. One-dimensional bargainers believe that negotiation is mainly what happens *at the table*. To them, preparation and execution are mainly about process and tactics.

But all too often, this one-dimensional approach leaves money on the table. It is inadequate for the tough negotiations in which the other side seems to hold all the cards. It isn't well-suited to common deal-making challenges such as multiple—not just two—parties, tricky internal as well as external negotiations, and shifting agendas. It leads to suboptimal deals, creates needless impasses, and fosters conflicts that could have been avoided.

We have a better approach—one that encourages you to negotiate in three dimensions, not one. We've coined the phrase *3-D Negotiation* to describe our approach, and to distinguish it from most of the negotiations that go on out there.

Our first dimension—*tactics*—is familiar territory. Tactics are the persuasive moves you make and the back-and-forth process you choose for dealing directly with the other side, at the table. Good tactics can make a deal; bad ones can break it.

Our second dimension—*deal design*—includes more than the obvious, face-to-face aspects of negotiation. Deal designers know how to probe below this surface to uncover the sources of economic *and* noneconomic value. To unlock that value for the parties, they have a systematic approach to envision and structure creative agreements.

Our third dimension—*setup*—extends to actions *away from the table* that shape and reshape the situation to the 3-D Negotiator's advantage. In deal after deal we've seen the same result: once the parties and issues are fixed and the negotiating table has otherwise been set, much of the game has already been played. In contrast, before even showing up at the conference room, 3-D Negotiators take the initiative. They act away from the table to set up the most promising possible situation, ready for tactical interplay. They "set the table"—ensuring that the *right parties* have been approached, in the *right sequence,* to deal with the *right issues* that engage the *right set of interests,* at the *right table or tables,* at the *right time,* under the *right expectations,* and facing the *right consequences of walking away if there is no deal.* If the *setup* at the table isn't promising, this calls for moves to *reset* it more favorably. As we'll show you, a superior setup *plus* the right tactics can yield remarkable results that would be unattainable by purely tactical means, however skillful.

So *3-D Negotiation* is our effort to crystallize this very different set of insights and skills about setup and deal design, as well as tactics. These ideas come from the field—where *you* are—but they are scrutinized and tested by a wide range of people with strong ideas about negotiation, or lots of practical experience, or both. We are confident that *3-D Negotiation*—based on this combination of field-testing and rigorous academic scrutiny—can help *you.*

We begin with an overview of the whole approach, "3-D Negotiation in a Nutshell." After an initial chapter that describes our three dimensions, the next two chapters are intended to get you familiar and comfortable with a couple of key processes:

- Identifying barriers to agreement

- Taking action to overcome those barriers

Using this "3-D barriers audit," we'll show you the coordinated moves both *at* and *away from* the table that give you the best shot at overcoming the barriers you've identified.

After the "nutshell chapters" (1 to 3), we move to multichapter sections, each addressing one of our dimensions, but moving in reverse order (3-2-1) to reflect how a 3-D Negotiator typically approaches a tough deal-making situation. In chapters 4 to 7, we show you how to act away from the table to get the setup right (the third dimension). The following section (chapters 8 to 11) shows you how to design value-creating deals on the drawing board (the second dimension). Chapters 12 and 13 show you how to bring these deals into being at the table by stressing problem-solving tactics (the first dimension). Our final section (chapters 14 and 15) demonstrates how to put it all together with a deeper look at 3-D strategies in practice. Throughout this book, you will find that we frequently draw on our advisory experience and on real cases that we know well to illustrate the practical use of virtually every aspect of our 3-D framework. While confidentiality concerns sometimes led us to disguise or alter aspects of these negotiations, we've preserved their essentials—and broader lessons.

As you read, you'll very quickly see a distinctive aspect of 3-D Negotiation: a problem in one dimension may call for a solution in another. By analogy, you will readily understand that the answer to a particular business problem sometimes comes from a seemingly unrelated realm: for example, an operations problem can turn out to be a finance problem, or vice versa. You'll find the equivalent in 3-D Negotiation: if you mainly focus on what to do at the table, you may have too few arrows in your quiver. Pushing harder on your tactics and face-to-face dealings, for example, may not work. It may even be counterproductive if the underlying problem is a flawed setup requiring actions away from the table.

If you don't see all three dimensions of negotiation, you may end up stuck as a 1-D player in a 3-D world. You may never find the right answers to your most important negotiation problems. But when both eyes open to a wider 3-D view, the odds for your success go up. If you know where to look, and what you're looking for, you'll often find great agreements and the strategies to make them real. We've written this book to be your guide.

Part One

Overview

3-D Negotiation in a Nutshell

Chapter One

Negotiate in Three Dimensions

WHY ARE WE BORN with two eyes? One reason, of course, is redundancy: it's good to have a backup, in case we lose an eye to an accident or illness. But there's another consideration. Having two eyes is different from having, say, two kidneys, or two lungs. Having two eyes gives us the extraordinary ability to see the world *in three dimensions*. Yes, it's certainly possible to get along in the world with only one eye—and many people do—but "binocular" vision gives us the enormous advantage of depth perception. When seen with two eyes rather than one, a formerly flat world acquires all kinds of useful complexity.

This is a book about seeing the world in three dimensions. More specifically, it's about learning to negotiate in ways that recognize—and take advantage of—the rich complexities of human interactions. We call our approach *3-D Negotiation* because it draws on three distinct dimensions to achieve great outcomes. But before getting into the specifics of our approach, let's look at the alternative, which we'll refer to as *one-dimensional negotiation*.

Negotiating in One Dimension

There are many kinds of one-dimensional negotiators; in fact, the world is full of them. But most fall into one of two broad categories, which for the purposes of this overview chapter we'll call "win-lose" and "win-win" negotiators. Whether you're a pro or a novice, you'll instantly recognize these two types. They offer competing seminars. They do battle in academic journals. And in many cases, they engage at the table.

Win-lose bargainers are from the old school, although you can certainly still find plenty of them plying their trade in the boardrooms, town hall basements, rented conference facilities, and the other venues where negotiations take place. Their bookshelves bulge with manuals on adversarial ploys, such as Robert J. Ringer's *Winning Through Intimidation* and Jim Camp's *Start with No*. They battle and scrap for the best price, the biggest share of the pie, and so on. They sit down at the bargaining table intending to walk away not only with their share of the goodies, but most of yours, too.

Win-win negotiators, by contrast, have for some time now represented the new way. They promise innovative solutions, more value, and better relationships. The win-win library consists of books that emphasize the cooperative potential of negotiation, including valuable ones like *Getting to Yes* and *Getting Past No*.[1] Win-win types don't sit around cooking up unilateral ways to get more than their fair share at the table; they'd rather engage in joint brainstorming sessions to come up with creative solutions that "make the pie bigger" for all.

Experience has probably given you an intuitive feel for the pluses and minuses inherent in each approach. Yes, the aggressive win-lose negotiator gets a better deal some of the time. But he or she may damage relationships in the process, may overlook more creative agreements, and may even precipitate a deadlock, thereby causing promising discussions to break down unnecessarily. (Although, as we will emphasize in later chapters, some discussions *deserve* to break down.)

The earnest win-win player may be more focused on creativity—and almost certainly has more friends—but may come up short in tough encounters. It's a trade-off, and not always a beneficial one. In the name of long-term relationships, naive win-win negotiators may give up achievable gains in the here and now.

So win-lose and win-win negotiators couldn't be more different, right? Well, no. In fact, we see them as being very similar in a fundamental way: they are both one-dimensional negotiators. They both concentrate almost exclusively on the *face-to-face* and *tactical* aspects of negotiation. They view the negotiating process mainly in terms of actions *at the bargaining table*, which of course comprises not only the conference room, but virtual tables (phone, fax, e-mail, etc.).

Negotiating advice from both camps focuses mainly on how best to deal *directly* with the other side. From the win-lose side of the house, this means tips on how to size up your opponent's weak spots; who should make the first offer;

how much to demand; how to persuasively overcome objections, decipher body language, and threaten to walk away; and how to profit from various ploys—the "powerless agent" story, the "good cop, bad cop" routine, and so on.

Meanwhile, the win-win playbook shows how to build trust, communicate clearly, probe for real interests behind bargaining positions, brainstorm new options, avoid cross-cultural gaffes, and successfully counter the ploys used by their hardball counterparts. But note again that the focus is on the tactical. The players are predetermined, the chess board is set up; all that remains is for the game to be played there and then, whatever the choice of approaches may be.

In our experience, most people consider negotiations to be one or the other of these approaches, or a blend of the two. And obviously, win-win negotiators and their win-lose counterparts do more than interact at the table; they also prepare before they get there. But mainly, they prepare by planning their face-to-face approach and tactics. Take a look, for example, at the many negotiation seminars offered by the venerable American Management Association, which are mostly listed under the category "Communication and Interpersonal Skills": *Negotiating is what happens at the table. It is about tactics and dealing directly with the other side.*

Years of doing deals and analyzing negotiations have persuaded us that this apparently commonsense focus on the table often fails. It routinely misses the larger potential game that can really drive the outcome. Even if they don't recognize it or acknowledge it, one-dimensional negotiators are actually playing in a 3-D world, and they often pay a steep price for their very limited approach. They, or the people whom they represent, are the losers.

The 3-D Negotiation Alternative

So what *is* this larger 3-D game? Like any good bargainer, a 3-D Negotiator must master the tactical, at-the-table, face-to-face techniques that rely on effective communications and interpersonal skills. But as we've said, 3-D Negotiation involves not one, but *three* dimensions, all of which are in play more or less concurrently throughout an effective negotiation. The three dimensions are:

1. Tactics

2. Deal design

3. Setup

By now, you've already got a sense of tactics—at least of the win-win and win-lose kind. The second dimension, deal design, will likely be somewhat familiar to you as we begin to shift our focus away from one-dimensional moves at the table. So let's look at deal design before getting into our much less well-understood—and most powerful—third dimension.

The 3-D Focus on Deal Design

Here is deal design in a nutshell: *negotiation involves the art and science of drawing up deals that create lasting value.* Deal design employs a good old-fashioned tool—the *drawing board*—in new and productive ways. This is where the win-lose negotiator, in particular, comes up short. In the win-lose mind-set, the broad outlines of the deal are self-evident. So the core challenge of negotiating lies in choosing the best tactics to *win*—the best price, the most generous terms, or whatever.

Here's what *we* mean by a systematic approach to deal design: when a proposed deal does not offer enough value to all sides, or when its structure won't achieve its purposes, deal designers must go to work on the drawing board, sometimes on your own, sometimes with your team, and sometimes in concert with the other party. Their deal designs create value, often unexpectedly, guided by general principles and specific techniques that we'll demonstrate to you in chapters 8 through 11.

Maybe we need to make a definitional aside as we introduce this term. "Back to the drawing board" sometimes has a negative connotation—that is, scrapping a failed project and having to start over—that we don't intend. Rather, we use the drawing-board metaphor to invoke notions of creativity, invention, and fresh thinking guided by potent underlying deal-design principles.

Smart people working at the drawing board can sometimes discover hidden sources of economic and noneconomic value, then craft agreements—design deals—that unlock that value for the parties involved. For example: Is it *really* a pure price deal? Does some sort of trade between sides make sense and, if so, on what terms? Can we unbundle different aspects of what looks like a single issue and give to each side what it values most? Should it be a staged agreement, perhaps with contingencies and risk-sharing provisions? If there's a contract involved, should it be an unusual kind of contract—one with a more creative concept and structure than we've used before? One that meets ego needs as well as economic ones?

A Few Deal-Design Examples

Conventional wisdom says that we negotiate to overcome the differences that divide us. So, typically, we're advised to find win-win agreements by searching for common ground. While identifying common ground almost always helps, many of the most frequently overlooked sources of value in agreement arise from *differences* among the parties. Deal-design principles can systematically point to agreements that create value by dovetailing differences.

For example, when Egypt and Israel were negotiating over the Sinai, their positions on where to draw the boundary were incompatible. When negotiators went beyond the opposing positions, however, they uncovered a vital difference of underlying interest and priority: the Israelis cared more about security, while the Egyptians cared more about sovereignty. The solution was a demilitarized zone under the Egyptian flag.

Differences of interest or priority can open the door to unbundling different elements and giving each party what it values the most at the least cost to the other (as the Egyptians and Israelis did): a core principle of deal design. A good win-win negotiator may well come up with such creative agreements through focusing on *interests*, not positions, and brainstorming options. The distinctive contribution of deal design, however, is to crystallize and much more systematically develop the underlying principles.[2]

Let's look at an example of another kind of difference, focusing on how divergent *forecasts* can fuel joint gains. Suppose an entrepreneur who is genuinely optimistic about the prospects of her fast-growing electronics-components company faces a potential buyer who likes the company but is much more skeptical than the entrepreneur/owner about the company's future cash flow. They negotiate in good faith, but at the end of the day, the two sides sharply disagree on the likely future of the company and so cannot find an acceptable sale price.

Instead of seeing these different forecasts as a barrier, a savvy deal designer would perceive opportunities to bridge the "value gap." One option would be a deal in which the buyer pays a fixed amount now and a contingent amount later, with the latter amount determined by the future performance of the company. Properly structured, with adequate incentives and monitoring mechanisms, such a contingent payment (or "earn-out") can appear quite valuable to the optimistic seller—who expects to get that earn-out—but not very costly to the less optimistic buyer. The seller's willingness to accept such a contingent deal, moreover, may give the buyer the confidence he or she needs to go through with the deal. The two-step payment process may make the deal suffi-ciently attractive to both parties—and more attractive than walking away.

As we will demonstrate in later chapters, a host of other differences make up the raw material that skilled deal designers transform into joint gains. For example, a less risk-averse party can "insure" a more risk-averse one. A more impatient party can get more of the early money, while his more patient coun-terpart can get considerably more over a longer period. Differences in cost or revenue structure, tax status, or regulatory arrangements between two parties can be converted into gains for both. If one party mainly cares about how a deal looks to a key constituency, while the other focuses on substance, the right deal design can create value for both. Indeed, for a savvy deal designer, conducting a disciplined "differences inventory" is at least as important a task as identifying areas of common ground.

By now, you should be getting a better sense of what we mean by the sec-ond dimension in our 3-D scheme: deal design on the drawing board. While our first dimension, tactics, focuses mainly on the interpersonal *process* at the table, deal design shifts toward *substance and outcomes*, often significantly away from the table itself.

The 3-D Focus on Setup

The third dimension, setup moves—often the most potent actions a 3-D Nego-tiator can take—completes the shift in focus. These moves take place entirely *away* from the table. In a nutshell, here is what we mean by setup: *negotiation involves moves away from the table to set up the most promising situation once you're at the table.* Before taking a seat at the table, the 3-D Negotiator has taken advantage of powerful negotiation principles—carefully developed in later chapters—to create the optimum conditions before the parties face each other directly. In other words, the table has been set well before the tactical interplay (the focus of win-win and win-lose negotiators) begins.

What does "setting the table" mean in this context? Simply put, it means act-ing to ensure that the *right parties* have been involved, in the *right sequence*, to deal with the *right issues* that engage the *right set of interests*, at the *right table or tables*, at the *right time*, under the *right expectations*, and facing the *right conse-quences of walking away if there is no deal*. Before worrying too much about tactics, the 3-D setup architect works hard to optimize these elements—the scope, sequence, and choices about the process itself—within which interper-sonal dealing will play out.

If the setup at the table isn't promising, the 3-D Negotiator doesn't merely resort to bullying (like the win-lose type) or turning up the empathy and personal charm (like the win-win negotiator). Instead, he or she takes action away from the table to *reset* the table more favorably. The 3-D Negotiator understands that a bad setup makes tactics at the table more or less irrelevant—and that a great setup, conversely, makes good tactics all the more effective. In fact, it can help the tactician achieve otherwise impossible results.

Financing Staples: Getting the Scope and Sequence Right

The 3-D Negotiator pays careful attention to optimizing the *scope* (the parties, interests, no-deal options) and *sequence* by which different potential parties are involved in order to create the most promising possible setup. Let's look at an interesting case to give you a clear illustration of what we mean by a better setup.

The case involves Thomas Stemberg, the founder of Staples, the original big-box office supply store.[3] Thanks to a first round of financing received from Stemberg's initial venture capital (VC) backers, the Staples concept—rock-bottom prices on office supplies for small businesses—appeared increasingly compelling, beating early sales targets by 50 percent. With these positive early results in hand, and with the threat of new competitors like Office Depot jumping into the market that Staples had started to create, Stemberg urgently needed expansion capital. Logically enough, he went back to the same well: the venture capitalists that had helped get Staples off the ground in the first place.

But during the hunt for second-round financing, the question of *valuation* emerged as a potential stumbling block. From Staples's side of the table, it appeared that the VCs were closing ranks, stonewalling Stemberg, and refusing to value Staples as highly as he'd hoped. Not a novel tactic, certainly—offering less capital while demanding a bigger piece of Staples's equity—but surprising in its monolithic nature. No matter where he went in the venture capital community, Stemberg heard more or less the same thing.

So what was the best negotiating stance for Stemberg to adopt at this point, to (in his words) "break the venture capitalist cartel"? Was the answer to be found in being a better tactician at the conference table? If so, should Stemberg concentrate on being a better win-lose negotiator of the old school? In other words, should he try harder to unflinchingly look the bankers in the eye or decipher their body language? Should he resolve to lock everyone in a room until the positive result he was looking for finally emerged? Should he just say "no"? Refuse to budge? Wear them down until he wore them out? Or, alternatively, should he resolve to be a more effective win-win player? That is, should he listen actively? Brainstorm options? Focus on what would be fair?

In a word, *no*—on all counts. From the 3-D Negotiator's perspective, the best way to deal with this hardball stance was *not* to focus on tactics and process at the table. Instead, we would argue, Stemberg needed a more promising setup, involving the *right new parties and interests*, that would be more receptive to the particular deal he was seeking.

Going out to generate a better financing offer would be a good move here, in line with standard negotiation advice. And Stemberg did just that. He initiated conversations with Goldman Sachs: an investment bank, rather than a venture capital firm. After talking to its venture contacts, however, Goldman initially proposed *exactly the same valuation* as the VCs. Rather than weakening, it appeared that the "cartel" was broadening. *Now* what?

In a case like this, a good 3-D Negotiator would routinely ask a series of questions (we'll develop these for you later) in order to generate a more promising setup. Here's one such line of questioning: "Who are the potential 'high-value players' here? What parties are not now involved who might value this agreement more highly than those in the current setup?"

To answer these questions—to overcome the cartel he perceived—Stemberg visited Harvard Business School and sought out one of our colleagues, Professor Bill Sahlman, who is an expert on venture firms and the financing of entrepreneurial start-ups. Stemberg asked: "How do you break this?" Sahlman's answer: "Go *directly* to the institutions: the pension funds and insurance companies . . . They may be limited partners of the venture capital firms, but they often resent handing off 20 percent of the profits and a hefty management fee, instead of keeping it themselves."[4]

To a 3-D Negotiator in Stemberg's case, these institutions were potential "high-value players." If brought directly into the deal, they would see 20-plus percent higher returns than if they invested indirectly through venture capital partnerships. By following this advice, Stemberg found his funding options greatly expanded, as several limited partners of the venture funds offered to put up their *own money* at Stemberg's price.

Meanwhile, who else might be a high-value player, for different reasons? Stemberg decided that he should also make an appeal to high-net-worth individuals with independent perspectives who might support a higher valuation than the VCs. For example, he approached Marty Trust, head of Mast Industries, whose office was literally across the street from Staples's second store.

Trust could see Staples's remarkable results for himself. He had the retailing background to recognize its potential. And he understood that Stemberg had to act *fast*, since clone competitors like Office Depot were opening stores like mad. As Stemberg later recalled, "When [Marty Trust] said he wanted 10 percent of the company, we'd say, 'Fine, that'll be $3 million.' And he'd say 'Fine'— and like magic, the company had a value."

Does this story surprise you as an example of 3-D Negotiation? Didn't the negotiations with the venture capitalists break down? Is *that* an example of successful negotiations?

"Yes" to both of those last two questions. This is an example of exactly how 3-D Negotiators think. How so? Because Stemberg didn't rely on face-to-face tactics to change the minds of his initial backers, whom he considered to be overly greedy. (That would have been standard, one-dimensional kind of thinking.) Instead, he changed the *scope* of the negotiation (the parties, their interests, the no-deal options). He favorably reset the table with right new parties whose interests were far more aligned with *the deal he wanted to do*. And, as we'll see, he then sequenced the process.

Now, the generic advice in this particular story—that is, to shop around for other options—is pretty standard and pretty good guidance, and it should hardly surprise you. Yet if Stemberg had spent his time indiscriminately pitching other investment bankers, commercial bankers, or many other potential capital sources, he would likely have come up empty-handed, while burning up precious time. Why? Because although these were alternatives to the VCs, in practical terms, they were not the *right* players.

By applying the principles of 3-D Negotiation in a systematic, disciplined way, you can learn to zero in on potential high-value players—those parties not now involved who might value a desired agreement more highly than those in the current setup—and thereby achieve a better setup, and a better outcome. In the Staples case, the right players were the high-value ones; in other cases, we'll show you how *other* kinds of players are the right ones to enhance the setup. Examples would include direct or indirect influence, a key role in deal approval or implementation, and so on.

The setup also improved in other ways as a result of Stemberg's away-from-the-table moves. Even as he went out to the new sources suggested by Sahlman and pushed Goldman Sachs to sweeten its offer, Stemberg continued negotiating with the venture firms—but with better options in case the VCs ultimately said "no." Meanwhile, of course, Stemberg's effective maneuvers sharply worsened the VCs' no-deal options. When he went back to his first-round backers, he was able to present alarming news to them. Not only were they now in the unaccustomed role of middlemen—at risk of being cut out by their own limited partners—but it began to look like they might be crowded out altogether as other investors piled in. "This thing's filling up fast," Stemberg declared flatly. "Do you guys want to play or not?"

It worked . . . on his terms. Despite its tough aspects, Stemberg's approach did not rupture relationships with his venture investors; for example, Bain's Mitt Romney served on the Staples board for years. And the ultimate success of his table-resetting effort would also have a beneficial impact the next time he approached potential financial backers. *(Hey, guys—I've already proven I can get the money somewhere else. Do you want to play more reasonably or not?)*

Of course, there's a lot more to getting the right *scope* (parties, interests, no-deal options) and *sequence* than we've included here. But you get the general idea. Don't just focus on tactics at the table; be sure the setup is right. If you don't like the way the table is set, reset it by attacking the scope and sequence of the negotiations.

Creating and Claiming Value

Let's back up a step and ask a fundamental question whose answer underlies our approach: whether we act in one, two, or three dimensions, what are we actually trying to do by negotiating? On one level, everyone will answer this question differently, depending on the specifics of the negotiations at hand. (On this level, Tom Stemberg would have said, "The point of negotiating is to get the money I need quickly and on terms that I consider fair.") But on a deeper level, the answer to our rhetorical question is always the same: *Your negotiating objective should be to create and claim value for the long term by crafting and implementing a deal that is satisfactory for both (or all) parties.*

What is *value*? Of course, many negotiations center on economic value—that is, potential financial gains to the negotiating parties. Suppose that we own a patent that could dramatically boost the value of your products in a market segment in which our firm has no interest in competing. A licensing deal could create economic value for both of us and would certainly be more appealing than the no-deal alternative.

But value can—and in many cases, should—be understood more broadly. Think of the example of Egypt and Israel negotiating over the Sinai described earlier. Rather than a zero-sum battle over where to draw a line in the sand, they came up with a demilitarized zone under the Egyptian flag; the kinds of value they created were not mainly economic, but involving security for the Israelis and sovereignty for the Egyptians. The idea of value can go farther still; as long as one or more parties care strongly about some aspect of the process or outcome, that aspect is a potential source of value in the negotiation. So, yes, "value" can mean a discounted cash flow. But it can also mean precedent, relationships, reputation, political appearance, fairness, or even how the other side's self-image fares in the process. The 3-D Negotiator is a master at the kinds of cooperative, problem-solving skills that uncover joint gains, and thereby create value for all sides relative to no deal. Value-creation falls into the "win-win," or "non-zero-sum" aspect of the process, because value creation benefits all parties.

But that's only half the story. The 3-D Negotiator is also a master at *claiming* value. This is the competitive, win-lose part of the negotiation, in which one side seeks to claim a full share of the "value pie." Obviously, there's an inherent tension between the cooperative moves needed to create value jointly and the competitive moves that enable you claim value individually. Managing that tension is at the very heart of the art and science of negotiation. When those contradictory tugs are badly managed, things tend to break down quickly. Hardball moves to claim value can short-circuit the moves needed to create value. Impasses arise unnecessarily, and money gets left on the table. The 3-D Negotiation techniques described throughout this book will help you solve all three of these challenges. They will help you create value, claim value, and productively manage the tension between creating and claiming.

There's one more point to make here: negotiators need to think in the long term when creating and claiming value. Yes, there are many kinds of one-shot negotiations after which it is highly unlikely that the two parties will ever sit down to bargain together again. Most likely, you will only sell your company once. If you sell a series of houses or used cars over your lifetime, you'll almost certainly be dealing with a different individual each time. These are important deals, and in the following chapters we will offer you a great deal of advice for managing one-shot negotiations, which—by definition—don't require a long-term perspective.

But in negotiations that aren't one-shots, keeping the long term in mind when creating and claiming value is important for at least three reasons. First, many negotiations are only a single chapter in a larger, ongoing relationship that could be damaged by adversarial tactics, making it harder to strike good deals in the future. Second, many agreements deliver their value only when all parties live up to their respective sides of the bargain in the intended spirit. If parties to the agreement feel that they have been exploited or otherwise dealt with unfairly, they may live up to their side of the bargain only halfheartedly— or they may even repudiate the agreement. Third, even in the case of a true one-shot, stand-alone agreement, your approach to deal making can affect your reputation beyond the confines of that one deal. The business and personal networks within which we all interact are becoming ever more tightly connected. People talk. If you get a reputation for dealing unfairly or adversarially, it may come back to haunt you.

We stress the overall negotiating objective—to create and claim value for the long term—since this objective directly informs both how you perform a 3-D barriers audit (the subject of our next chapter) and how you craft a 3-D strategy to overcome the barriers you've identified (the subject of chapter 3). As we analyze what is difficult about a given negotiation, we will often ask two more precise questions:

- What are the barriers to creating value?

- What are the barriers to claiming value?

Similarly, in talking about crafting a 3-D strategy, we will focus on the setup, deal design, and tactical moves that will (1) create the maximum possible value, and (2) claim a full share of that value—on a long-term basis.

Not One Dimension, but *Three* Dimensions

To summarize, the 3-D Negotiator plays a more complete game than either the old school win-lose negotiator, the trendy win-win negotiator, or their many close cousins who cluster around the bargaining table. That's why we've come to use the metaphor of "dimensions" to describe the three different—and mutually reinforcing—classes of negotiating moves that comprise the 3-D Negotiator's arsenal: tactics, deal design, and setup. Table 1-1 summarizes each of our three dimensions. By putting these pieces together, this book will show you precisely what it means to be a 3-D Negotiator, playing the *whole* negotiating game rather than just the at-the-table part of it.

A final word: in most negotiations, *the stakes are high*. This is true whether you're trying to secure second-round financing, broker a peace between warring states, or close a key business deal. True, these are very different negotiating contexts, with very different sorts of things hanging in the balance: lives, profits, individual dreams. But in all of them, the people at the table care very deeply about the outcome of the bargaining process. Unfortunately, when it comes to

TABLE 1-1

Individual dimensions that make up an overall 3-D approach

Dimension	Nickname	Where	Focus	Sample Moves
First	Tactics	"At the table"	People, process	Improve communication, build trust, counter hardball ploys, bridge cross-cultural divides
Second	Deal design	"On the drawing board"	Value, substance, outcomes	Invent and structure agreements that create greater value, meet objectives better, are more sustainable
Third	Setup	"Away from the table"	Architecture	Ensure most favorable scope (right parties, interests, no-deal options), sequence, and basic process choices

negotiating success, caring deeply doesn't make the difference. Only *effective preparation and focused action* make the difference—and in our experience, the best preparation is mastering the principles of 3-D Negotiation. The very first part of preparation is understanding what you're really up against. To us, that means the barriers that stand between you and the deal you want. Diagnosing those barriers is our next order of business, as we move to chapter 2.

Chapter Two

Do a 3-D Audit of Barriers to Agreement

H OW DO YOU GET the agreement you want? Start with a clear understanding of what you want. What are the broad outlines of the deal you hope to do? Then, you develop a clear picture of where things stand today. Based on that picture, you ask and answer the question: what stands between you and reaching the full potential of the agreement you have in mind? Then you work backward from your understanding of those barriers to develop a negotiating strategy. To address the basic barriers question, "What's in the way of the ideal agreement?" let's use the terminology from the last chapter: Are setup flaws blocking your desired agreement? Deal-design issues? People problems?

Don't jump to the conclusion that it's purely a price gap, or that cultural differences are getting in the way, or that those people across the table are simply unreasonable. Without an accurate barriers assessment—what we call a *3-D barriers audit*—your strategy and tactics may address the wrong problems.[1] We use the term *audit* to underscore the fact that what's needed is a *systematic* assessment of the situation in terms of its setup, deal design, and tactics. In this chapter, we'll show you how to perform this kind of assessment. But first, let's look at a negotiation that didn't have the benefit of a 3-D audit—and suffered as a result.

LockStore: The 3-D Audit That Should Have Happened

This case is based on a real story: the deal-making saga of a technology company that we'll call LockStore Systems, Inc. LockStore had developed a technology for detecting leaks in underground gas storage tanks—a "sniffer" that was one hundred times more accurate, faster, and substantially cheaper than competing technologies.

At that time, the Environmental Protection Agency was promulgating standards that would require underground tanks be continuously tested to protect groundwater supplies. Although LockStore made no effort to help shape the new regulations, it followed the drafting process with great interest. When the new standards were implemented, LockStore was sure it had a winner: not only faster, cheaper, and better, but now *mandated!* Its sales engineers began negotiating with potential buyers—and were astonished to receive a grand total of *one order* in the marketplace. One after another, potential customers walked away from the table.

What went wrong? More precisely, what were the barriers to agreement?

We usually advise starting a 3-D audit with a look at the setup, the third dimension that generally encompasses the others. For now, however, let's reverse the order and start with the more familiar first dimension: tactics and interpersonal factors at the table.

In LockStore's case, were dull engineering personalities the culprits? Not knowing just the moment to look the buyer right in the eye and drive to close? No. These interpersonal issues (it later became clear) had nothing to do with the string of turndowns.

Think for a moment about how target buyers might see *their* interests in the device—especially in light of the fact that EPA regulations still permitted multiple-gallon leaks, while the new technology would unfailingly pick up a leak that would barely fill a drinking glass. LockStore's device was simply *too* good. "What a technological tour de force," the potential buyers all agreed— sometimes within earshot of the LockStore's sales engineers. "Great price, too. But the truth is, this handy new device will almost certainly get me into needless, expensive regulatory and legal trouble—and create PR headaches, too. I think I'll pass. But come to think of it, my *competition* should definitely have the benefit of this new technology!" From LockStore's perspective, then, "faster, better, cheaper" added up to a sure sale; to the other side, it looked like a sure headache. No deal.

The first, and killer, tactical barrier was LockStore's myopic focus. Stuck in their own perspective, LockStore's sales engineers did not think very hard about how "faster, better, cheaper" would look to the *other* side. And remember, it is the *other side's* choice—to say yes or no—that you're trying to influence in your negotiations.

Getting this basic interpersonal piece right would have been useful for Lock-Store. Unfortunately, better probing and listening would mainly have served to uncover a deal-related barrier: the necessary value was simply not there for the buyer. Indeed, this hypersensitive device would have created needless costs and risks for the intended user. This represents a classic barrier, which we call an *adverse deal/no-deal balance*; it simply means that "no-deal" looks better than "yes" for one or more of the parties.

It would be pretty hard to shift this deal/no-deal balance by tinkering with possible contracts. So, short of purposely degrading the accuracy of the new devices while keeping their costs low and installation easy, what might be done?

As our audit of tactical and deal-design barriers suggests, neither silver-tongued persuaders nor artful deal designers would have been likely to succeed. Had we been involved, we would have counseled LockStore to look *away from the table* for a solution. The real barrier to success involved the *setup* itself, which was limited to company-customer sales negotiation.

LockStore was simply negotiating with the wrong people. It should have put far more energy into persuading the government to *require* the higher level of compliance that its device could deliver. On the merits, this outcome would have had lower compliance costs and offered better environmental results for all. Maybe LockStore could have joined forces with its suppliers to achieve this outcome. Maybe it could have proposed licensing deals with existing competitors, to bring them on board. Maybe it could even have persuaded a few major potential customers to join this coalition. (None of these customers wanted to be the *only* one to incur the higher remediation costs that the LockStore device would have generated, but perhaps most or all of them would have been happy to use LockStore sniffers if *everybody* with gas-storage tanks had to hit the same high standard.) If the EPA had mandated the use of the best available technology to monitor storage tanks *across the board*, LockStore could have enjoyed enormous sales to a broad range of industrial customers.

This postmortem 3-D audit suggests that LockStore faced a self-inflicted tactical barrier by keeping an inward focus and being guilty of the all-too-common failure to probe the other side's real interests. But even a more effective interpersonal approach would only have revealed the unhappy deal-related barrier—that no zone of agreement existed—but at least would have clarified the daunting setup barriers to a deal.

To overcome this barrier, LockStore had to change the setup from an unpromising one to a higher-potential one, with potentially huge financial and environmental payoffs. When LockStore mapped the parties to the negotiation, its focus was limited to those already at the table. But a 3-D Negotiator also looks for *potentially* involved parties, in order to set up the most promising situation. LockStore failed to do so, and, as a result, paid a high price.

And, of course, doing a *prospective* 3-D barriers audit to guide your negotiating strategy sure beats doing an autopsy to find out why it didn't work. With the illustrative LockStore case in mind, we'll work through a more systematic barriers audit, starting with the setup.

Assessing Setup Barriers

A flawed setup means less fertile ground for the kind of agreement you want. Setup problems can involve three aspects of the negotiation: scope, sequence, and basic process choices.

Scope flaws mean the wrong parties, interests, and/or no-deal options. Experience teaches us that getting the scope right calls for more than a mechanical list; it requires a disciplined kind of imagination that the 3-D approach will help you develop. Tom Stemberg realized that the original scope of his Staples financing negotiation presented insuperable barriers. He succeeded by bringing in new parties with different interests that improved his walk-away options and worsened those of the VCs. LockStore management did not—and failed.

Sequence flaws, by contrast, are problems with the order in which the negotiation is to unfold. Mistakes can be made, for example, as to which parties are approached first or the order in which issues are dealt with, that can stymie or kill an unfolding negotiation.

And finally, basic *process choice* flaws can include problems with the way a negotiation is organized. For example, there may be no provision for useful joint fact finding or for a third party, such as a mediator, to support the process, when such features could have been helpful.

Each of these three categories of flaws calls for its own countermeasures. First, you should map the scope: all the parties, their interests, and their no-deal options. Second, you should check the sequence. And third, you should check basic process choices for hidden flaws. Let's look at each in turn.

Mapping All the Parties and Their No-Deal Options

Mapping the parties and their interests is a vital step that many would-be negotiators tend to rush by. How hard can this be, they ask? There's me, and there's the guy across the table, and we're settling on the right price.

Who Are the Real Parties?

The truth is that *really understanding* the full set of interested parties—including those now in the picture, and those who may need to enter the picture—often requires a real act of imagination. Let's say you're the seller. Are you absolutely sure that the prospective buyers you have in mind are the most motivated buyers? Is there another way of looking at your product or service—another context in which it could be used—that would make it even more valuable to another kind of buyer? If you haven't fully explored these possibilities, you may leave money on the table.

In other cases, you may have the right parties, but you may not be negotiating at the most useful level. Even when you're dealing with a huge corporate or public-sector entity, most likely you're not dealing with a monolith, but with specific people, many of whom have their own agendas, perceptions, and interests. To tailor your negotiating approach most effectively, you need an accurate map of your counterparts and how they fit into their organization. What's the hierarchy? Who influences whom? And yes, where are the oil-and-water combinations that you need to be aware of? How might they influence the negotiations?

Less experienced negotiators sometimes become mesmerized by the aggregate economics of a deal and forget about the interests of players who are in a position to enable or torpedo it. When the boards of pharmaceutical giants Glaxo and SmithKline Beecham publicly announced their merger in 1998, for example, investors were thrilled, rapidly *increasing* the combined company's market capitalization by a stunning $20 billion. Yet despite prior agreement as to exactly who would occupy which top executive positions in the newly combined company, internal disagreements about management control and position resurfaced. These disagreements sank the announced deal, and the $20 billion evaporated.[2]

This episode confirms two related lessons about parties and interests. First, while favorable overall economics are generally *necessary*, they are often not *sufficient*. Second, keep all potentially influential internal players on your radar screen; don't lose sight of their interests or their capacity to affect the deal. What is "rational" for the whole may not be so for the parts.

What Is the Full Set of Their Interests?

The next part of mapping focuses on *interests*. Sometimes it's as easy as hitting the right price. In many cases, though, there are all sorts of other submerged interests that may not be put on the table, but which have the potential to affect negotiations profoundly. If there's a difference between what people say they want (their bargaining *position*) and what they really want (their *interests*), you need to figure out what that difference might be. Remember that what they value encompasses both economic and noneconomic factors, tangibles as well as intangibles.

For example, an English property development firm assembled most of the land in an area outside London needed to build a large regional hospital. Yet a key parcel remained, and its owner stubbornly resisted selling. Although the small property was appraised at a mere £80,000, the developer had successively offered £90,000, £100,000, then £120,000, and ultimately £200,000—all to no avail. The owner seemed to be well aware of the parcel's pivotal position, and seemed determined to exploit it. In desperation, with the project hanging in the balance, the firm's chief executive arranged a personal appointment with the owner. When the chief executive arrived in his chauffeured limousine at the property in question—a somewhat shabby but neat cottage—the owner, who turned out to be an elderly woman, invited him in and offered him a cup of tea.

Looking around, he noticed several framed pictures of a small dog. In the course of polite conversation, the owner—call her Mrs. Jones—sadly described how "dear Fluffy" had passed away three years ago and was buried in her garden behind the cottage. Eventually, the CEO asked to see her beloved pet's gravesite. Following a moment of quiet contemplation in the tiny garden, he delicately asked Mrs. Jones whether she had ever considered what would happen to this spot as the neighborhood changed over the years, as it was bound to do. Wouldn't a proper memorial, well-tended in perpetuity, be a more fitting remembrance of Fluffy?

Mrs. Jones agreed almost immediately. The development firm expedited arrangements for Fluffy's remains to be reinterred on the grounds of a prestigious pet cemetery, the cottage sale was closed for less than £100,000, and the hospital project was put back on track. On signing the sale papers, Mrs. Jones was heard to remark, "What use does a childless old woman like me have for more money, as long as I can rent a nice flat closer to Fluffy?"

While quirky, this episode illustrates a very much broader aspect of negotiating: the importance of probing behind apparently incompatible bargaining positions to understand the full set of real interests of the parties. Wayne Huizenga, veteran of more than a thousand deals that went into the building of Waste Management, Inc., AutoNation, and Blockbuster, distills his extensive experience into a kernel of sound advice: "In all my years of doing deals,"

Huizenga reflects, "a few rules and lessons have emerged. Most important, always try to put yourself in the other person's shoes. It's vital to try to understand in depth what the other side really wants out of the deal."[3]

This may seem like a lot of work—and a lot of *guesswork*, to boot. But in most cases, mapping the full set of parties and the full set of their interests—actual and potential—is time and money well spent. Why? Because getting the parties and interests right opens up possibilities for value-creating trades that increase the chances for a successful negotiation. What do those people across the table *really* want? What can I offer that gives them what they want, but doesn't cost me too much? It's not easy, and negotiators frequently fumble this vital task. But guidelines for mapping all the parties and their interests have emerged, based on both practical experience and academic research; we'll present those guidelines in subsequent chapters.

Assessing No-Deal Options

In any negotiation, you and the other parties involved face a fundamental and ongoing choice: between staying and walking, between striking a deal and not, between "yes" and "no." To say "yes" to a deal on the table, you need to understand how well that deal would serve your interests. But you can't make that calculation in a vacuum. The real question is, "How well does it serve my interests, *compared to what*?"

This is the *deal/no-deal* balance. On one side of the balance, you have the proposed deal; on the other, you have your "walk-away" option—sometimes called your *best alternative to a negotiated agreement*, or *BATNA*.[4] Can you find another buyer? Is there an alternative supplier or alliance partners? Can you go to court? Can you take a strike? Can you risk another war with Egypt? Is there another course of action that's more likely to serve your interests than the deal that is on the table? Your alternative to cutting a deal sets the bar, in value terms, that any proposed deal has to clear. If the proposed deal is worth less to you than the alternative, you will leave the table.

Understanding the deal/no-deal balance requires a two-part assessment by each party: first, the assessment of your own position, as noted above, and second, the assessment of the *other* party's alternatives, insofar as you can understand them. Why? Because part of a successful negotiating strategy is shaping your counterparts' perception of *their* deal/no-deal balance in order to get them to say "yes" to the deal that *you* want. They have to decide for themselves that the deal you're offering is better than any of the alternatives, including no deal at all. To get them to reach that decision may require a number of concurrent actions on your part, including: improving the value of the deal to them, getting them to see their best no-deal alternative as bad (and getting worse), and getting them to see your best no-deal alternative as good (and improving).

The deal/no-deal calculations should take place on two levels: the individual and the aggregate. Think back to how you mapped all the parties. Each player is potentially important—or that player wouldn't be on your map—but *combinations* of players are also key. How will a potential winning or blocking coalition assess this particular deal/no-deal choice?

Note, too, that calculating the deal/no-deal balance is likely to be an ongoing process. No-deal options are likely to evolve and shift (in part through your efforts). Just as a skilled medical team continually monitors its patient's vital signs, effective negotiators monitor both sides' perceptions of how the deal/no-deal balance is currently tilting—and then take steps to alter the balance, as necessary. In many cases, this monitoring continues even after the agreement is inked: are all sides continuing to see compliance with the deal as preferable to their no-deal alternatives?

In complex negotiations involving multiple parties, the assessment of no-deal alternatives can be extremely challenging—and all the more important. Without such an assessment, you can't know whether enough (and the right) parties are on board to make a deal. Here's a place where the all-party map pays off. Mentally assign colors to the various parties in the negotiation: green for those who appear to be leaning toward a deal, yellow for those who appear to be genuinely undecided, and red for those apparently leaning toward their no-deal alternatives. How many "reds" are lurking out there? Are they numerous and well-placed enough to form a blocking coalition? If so, what's your best hope of converting, sidestepping, co-opting, or overcoming some or all of them?

Assessing the other party's best no-deal option can turn up some surprises. In one instance, we advised a senior executive of a global consumer products company. He had hoped to sell a poorly performing division for a bit more than its depreciated asset value of $7 million to one of two potential buyers. After we mapped the parties and the full set of their interests, the fierce rivalry of these two potential buyers in other markets became more obvious. It seemed likely that, prodded by the right negotiating strategy, each party might see the other as the seller's (very credible) no-deal option and might be willing to pay an inflated price to keep the other from getting the division. So we made sure that each suitor knew the other was actively looking, kept both sides "warm" throughout the process, and carefully stimulated the interest of both. After a heated auction-like negotiation, the division sold for $45 million.

So you need to smoke out the interests of the other side and understand its best walk-away option. Meanwhile, of course, you need to cultivate your own. A strong walk-away option is an important negotiation tool. Many people think that it's the ability to inflict or withstand damage that translates into bargaining power, but in fact, your ability to walk away to an apparently good alternative is often more important. The better your no-deal possibilities appear both to you and to the other party, the more credible your threat to walk away becomes, and the more these possibilities can serve as leverage to improve the deal. Our colleague Roger Fisher has dramatized this point by asking which you would prefer to have in your back pocket during a compensation negotiation with your boss: a gun, or a terrific job offer from a desirable employer who is also one of your company's serious competitors?

Checking the Sequence and Process Choices

Having mapped the full set of parties, their interests, and no-deal options, the 3-D Negotiator looks for barriers associated with the sequence in which different parties are involved, and the basic process choices on how the negotiation is to unfold. Ideally, you will put in place the best sequence by which different potential parties are involved, in order to create the most promising possible setup. The way you orchestrate the process—its timing, whether it is framed cooperatively or competitively, the possible involvement of third parties such as mediators, and so on—can significantly affect the outcome. Significant barriers arise by getting these elements wrong.

Imagine that you need to generate internal support for a new product or sales initiative. Maybe you're inclined to follow the old prescription to "get your allies on board first." If so, you might want to think again, because this is not always the best sequence.

When the United States sought to build a global anti-Iraq coalition following that country's 1990 invasion of Kuwait, Israel was the United States' strongest ally in the region. Yet the Israelis were pointedly excluded from the coalition. Why? Because Israel's formal inclusion would have discouraged, or even precluded, most Arab states from signing on. An alternative sequence—starting with the moderate Arab states and assuming tacit Israeli membership—completely sidestepped this problem.

Another standard prescription for sequencing is to get your own house in order first by developing an internal consensus before dealing with outsiders. But it's not always the best choice. For example, when preparing for the first Gulf War, President George H. W. Bush first committed U.S. troops to the region. Then he engaged in exhaustive negotiations to build an external UN coalition behind a Security Council Resolution that authorized "all necessary means" to eject Iraq from Kuwait. Only then did he begin negotiating seriously for U.S. congressional authorization to use force in the Gulf.

Had Bush started by seeking the "internal" approval of a deeply skeptical U.S. Congress, agreement would have been elusive. And if he had first tried and failed to win congressional approval, any subsequent American-led international (or "external") coalition-building enterprise would have been hobbled. As National Security Advisor General Brent Scowcroft observed: "There has been some criticism of us for, in effect, pressuring Congress by building an international coalition and then making the argument, 'You mean, Congressman, you're not going to support the President, but the President of Ethiopia is supporting him' . . . If there had been no coalition and no UN vote, we would never have gotten Congress."[5]

In short, getting the negotiating sequence right opened the door to success, while getting it wrong would have led to failure. This kind of sequential reasoning is not limited to high diplomatic or military negotiations. Getting buy-in from the participants on a task force or a cross-functional team may depend on the order of consultation. Even getting the "right" participants to sign up for a party, a seminar, a panel, or a charity event can raise elaborate sequencing choices: Whom should I involve first? How should I frame the approach? Based on that outcome, whom should I call next? Then what?

Assessing Deal-Design Barriers

An inadequate deal design can impede, or even preclude, progress.

In chapter 1, we described several cases in which the original agreement being negotiated could not possibly lead to success. Recall, for example, our recounting of the bargaining around the proposed sale of an electronics-components company—a bargaining process that was ultimately resolved with the introduction of a contingent "earn-out." But in the early stages of the bargaining process—*before* that solution possibility was raised—there was a serious deal-design barrier: the two parties' differing views of the longer-term prospects of the company, which led to substantially different valuations of the company. The earn-out represented a significant rewriting of the original deal that was on the table. That rewriting was based on an audit of inherent deal-design barriers, and a successful invention process in the wake of that audit.

Similarly, LockStore's proposed deal—selling oversensitive leak-detection devices—was a nonstarter relative to the no-deal options of its target customers. A barrier audit would most likely have revealed that fact and forced LockStore to rethink its bargaining position.

What happens when a barriers audit turns up a flawed deal design? As implied above, one or both parties can walk away from the table, or they can attempt to fix or get around that flaw. Working solo or jointly at the drawing board, negotiators can sometimes discover hidden sources of economic and noneconomic value, then craft agreements that unlock that value for the parties involved and overcome the barrier that has grown out of the poor deal design. We'll explore deal design in more depth in part 3 of this book.

Assessing Tactical and Interpersonal Barriers

"What we've got here is failure to communicate," says the authoritarian Captain in the 1967 film *Cool Hand Luke*, after Luke's failed escape attempt. "Some men you just can't reach."

When negotiations aren't going well, you may find yourself arriving at the same conclusion as the Captain, unsympathetic as he was: *some people you just can't reach!* Those characters on the other side of the table (you find yourself thinking) must be especially dense. They just aren't recognizing the sheer compellingness of the case we're presenting. You may find yourself starting to talk a little louder, and a little more urgently, in an effort to "reach" those slow-witted characters, just as many people raise their voices or speak more slowly when they're talking to someone who *literally* doesn't speak their language—as if talking louder will make the speakers' words more comprehensible. It doesn't, of course. In fact, it's highly likely to make these speakers appear more obnoxious to that uncomprehending listener, who therefore becomes less interested in trying to figure out what's being said.

Communication barriers are something that most of us—including non-negotiators—deal with every day. They're therefore more familiar to us, and need less explanation in this context. But let's touch on them briefly here, and then discuss them in depth in later chapters.

In negotiation, the most common communication problems involve the strong sense on one or both sides that, somehow, intended perspectives and interests are not coming across effectively; the other side just doesn't seem to understand key concerns, priorities, or limits. This difficulty may result from your lack of clarity in presentation, or your failure to frame points effectively, or from either side's poor listening skills (good, "active" listening is something that people tend to take for granted; in fact, it's an acquired skill). It may also be a function of the bargaining approach; for example, each side may do little more than reemphasize its immovable position.

Communication barriers may also result from a failure to put the proper cultural filters in place. The classic example is the "yes" that the American negotiator extracts from his or her Japanese counterpart. The American hears the Japanese saying, "Yes, I agree to the deal." But there's a good chance that the Japanese negotiator is merely saying, "Yes, I *heard* you." When the inevitable crunch comes in the wake of this misunderstanding, the American thinks the Japanese can't be trusted, and the Japanese thinks the American must be astoundingly obtuse. Neither conclusion does much to help subsequent communications!

While we've illustrated tactical barriers at the table mainly with communication issues, there are plenty of others. In our experience, some of the most potent tactical barriers result from each side's overemphasis on *claiming* value, rather than creating it. We're all familiar with hardball moves, put-downs, last-minute demands, pressure tactics, hiding information, walk-away threats, and the like. These *do* need to be part of your audit of tactical barriers. With each side aggressively pushing for more, the risk of poor deals, needless impasses, and conflict goes up dramatically.

Two Cross-Cutting Barriers to Be on Guard Against

Up to this point, we've described a barriers audit in a compartmentalized way: first in the setup dimension, then in the deal-design dimension, and finally in the tactical/communications dimension. We should emphasize, however, that most real-life negotiations—at least the complex ones—involve potential barriers in more than one dimension. Two of these merit special attention.

AN ADVERSE DEAL/NO-DEAL BALANCE. We've already introduced this major barrier in the context of the setup. If the deal isn't good enough for one or more of the parties—if there isn't enough value in it relative to no deal—the negotiation may be doomed. The reverberations are likely to carry across all of our 3-D dimensions: setup, deal design, and tactics. So favorably redressing an adverse deal/no-deal balance may require a number of concurrent tactics on your part, including: improving the value of the deal to the other side and getting them to see their no-deal alternative as bad (and getting worse). We will look at possible responses in a more sustained way in subsequent chapters.

INCOMPLETE OR BLURRY INFORMATION. Bad or missing data can also serve as a cross-cutting barrier. Without accurate information on the key elements of a negotiation—including the parties, their interests, and no-deal options—it is difficult to create and claim value effectively. Are there holes in your knowledge? Do you have only a fragmentary understanding of the motivations around the table?

To surmount this common barrier, an effective 3-D strategy will need to contain an information-gathering component. And when decisions must be made on the basis of complex data with lots of contingencies involved—*if this, then that*—then all of the parties may need to develop a baseline of agreed-upon information. Otherwise, they may argue incessantly about the facts of the situation, rather than what to *do* with the facts.

Getting from Here to There

Before you can negotiate effectively, you need to understand two things:

- Where you want the negotiations to wind up
- What stands in the way of your getting there

Presumably, the shape of the deal you want to cut has grown out of ongoing discussions within your organization: the price and broader terms you need to realize for your product or your company, the price you're willing to pay to secure financing for your next stage of growth, the borders you want to establish to guarantee your nation's security, and so on. You then have to figure out what might prevent that overriding goal from being attained.

This is the function of the 3-D barriers audit. If you're about to go into negotiations—or if you're already involved in bargaining that doesn't seem to be going where you want it to go—a barriers audit is crucial. It should comprise all three of our 3-D dimensions (setup, deal design, and tactics), and also reflect the realities of cross-cutting barriers.

Based on what you learn from your audit, you should be prepared to craft a 3-D strategy to overcome them. That's the subject of our next chapter.

- With a provisional agreement in mind, do a 3-D barriers audit.

  - What prevents you from reaching the potential of the deal you want?

  - Wrong parties? Wrong interests? Wrong no-deal options? Wrong sequence? Wrong basic process choices? Wrong deal design? Adverse tactics or interpersonal approach?

- Assess setup barriers.

  - Have you mapped all the parties, their interests, and best no-deal options?

  - Have you assessed the full set of actually and potentially involved parties?

  - Have you probed the full set of interests at stake, yours and theirs, going behind bargaining positions?

  - Have you assessed each side's best no-deal option, which sets the bar for any acceptable deal and influences negotiating "power"?

  - Have you checked the sequence and basic process choices?

- Assess deal-design barriers.

  - Does the proposed agreement create the maximum possible value?

  - Does it meet the requirements and objectives of the parties?

- Assess tactical and interpersonal barriers.

  - Do you face hardball or other difficult tactics?

  - Are there communication, trust, personality, style, or cross-cultural issues?

- Watch for cross-cutting barriers.

  - An adverse deal/no-deal balance?

  - Missing or blurry information?

Chapter Three

Craft a 3-D Strategy to Overcome the Barriers

HERE'S A TOUGH NEGOTIATING CHALLENGE for you, straight from the docks and boardrooms of the U.S. West Coast.

In 1999, the Pacific Maritime Association (PMA), an association of seventy-two diverse shipping lines and terminal operators in West Coast ports from San Diego to Seattle, sought an agreement with the International Longshore and Warehouse Union (ILWU) to introduce new information technologies that would enhance shipping efficiency and increase the capacity of often-clogged West Coast ports.[1] Because the longshore and clerk divisions of the ILWU had been steadily losing jobs because of containerization and other technological changes (shrinking from a workforce of approximately 100,000 in the 1950s to about 10,500 in 2002), the union, not surprisingly, feared that these technologies would cause further losses to its diminishing ranks.[2]

Though reduced in numbers, the longshoremen still wielded awesome power, enough to effectively stop U.S. seaborne trade flowing through the West Coast—trade worth some *$6 billion per week*. So, in response to the perceived threat, the union flatly turned down the PMA proposal and began an informal job slowdown. Lines of loaded container ships backed up in West Coast harbors, causing massive supply chain disruptions nationwide. Those dependent on ocean shipping, from Wal-Mart and Home Depot to time-sensitive agricultural interests, pressured the PMA to make a deal—*any* deal. The PMA, a fragmented organization of both huge and minor shipping players, soon dropped its technology demands, but vowed to reintroduce them in the 2002 talks.

Unfortunately for PMA's resolve to try again, the union remained a formidable opponent. One result of this clout was high compensation: by 2002, union members were among the elite of U.S. workers. Annual wages, including overtime, averaged $83,000 for longshoremen, $118,000 for clerks, and a princely $158,000 for foremen.[3] As University of Michigan labor expert Howard Kimeldorf put it, "Among workers who work with their hands in America, there is probably nobody paid better than the longshoremen . . . In terms of economic muscle, [the ILWU] may be the strongest union in the country."[4] When the talks came around, ILWU continued to wield its slowdown/strike weapon.

Against this backdrop, imagine that you are Joseph Miniace, PMA's president and CEO, licking your wounds shortly after the 1999 debacle. You are now contemplating the upcoming 2002 negotiations, during which you plan to make a second run at a new technology agreement with the union. If you were to do a 3-D barriers audit, what would it turn up?

Maybe you would conclude that something was badly wrong with your negotiating style, and maybe you'd be right. Maybe your tactical and interpersonal approaches *do* need help. Maybe you'd enroll in a seminar to make you into a better listener, a more insightful interpreter of body language, and a much more persuasive communicator. And maybe your instructor would extol the virtues of the "win-win" approach to negotiations, relative to the "win-lose" game that your union counterparts seem bent on playing. Maybe you'd conclude that joint brainstorming for creative solutions on electronic whiteboards has potential. Most likely, though, a little voice somewhere inside your brain would probably be telling you that the union's capacity to shut down $6 billion worth of U.S. foreign trade per week would again triumph over new negotiation skills and new approaches to the whiteboard.

And this little voice would be *right*.

So what to do instead? As Miniace contemplated the 2002 talks, he faced deep distrust and other interpersonal barriers posed by a powerful, wary union counterpart. More fundamentally, though, he faced a nasty setup barrier to the deal the PMA sought. (We have clinically referred to this barrier as an "adverse deal/no-deal balance.") Specifically, he faced the threat of another devastating union slowdown or strike, which—as he knew from past experience—would quickly lead to virtually irresistible demands from his own PMA members to do *anything* to get the cargo flowing and the supply chains operating.

What might a 3-D strategy look like in a hardball case like this? We'll soon turn back to the specific problem facing Miniace. But first let's consult Daniel Vare, an Italian diplomat and author who lived in the early twentieth century.

Vare came up with a pithy (and useful) characterization of successful diplomacy: the "art of letting *them* have *your* way" [our emphasis].[5]

On the face of it, this may sound like a thinly disguised call for manipulation. But we think Vare's advice can mean much more—and serve much better purposes—than that. At its best, letting them have your way means *finding an agreement that meets your counterparts' real interests, as a way of meeting yours.* It means shaping how the other side sees the basic choice—between yes and no—so that the "yes" they choose for *their* reasons yields the deal *you* want for yours.

This is no easy task. It requires you to craft a 3-D Negotiation strategy: a plan for getting from where you are today to where you need to be tomorrow. We began the last chapter by asking a simple question to help you get there: *what stands between you and the agreement you want?* Answering that question calls for the 3-D barriers audit that we described in chapter 2. This requires you to map all of the parties, their interests, and no-deal options. You must assess the sequence and basic process choices. You should probe the deal/no-deal balance along with the people side of the equation. Completing a barriers audit means paying careful attention to problems in all three dimensions of our 3-D scheme: the setup, the deal design, and the tactics. Then, based on that audit, you figure out how to get from today's reality to a successfully concluded negotiation. This involves crafting a 3-D strategy to overcome those barriers, and that's the subject of this third and final introductory chapter.

3-D Strategy: The Basics

Now we want to give you a clearer sense of how a 3-D strategy actually works to overcome the barriers that you've carefully sized up. Such a strategy calls for three mutually reinforcing activities—our three dimensions—designed to let them have your way:

- Setting up the right negotiation

- Designing value-creating deals

- Stressing problem-solving tactics

As you read the following sections, think of these activities as pieces of a bigger puzzle to be put together by you as the picture begins to take shape. As a 3-D Negotiator you are nimble, flexible, and opportunistic. In addressing the barriers, you don't hesitate to reshuffle the deck or reset the table in order to mold how the other side weighs "yes" versus "no." Your moves away from the table, on the drawing board, and at the table combine—in various proportions—to induce your counterparts, for *their* reasons, to opt for the agreement you want.

Basically, we contend that by establishing and maintaining multiple perspectives on a bargaining process, you will be a far more successful negotiator. The dimensions we refer to may come into play at different times—for example, setting up naturally precedes designing good deals, and design is usually separate from getting your tactics straight—but in most cases, the three dimensions are capabilities that are drawn upon concurrently or alternately.

A rough analogy would be the way we use our senses; the more senses—seeing, hearing, tasting, and so on—we can bring to bear on a situation, the better off we're likely to be. This is the essence of 3-D Negotiation: bringing the broadest possible knowledge base and skill set to bear on the bargaining process, in ways that enhance your chances of success.

Before we get into the specifics, we want to stress one key point that flows from our 3-D approach. *A problem encountered in one dimension can often push you into other dimensions for a solution.* For example, in the LockStore case example, cited in the previous chapter, what looked like a tactical failure was actually a setup failure. This is a very important aspect of 3-D Negotiation, and it's a characteristic that distinguishes our approach from other negotiation approaches.

Think back as well to the example of Tom Stemberg's hunt for financing, as described in chapter 1. Faced with stonewalling *tactics* by the venture community, Stemberg simply couldn't come up with the deal he sought by using counter-tactics at the table. Instead, he went in search of a new *setup* involving new parties and interests that might be more inclined to take the deal he was offering. In other words, he reset the table and launched new negotiations based on that new setup. Meanwhile, of course, he continued with the other negotiations, in hopes that the original players might decide that their own no-deal options were changing for the worse. Ultimately, faced with the deal/no-deal choice crafted by Stemberg in the new setup, his counterparts said "yes."

As these examples show, if you think of negotiation mainly in terms of people and tactics at the table, you limit yourself to interpersonal and tactical responses. Faced with the variety of roadblocks that negotiations put in your intended path, you'll be stuck as a 1-D player in a 3-D world. 3-D Negotiation offers a productive way out. Now you must make the transition into the heart of 3-D strategy—overcoming the barriers that your 3-D audit has identified by crafting an aligned combination of all three dimensions. In the right proportions for the challenge at hand, you must set up the right negotiation, design value-creating deals, and stress problem-solving tactics. Here's a bit about each process, followed by a challenging case that puts it all together.

Set Up the Right Negotiation

So let's start with the setup. To rephrase our original definition, this consists largely of moves away from the table, aimed at ensuring that the right parties, approached in the right sequence, deal with the right issues using the right process in the context of the right expectations, with the right no-deal alternatives in the back of their minds: *right, right, right, right, right,* and *right.* Since a flawed setup will complicate (or even kill) a negotiation, the prenegotiating arrangements—the rules of engagement, to borrow a military phrase—have to be set up with great care.

For the purposes of this chapter, some of the key setup challenges can be captured in a few bullet points, as follows:

- Scan widely for potentially advantageous elements; don't accept the current setup as fixed.

- Envision the most promising *scope, sequence,* and basic *process choices.*

- To find the best path to this most promising setup, *map backward* from the ideal to the current setup.

- Involve issues and parties with the potential to create value; avoid pure value-claiming battles where possible.

- Ensure that the elements of a potential winning coalition are present and that your setup doesn't empower potential blockers.

To illustrate, let's go back to the unfavorable setup facing Joseph Miniace at the helm of the PMA. He hoped to negotiate a new technology deal with the longshoremen's union that had rolled him and the PMA in their last encounter. He had correctly identified the overwhelming barrier to the agreement: historically, faced with a proposal it didn't like, the union could say "no" and make its no-deal option stick through an extraordinarily costly slowdown or strike. How could he act to redress this adverse deal/no-deal balance and set up a more promising situation? In particular, how could he reset the

table so that, to the longshoremen, a "yes" to the proposal would look better
than a "no"?

Investing months visiting the PMA's seventy-two member firms, Miniace
began with a concentrated *internal* campaign to restructure PMA's unwieldy
board, which had traditionally operated by consensus. The new board would
comprise "fewer labor relations executives—who had a vested interest in making sure contract negotiations ran smoothly—and . . . more operating executives who understood the economic consequences of repeated concessions. It
also meant getting the biggest players on the board."[6] With top-level executive
members on the restructured board—whose votes were weighted by shipping
tonnage, so the major players had decisive influence—and an extensive internal educational campaign on the critical future importance of the new technology, Miniace began an external outreach effort.

He first coordinated closely with Robin Lanier, former president of the
International Mass Retail Association, who had close ties to shippers, large
importers, and retailers such as Wal-Mart. Lanier voiced the concerns that her
constituency repeatedly expressed in regard to port technology:

> *We had a congestion problem; we had an infrastructure problem . . . here
> were these very sophisticated importers who have Web-based and EDI-
> based supply chain management systems, and you got to the port and it all
> kind of fell apart. If . . . you [wanted] to know where your container is at all
> times, once it got to the port [your efforts were thwarted] because of a lack
> of information technology . . . We had no idea how labor worked at the port.
> We did not go into this thinking we're going to pick a fight with labor.[7]*

Then Miniace and his team arranged visits to the Departments of Commerce, Treasury, Labor, Transportation, and Homeland Security, and the
Office of the U.S. Trade Representative. According to Miniace, PMA's message,
as delivered in the nation's capital, was consistent:

> *We told every single person [we met with] that we want nothing from
> them. We want you to understand what we are doing. We explained what
> happened to us in the last negotiations. This was the impact. This is what is
> on the table this time, and why it is important. We warned them that we
> could not take a slowdown this time. If [the union opts for a slowdown],
> we'll have to shut it down.[8]*

Finally, the PMA hired public relations help to start getting its message out
to the media and the wider public. If push came to shove, a better-informed
and restructured board along with energized business and political allies would

put the PMA in a far stronger position, despite belated PR efforts by the union in response.

Indeed, following these initiatives, and in response to a union slowdown and port lockout by the PMA, President Bush invoked the Taft-Hartley Act to force the parties back to work and to submit to federal mediation. This effectively blunted the union's slowdown/strike weapon.

In this dramatically more favorable setup, Miniace and his team worked hard with the union to craft a workable deal. Ultimately, the PMA won a much better technology agreement after a negotiating drama that entailed many steps, missteps, some arguably needless confrontations, and a remarkable call to the longshoremen by U.S. Homeland Security chief, Tom Ridge. The top union negotiator interpreted Ridge as saying, "If you stall this [negotiation], you're going to be viewed as economic terrorists."[9] In a post-9/11 world, that was a powerful message.

In this case a barriers diagnosis pointed up the central challenges for the PMA: a hardball-playing opponent and a negotiating setup with a highly adverse deal/no-deal balance. A purely tactical response at the table, focused on the interpersonal, would have failed. So Miniace's group launched multiple efforts, both internal and external, to redress this balance, and those efforts proved decisive. As the lead union negotiator for the longshoremen ruefully observed, "It used to be that the negotiation took place at the table."[10]

As further evidence that setup and deal design are vital, consider the fact that some of the major players were the same during both confrontations. Joseph Miniace had been hired as the shippers' CEO well in advance of the 1999 negotiations. But when preparing for these disastrous talks, he had taken *none* of the steps we described. Only after this searing experience did he embrace actions to set up a more promising situation for the PMA. And then, as an effective 3-D strategist, he set up the right negotiation, extending to the internal, external, actual, and potential players; their interests; as well as their no-deal options.

Design Value-Creating Deals

Nothing will kill an otherwise good deal as quickly as a value gap—that is, a gap between the deal and the no-deal alternatives of one or more parties. The deal has to put enough value on the table for all parties. And, of course, that value has to be sustained over time. It's far better to arrive at a self-enforcing agreement than one that has to be enforced externally—usually at considerable expense and with no guarantee of effectiveness.

Here are four key principles to observe when designing value-creating deals:

- Focus on maximizing the total net pie that can be created through agreement.

- Seek issues that are relatively easy for one party to give and valuable for the other party to get; dovetail these core issues with complementary issues. (It's the differences of interests that lead to joint gains.) Seek other value-creating differences: in forecasts, in attitudes toward risk and time, and so on. As a deal designer, think high benefit, low cost.

- Design deals that are robust and sustainable; project how a continued agreement will look relative to future no-deal alternatives.

- Negotiate the "spirit of the deal" in tandem with its "letter"; productively align the social contract with the economic contract.

Let's return briefly to the shippers' contract with the longshoremen, finally negotiated in a much more favorable setup for the shippers (with the invocation of Taft-Hartley forcing the ports to open and the union back to work). Hammered out with the tireless and creative assistance of federal mediators, the ultimate deal did not simply coerce the union to accept the new technology. Instead, perhaps realizing that the two sides would have to live with each other for the long term, both parties engaged in a back-and-forth process that led to a more balanced package deal. While management won its top-priority right to implement labor-saving technology on the docks and a new arbitration mechanism to oversee this right, the ILWU would retain what it regarded as a core prerogative: jurisdiction over all remaining and newly created work, as well as all rail and yard planning functions. This effectively meant a lifetime employment guarantee for key classes of union members. Pension plans were more adequately funded, and wage increases were provided.

As the design of the overall deal crystallized, its advantages to each side led to an unexpected provision: a *six*-year contract, rather than the *three*-year period of previous contracts. Within eighteen months after the new contract was signed, coastwide container throughput increased by 10 percent. With this volume increase came a reversal of the union's longtime membership decline; in Southern California alone, more than eight hundred new longshore workers were registered.[11] The design of the deal created lasting value for both sides.

For further perspective on deal design, let's look at a dispute in the midwestern United States, in which environmentalists and farmers opposed a power company's plans to build a dam. From all appearances, the parties had deeply felt, irreconcilable positions: "absolutely yes" versus "no way."

And yet, there was a superior deal design waiting to be teased out, if the parties could get past their bargaining positions to their underlying interests. In reality, the farmers were worried about reduced water flow below the dam, the environmentalists were focused on the downstream habitat of several whooping cranes—an endangered species—and the power company needed both new capacity soon and a greener image. After a costly legal stalemate, the three groups devised an interest-driven agreement that all of them considered preferable to continued court warfare. The carefully designed and mutually beneficial agreement—involving a completely new set of issues and interests— included a smaller dam built on a fast track, water flow guarantees, down-stream habitat protection, and a trust fund to enhance whooping crane habitats elsewhere.

Do potentially complementary differences of interest, priority, cost, or value exist? If not, can the scope of the negotiations be enlarged to enable value-creating deal designs? In other words, can changes in the setup lead to better deals? As we can see from the cases described above, the answer is yes, remind-ing us that the components of 3-D strategies often interact. To see another example that involves an even broader scope, look to the diplomatic realm, in which potentially valuable bilateral deals can sometimes be impossible unless a third party with complementary differences of interest can be included. Con-sider the result of Henry Kissinger's move to add the United States as another party to a negotiation that was stuck when it involved only Egypt and Israel:

> [T]he circular structure of payment was essential to promoting agreement among the parties: Egypt improved the image of the United States in the Arab world, especially among the oil-producing states; the United States gave Israel large amounts of military and financial aid; and Israel supplied Egypt with territory. Indeed a bilateral exchange between Egypt and Israel would not have succeeded since each did not want what the other could supply.[12]

In *Co-opetition*, their influential book on business strategy, Adam Branden-burger and Barry Nalebuff explored the concept of the "value net," or the col-lection of players whose potential combination and agreement can create value.[13] Setup moves can often be understood as "weaving" the possible value net by scanning beyond the limits of a contemplated transaction for compati-ble players with complementary capabilities or valuations. Such moves to reset the table may enable value-creating deal designs that profitably incorpo-rate these additional players.

Stress Problem-Solving Tactics

Most people think of tactics when they think about "negotiations": What happens at the table? What moves are likely to create the maximum possible value while capturing a full share of that value for your side?

In answer, we make two observations: first, focusing on only one dimension of 3-D Negotiation is a mistake, for the reasons outlined previously. You wouldn't study a physical phenomenon by first closing one eye. Success in negotiations requires all of the skills that a negotiator can bring to bear. Second, most successful negotiations aren't driven by flashy, dazzling, or Byzantine tactics. They are driven by behavior that is serious, substance oriented, and reasonably predictable. People who sit down across the table from you don't necessarily expect to deal with Mother Teresa, but they don't want to deal with Machiavelli, either. They expect you to earn their trust—and vice versa.

In subsequent chapters, we'll have a lot to say about tactics. Here's a representative foreshadowing:

- For pure value-claiming (i.e., price) deals, accurately assess and favorably shape perceptions of what we call the "zone of possible agreement," set aggressive targets, shape the other side's perceptions advantageously, make credible commitments, and seek attractive "fairness principles" to resolve the distributive problem.

- In order to both create and claim value, push to get behind incompatible positions to understand deeper interests, build trust, improve communication, share information, foster creativity, and seek an orientation in which the parties are side-by-side against the problem, rather than face-to-face against each other.

- Listen, learn, and adopt a persuasive style that is both empathetic and assertive.

- Foster an appealing and productive negotiation process and atmosphere.

- Take steps to productively manage the tension between the cooperative moves that are necessary to create value jointly and the individual moves that are needed to claim value unilaterally.

Putting It Together: Acquiring a Division

We've now looked at the *individual* components of a 3-D strategy: setting up the right negotiation, designing value-creating deals, and stressing problem-solving tactics. To see these three elements aligned in a 3-D strategy *as a whole*, let's leave behind the classic "old economy" union-management confrontation we described above, and examine the approach of a large biotech firm eyeing an acquisition.

In this case, we advised the head of business development for the biotech firm concerning an acquisition opportunity—a division of an agribusiness firm—that he had identified as potentially quite attractive on scientific grounds. After preliminary research and inquiries, he sketched a quick party map and took a quick cut at interests, no-deal options, and potential deals (see figure 3-1). The assessment of the likely deal/no-deal balance for each party revealed a risk: both *internal* and *external* blocking coalitions could easily form if the business development head simply announced his potential interest in the acquisition.

Inside the biotech firm, for example, the relevant research chief might see the agribusiness division's approach as competitive to the route his own group was taking, and potentially even a source of embarrassment (i.e., buying this division might seem to cast doubt on the wisdom of the internal R&D group's chosen strategy). Meanwhile, given that cash was tight, the biotech firm's CFO—and most likely its CEO—would probably balk at the prospect of this deal. On the external front, the CEO of the agribusiness firm that contained the target division had recently praised that division in public and had committed significant resources to it. Across the party map, therefore, barriers

FIGURE 3-1

Party map with likely positions

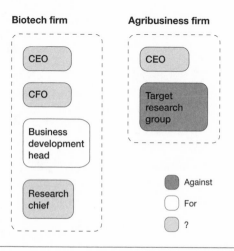

dotted the internal and external landscape: the *aggregate* deal/no-deal balance did not look promising, with potential internal and external blockers.

Here's a useful exercise. Try to visualize those parties whose current view of the deal/no-deal balance tilts toward their best no-deal options as flashing red, those who are cautious or negative as flashing yellow, and those who see a deal as the better choice as green. When our client, the business development head of the biotech firm, tried this, his party map looked like a mass of flashing yellow and red. How could he convert these to mostly greens? Specifically, how could he build a winning coalition on behalf of the deal—and preempt potential blockers?

To craft a 3-D strategy, we urged that the business development head think back to Daniele Vare's advice. How could he let "them"—his own CEO, other internal stakeholders, and, ultimately, the CEO of the agribusiness firm—have *his* way? We urged him to imagine what would have to be in each of their heads to elicit a "yes" to his deal, rather than the "no" that would surely result from the present situation.

To begin with, what would his own CEO have to see in order say "yes"? After puzzling about this question, the business development head decided that if his CFO and research head were on board, the CEO might look favorably on the acquisition. Then, a conversation with his firm's research head elicited the fact that the agribusiness unit was pursuing a complementary scientific approach on an underlying genetic mechanism. In this conversation, it became clear that the target agricultural group's approach could be independently attractive, at a minimum, as a scientific hedge. Even without the agricultural applications, the biotech possibilities for human use were quite attractive. As the business development head talked with his research colleague, the research head became more and more positive on the possibilities—and less concerned with his group looking bad—especially if the proposed deal could be sold as the research head's own initiative.

Meanwhile, the CFO, learning of the research group's enthusiasm, said he'd approve of the deal if it could be structured mainly as a stock transaction, to preserve scarce cash. With the CFO and research head provisionally on board, the business development executive pitched to the CEO, who quickly threw his support behind the proposal.

Indeed, the CEO was keen to pick up the phone then and there, to pitch his counterpart CEO on the possibility. We urged him to reconsider this impulse. Based on our assessment, if approached "cold," the target CEO would likely see the potential deal/no-deal balance adversely and quickly dismiss the possibility.

As far as we could determine, he saw this research division as a source of future competitive advantage (picture a flashing red light here, too!). Thus we counseled "our" CEO against getting right into serious talks. Was there a better approach, one with a more promising setup? Specifically, how could we "let the target CEO have our way"?

We then imagined what conditions would maximize the chances of the target CEO saying "yes." The odds seemed highest if we could get his CFO on board and also get his research scientists enthused about the possibility. How should we orchestrate a 3-D strategy for accomplishing these goals? Mapping backward from our main objective—a "yes" from the target CEO—we decided to start by encouraging our biotech scientists to meet their agribusiness research counterparts at an upcoming professional meeting. Ideally, this would help develop some rapport and a better understanding of their approach, which turned out to be almost exclusively focused on livestock applications.

As these technical conversations proceeded, an idea for a revised deal design began to take shape. What about a research collaboration on the underlying genetic mechanisms? Each side could contribute intellectual property, the use of specialized facilities, and the time of key scientists. Any resulting human applications could be carved out for exclusive use by the biotech firm, and any purely animal-oriented applications could be reserved for the agribusiness corporation. While the proposal was discussed only in very general, hypothetical terms, the scientists on both sides seemed quite positive about the concept. They also appeared to get along with each other personally and to clearly respect the quality of each other's work (although confidentiality concerns sharply limited specific disclosures).

While the scientists were becoming acquainted with each other, we asked around to learn whose opinion the agribusiness firm's CEO valued regarding acquisitions and related deals. We worked backward from the CFO and turned up an analyst in the finance department whom the CFO deeply respected. Given her technical and finance background, this analyst would almost certainly do the valuation work on this difficult-to-value and somewhat unorthodox deal. After all, if the deal could only count on stock as a "balancing currency"—a prerequisite of our "own" CFO—there would be lots of tricky questions about how to value things like intellectual property, facilities use, scientific time, and development rights.

So after initial "very exploratory" contact with the target CEO, we created a legitimate rationale for extensively meeting with this key analyst. We invested enormous time in ensuring that she *endorsed* the deal concept, and into the unusual way we thought the potential contributions to the collaboration should be valued. In this way, when "serious" negotiations began at the CEO level, the ground was prepared. The CEO turned both to his scientists and to his CFO, who turned to his key analyst, who essentially made the desired case for us—from the inside. In other words, careful sequencing and reconfiguring of the deal transformed flashing red and yellow—potential blocking coalitions in both firms—into "green" members of a winning coalition. (See figure 3-2 for a summary of this sequential approach.)

In later chapters, we will dig much more deeply into the logic of backward mapping—that is, sequentially building a winning coalition and forestalling potential blocking ones. The inputs to this analysis are informed assessments, continually refined, of how each party sees the deal/no-deal balance, both individually and in the aggregate. The output of this thinking can be a 3-D strategy, leading to a setup with a more promising scope and sequence, including a much more favorable overall deal/no-deal balance.

FIGURE 3-2

Sequential approach to building a winning coalition

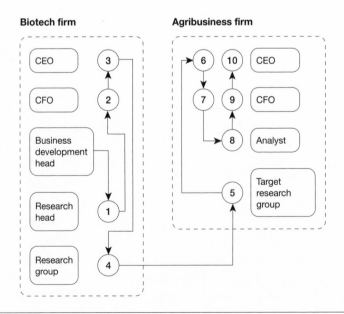

A Few Concluding Thoughts

In introducing you to 3-D strategies, we've already emphasized the fact that a problem encountered in one dimension can often push you into another dimension for a solution. This has two implications. First, if you mistake—for example—a setup flaw for a deal-design flaw, you're very likely to head down the wrong road for a solution. Second, even if you see a barrier for exactly what it is—for instance, a deal-design flaw that is, indeed, a deal-design flaw—you may have to look elsewhere for a remedy. So far we've used the Stemberg/Staples story, the case of LockStore, the longshoremen's contract, and the biotech-agribusiness case to illustrate this point; we'll present additional examples in subsequent chapters. Looking across dimensions for solutions to barriers is a very important aspect of 3-D Negotiation, and it's a characteristic that distinguishes our approach from most others. It's something like attacking a problem in your circulatory system by changing your diet: it's a promising approach only if you understand the underlying connections.

Our second concluding thought has to do with what might be called the *concurrency* of our three dimensions. In these introductory chapters, we've tried to present our ideas in the most logical sequence—specifically, first you *diagnose* (in the form of a barriers audit) and then you *act* (by developing a 3-D Negotiation strategy). But as you might suspect, the reality is a lot more complex. Negotiating effectively is not like following a recipe: step 1, step 2, . . . then you're done.

As you'll see, the essence of 3-D Negotiation is doing many things well, sometimes all at once.

Throughout this book, for narrative purposes, we're going to break things down into their component parts following a 3-2-1 "dimensional" logic from broadest architectural possibilities for the negotiation to narrowest face-to-face moves at the table: setup, deal design, then tactics. In that kind of deconstruction, it's easy to lose sight of the fact that in 3-D Negotiation, many things tend to "stay in play." Our approach bears only a general resemblance to building a house, where you pour the foundation first, and then—with confidence that it will stay put—you frame out the upper stories. It's more like flying a plane through unsettled weather patterns over challenging terrain. Yes, you chart a smart course with a destination in mind. But in flight, you spend a lot of time adjusting that plan, responding to challenges and opportunities that arise as you go.

Maybe you'll get to your original destination by a different route—or maybe you'll get to a different endpoint entirely, because that turns out to be where you need to go, or have to go.

- A 3-D strategy is an aligned combination of setup, deal design, and tactical moves to overcome barriers to agreement. It enables you to "let them have your way in 3-D." Following a barriers audit, it requires that you:

  - ➤ Set up the right negotiation.

  - ➤ Get the parties right. Get the interests right. Get no-deal options and the deal/no-deal balance right. Get the sequence of approach right. Get basic process choices right.

  - ➤ Design value-creating deals.

  - ➤ Stress problem-solving tactics.

- Remember that a barrier encountered in one dimension can often push you into other dimensions for a solution.

- While we present the elements of 3-D strategies as separate classes of moves "away from the table," "on the drawing board," and "at the table," they tend to happen more concurrently in practice.

Part Two

Set Up the Right Negotiation

"Away from the Table"

Chapter Four

Get All the Parties Right

H ERE'S A PRESCRIPTION that may at first sound self-evident: start preparations for a negotiation by thinking hard about the interested parties.

Well—you may be asking—how hard can *that* be? Aren't the "interested parties" just you and the other guy (or maybe your side and the other side)? If you're buying a car, isn't it just you and the car dealer? If you're looking to beef up your operating budget, isn't it just you and your boss? If you're under pressure to save money in the procurement process, isn't it just you and the vendor(s)?

The answer is "yes and no." In some cases, of course, the interested parties do indeed boil down pretty quickly to just a few. In the case of buying a car, it probably *is* just you and the dealer—but hold on, the relevant parties to the deal may actually be you, the sales rep, the sales manager, your spouse, and even your kids, not to mention the other dealers still in contention for your purchase. But there are many negotiations in which the interested parties are far from obvious—and if you don't identify them correctly, the negotiations may be in deep trouble from the start.

In previous chapters, we've already provided some illustrations of this challenge. Recall, for example, LockStore, the company with the slick new gasoline-leak "sniffing" technology. Its sales force was confidently—and pointlessly—dealing with the wrong customers. Or, think back to the more complex sets of parties that were key to success in the cases of Staples/ Stemberg, the shippers/longshoremen, or the biotech/agribusiness acquisition we just examined in the last chapter. As these examples illustrate, going with only with the obvious parties can obscure the real keys to the deal.

So in your new role as a sophisticated 3-D Negotiator, you need to concentrate on getting the setup right. You need to think through the *full set* of involved and influential parties: both actual and potential. Who is now missing from the table but should be there? Conversely, who is now at the table but *shouldn't* be there? For great negotiators, even those dealing with seemingly simple bargaining processes, getting the full set of parties right often calls for going well beyond a mechanical listing of the obvious. It calls for *the exercise of a disciplined imagination.* That's the focus of this chapter.

Practically speaking, it's impossible to separate thinking about the *parties* from thinking about their *interests* (the subject of our next chapter). So here we'll consider the two factors together, with a primary focus on the parties, before focusing primarily on interests in chapter 5.

Sketching the All-Party Map: The Seven Key Questions

In assessing the parties, we use the term *all-party map* as a way of describing what we're aiming for (and to some extent, how we aim to get there). Each of the three words has significance. "All" cautions against too narrow a view. "Party" implies a constituency that is more or less organized. And "Map" reminds us that we're looking for more than a simple list; we're looking to get the relationships among the parties right. The all-party map depicts the *full set* of those who are either actually or potentially involved in the discussions, as well as their relationships to each other. By *relationships*, we mean not only formal organizational relationships, but also how the parties are connected in the decision-making process, and how lines of influence run.

The best way to start the mapping process is through a series of seven organizing questions, the discussion of which serves as the core of this chapter. They are:

1. Does your all-party map include the *highest-value* players, to ensure that your deal can create the greatest possible value?

2. Does your all-party map include the full set of potentially influential players, including those who may be part of the "informal negotiation"?

3. To help identify potential blockers (as well as potential allies), does your all-party map include those involved in the internal decision-making and governance processes?

4. Does your all-party map pinpoint agents or representatives who may have the wrong incentives and the ability to shape the decisions of

other parties by distorting or selectively providing information in a self-serving way?

5. Does your all-party map anticipate potential negotiations with those who must approve the deal?

6. Does your all-party map take account of those who must implement the agreement?

7. Are too many parties unnecessarily complicating the negotiation?

Let's consider each of these questions in turn.

Have You Included the Highest-Value Players?

To illustrate what we mean by an all-party map, let's visit the owners of a niche packaging company with an innovative technology and a novel product. These owners are deep in price negotiations to sell the company to one of two potential "within-industry" buyers. Both potential buyers are larger than the company that is in play. Both have offered a low purchase price—so low, in fact, as to be barely credible.

The party map of figure 4-1 illustrates how the owners initially see (and, from their side of the table, are conducting) the negotiations.

At this point, the sellers ask the first of our key questions: *Does your all-party map include the "highest-value" players, to ensure that your deal can create the most possible value?* Frustrated by the two low bids and the lack of any upward movement, the selling company's managers decide to think more broadly. A brainstorming process suggests that one of the company's major customers—a large consumer goods firm—might place a high value on having exclusive access to the niche player's technologies and products. Based on

FIGURE 4-1

Party map with two potential industry buyers

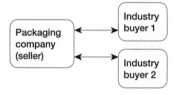

that hypothesis, the selling company's owners open negotiations on that front as well, leading to the party map shown in figure 4-2.

Including the potential higher-value player changes the whole dynamic of the situation. Industry buyers #1 and #2 must either raise their bids or risk losing access to a unique technology. Including the potential "high-value" player—the one that might value the deal the most and whose presence might lead to the greatest value creation as well as adding competition to the deal— was key to success.

This case, like the Staples example in chapter 1, should prompt your team to ask consistently, "*Who might value this deal the most, and is that player part of the negotiation?*" Answering this question often calls for a wider scan. But "wider scan" doesn't necessarily mean new *external* parties. Sometimes the answer can be found *inside* the company with which you are already negotiating. Consider the common situation of a supplier bargaining with an important customer. Suppose that both the supplier and client firms have made a very public point of developing a partnership in the interest of high quality, a reliable supply, and a good price (from the client's point of view); and a steady flow of orders (from the supplier's standpoint). But suppose, for the sake of argument, that somewhere deep down inside the ranks of the client company, the procurement agent is hammering on his counterparts at the favored supplier, grinding pennies out of them to help him meet his monthly targets.

On several occasions, frustrated suppliers have turned to us for negotiating help in dealing with such an individual, whom they tend to describe in unfriendly terms. (A "margin-shredding animal" is one of the colorful, yet printable, descriptions that we've heard.) "It's not fair," the suppliers'

FIGURE 4-2

Adding a potential higher-value player

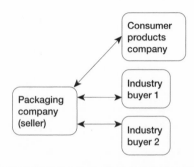

representatives say to us, in so many words. "Up at the CEO level, they're making happy talk and extolling the virtues of partnership—and meanwhile, down here on our level, they're beating us up!"

What is to be done? First, let's assume that the supplier offers *real value* to the customer (if you don't offer real value, even a 3-D approach won't save you!). In that case, the supplier has to make the most cogent, compelling case to the procurement agent. But in this example, even with a value-adding proposition, these conversations are going nowhere fast. What the supplier *also* has to do is find and nurture an influential internal champion elsewhere on the other side—one who really understands and benefits from the supplier's added quality and service (the internal higher-value player). Such a champion (or better yet, *team* of champions) can often be induced to help persuade, even pressure, the agent on the supplier's behalf—sometimes directly, and sometimes via links with senior management who have stake in the partnership.

The simple negotiation between the supplier and the purchasing agent can be represented by what we sometimes call a *naive party map*, as shown in figure 4-3; on this map, the supplier and the procurement agent could sit across the table from each other for a very long time. No amount of blustering or empathizing on the part of the supplier (i.e., tactics—the first of our three dimensions) is likely to have much of an impact.

Now let's look at an all-party map that depicts the supplier's cross-cutting coalition with the higher-value internal champion—an alliance that works against the procurement agent's tactics. This setup is shown in figure 4-4.

However, it's important to keep in mind that thinking of the internal champion as a classic "influencer," while not exactly wrong, is incomplete. An exclusive focus on the political dimension (i.e., "who has the chairman's ear?") can miss the real motivation for that influence. It's the uniquely high value that the supplier offers to the champion—value that is potentially at risk if there is no deal—that gives the internal high-value player a stake in the success of the negotiation.

FIGURE 4-3

Naive party map

FIGURE 4-4

All-party map with the internal champion as the higher-value player

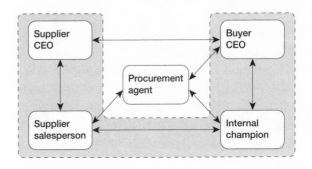

(Note to procurement people: Obviously, you want to head off such potential end runs, which you probably can do by focusing your one-on-one negotiations *on the merits* of the transaction. And, of course, generating real competition, often in the form of auctions, to get comparable value from alternative suppliers will help a great deal, too. More on this, and related points, later.)

To summarize: have you ensured that the high-value players are part of your negotiation? Finding them often requires a fresh look: outside traditional channels, inside your counterpart organization, in other parts of a fragmented value chain, or elsewhere. The logic of business strategy can be very helpful in this process.[1] Psychologists confirm that we often look too narrowly, mainly to familiar circles, in determining the parties with whom we should negotiate.[2] If you are not looking for new negotiating parties in a systematic, disciplined fashion, chances are that you won't find them. You may be stuck negotiating—maybe even negotiating with great skill—in the context of a setup that can't bear fruit.

Have You Mapped All the Potentially Influential Players?

On to the second of our seven questions: *Does your all-party map include the full set of potentially influential players, including those who may be part of the "informal negotiation"?* A friend of ours was interested in purchasing a very desirable house from its architect-owner, who—although he had designed and obviously loved the place—had put it on the market. The property was listed at a relatively high price. But from early interactions, it was pretty clear to our friend that simply trading price proposals wouldn't do the trick. It

FIGURE 4-5

Naive party map

began to look like the owner was actually reluctant to sell, sometimes taking the property off the market even when there were good offers on the table. Something else, it seemed, was going on. Figure 4-5 shows the naive party map of this situation.

So instead of just firing off more and higher offers to buy, and thus effectively bidding against himself, our friend tried to understand more about the underlying dynamics of the on-again, off-again deal. By talking with the real estate agent, our friend learned that the owner had recently remarried, and that his new spouse had two problems with the property in question. First, she saw it as an undesirable extension of his first wife, and second, she was concerned about an overall decline in the local housing market. In light of this information, a different approach seemed to make sense.

Now, rather than pushing for closure, our friend consciously *prolonged* the negotiation process. He also began accompanying his offers with a series of brief but compelling analyses of how the sale proceeds—if invested wisely—might grow handsomely in coming years, in contrast to the risks of leaving those same resources as equity in a house in a declining market. Through the tireless efforts of the real estate agent—who legally worked for the seller, but who only profited in the event of a sale—our friend made sure the spouse also saw, read, and thought carefully about these unusual offers/analyses. Figure 4-6 gives you a better idea of who needed to be involved to close this tricky negotiation.

FIGURE 4-6

All-party map with influential spouse included

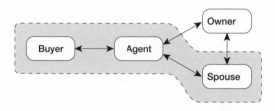

Will it surprise you to learn that the deal went through nicely, with a de facto coalition of the buyer, agent, and spouse all variously working on the reluctant architect-owner?

Effective salespeople use this approach all the time, even if they don't consciously draw up all-party maps. A great salesperson seeks to identify and win over the ultimate decision makers, who may be different from those at the table. In many settings, in fact, an informal negotiation can envelop and even overshadow the formal one. You should always be on the lookout for this "enveloping" process, mapping the parties who won't necessarily be involved in signing the contract or agreement, but who have influence nonetheless.

There may be cultural dimensions to this challenge. Negotiators in Japan, for example, need to pay careful attention to the large industrial/financial groups, the *keiretsu*, that are linked by a dense web of business ties and cross-shareholdings. Even though the companies have independent identities, knowledge of the broader relationships and their implications can be critical. Similarly, German financial giant Allianz is sometimes referred to as the "spider in the web" as a result of its widespread decision-making influence in that sector. In Italy, you ignore at your peril the economic decision-making role of powerful families and companies—the *salotto buono* ("good drawing room"). And of course influence can take more sinister form, such as the role of the Russian "mafia" and other protection/extortion rackets. In these and similar settings, good local advice can be critical to drawing up the right all-party map.

Even in the absence of these fairly fixed but informal webs of influence, an "informal" negotiating process may draw in a range of other players. The roles of such potential players can be obvious if you are looking for them—and a nasty shock if you are not. For example: Stone Container Corporation, a U.S. entity, was negotiating the terms of a major forest project in Honduras, a poor Central American country that had only recently democratized and had a long history of strained relationships with the U.S. government and U.S. multinationals. Formally, the deal had to be done with the Honduran president and his relevant ministries. As Jerry Freeman, the responsible Stone executive, explained, "We were down there dealing with who we thought had the power, the responsibility, the authority [i.e., the president]. Connected with that was their Forest Service, [which] had the scientific background. So, we had the science and they were going to be the quality control on the program that we did."[3]

This view was legally correct, but it was naive. Inadvertently—but quite predictably, to well-placed observers outside the process—Stone's narrow negotiating strategy triggered widespread suspicion. It forced the involvement of the Honduran Congress, labor unions, political parties, potential business competitors, and indigenous people in the affected region, as well as domestic and international environmental groups. Despite proposing what was arguably a very valuable project for virtually all concerned—especially relative to the likely alternatives—Stone became enmeshed in a complex, multiparty process. As Freeman later colorfully lamented, "We were caught in a drive-by shooting with no place to hide."[4]

He need not have been surprised. An informed assessment of Honduran history vis-à-vis U.S. corporations in natural resource projects, together with an understanding of the fragile status of the Honduran presidency, would have yielded a fuller and more accurate all-party map. It almost certainly would have pointed toward a less formal but more broadly based process, involving many additional parties from the outset.

Have You Included Those Involved in the Decision-Making and Governance Processes?

Less experienced negotiators sometimes become mesmerized by the aggregate economics of a deal and forget about the interests of players who may be in a position to torpedo it. That is the focus of our third question: *To help identify potential blockers (as well as potential allies), does your all-party map include those involved in the internal decision-making and governance processes?* Earlier, we discussed the proposed merger of pharmaceutical giants Glaxo and SmithKline Beecham. That merger went off the rails when insiders at both companies began working to block the deal—and something like $20 billion in added shareholder wealth disappeared when it looked like the deal was coming undone.

This episode highlights two related lessons. First, while favorable overall economics are generally necessary for a deal to succeed, they are often not sufficient, given the range of interests that may matter. Second, keep all potentially influential internal players on your radar screen—especially those who may wield blocking power. Don't lose sight of their interests or their capacity to affect the deal.

The question of who might potentially be involved in a deal, and who might have the power and inclination to block it, can have unexpected answers, especially in less familiar locales with distinctive decision processes, governance, and motivations. For those accustomed to North American shareholder-based corporate governance, for example, it may come as a surprise to encounter Germany's policy of "codetermination," which among other things calls for

50 percent labor representation on supervisory boards of directors. In another instance, a Canadian company that we worked with—which at that time was trying to cut a joint-venture deal with a privately owned Chinese manufacturer—was puzzled by the prominent role played by a local Communist Party official on the Chinese negotiating team.

More broadly, what is overwhelmingly "rational" for the whole may not be so for the parts. When dealing with "IBM" or the "Army," for example, remember that you are not dealing with a monolith. Instead, you face specific, idiosyncratic individuals, each enmeshed in a complex decision-making and governance structure, and each with his or her own interests and potential to hinder or help the deal you want.

Have You Mapped Influential Parties with the Wrong Incentives?

Now we address our fourth question: *Does your all-party map pinpoint agents or representatives who may have the wrong incentives, as well the capacity to filter information in a self-serving way?* In some cases, a representative or agent close to the process inherently has the wrong interests for your purposes. Suppose you're on the compensation committee of a company's board of directors, and you're trying to negotiate an appropriate salary for an incoming CEO. To whom should you turn for assistance?

To answer that question, let's look at a real-life case from the other side of the table. Joe Bachelder, an expert lawyer in executive pay deals, was representing a client who had been selected by a company to be its next chief executive and was working out his compensation package. After the first negotiating session, Mr. Bachelder took his client aside and confidently informed him that he would end up with everything he wanted from the negotiation—despite the board's discouragingly tough stance thus far. How could Bachelder be so confident of total victory? Because, he explained, the board had put the company's well-regarded internal general counsel in charge of the negotiations.

Why was this a mistake? It was not an issue of effectiveness: the company's general counsel was undoubtedly an honest and skilled negotiator at the table. Yet, as Mr. Bachelder happily informed his client, "When this is over, you're going to be that guy's boss. He knows that. He can't fight you too hard on anything."[5]

Obviously, the board put the wrong party in charge; it should have hired an outside specialist to help with this particular negotiation—one with properly aligned interests and incentives. No matter how good the firm's general counsel was at the table, and no matter how loyal he was to his board, he couldn't be expected to sacrifice his own long-term interests just to save the company some (relatively short) near-term money. (Moreover there is the experience and expertise factor: at most, the firm's general counsel may have done two or three CEO compensation deals, while Bachelder does them daily. Not only should the board's representative have the right interests, he or she should know all the tricks of this specialized kind of deal.)

Even a contract that appears to align economic incentives may fail to solve the wrong-agent problem. For example, after a small business suffered a fire, its owner decided that her insurance company was dragging its feet and hired an experienced consultant to negotiate the fire-damage claims on her behalf. The consultant would get a fixed fee, plus a sliding bonus based on the settlement amount.

The consultant very quickly negotiated a settlement, but after talking with other people who had filed similar claims, the owner became disenchanted with the amount. She realized that her agent, who had been dealing for years with the same small set of insurance companies, generally negotiated rapid claims settlements that were economical to the insurers. Why? Because it was far more valuable to the consultant to keep his overall practice going smoothly than to bargain harder to earn an incremental incentive fee from this one client—that would risk of disrupting the deal flow and inviting retaliation from the insurance firms. In effect, the business owner was a one-time bit player in a long-term, tacit "game" that powerfully aligned the interests of the insurance company with those of the consultant.

It can get worse. A very successful Australian executive once recounted to us how, decades before, as a young bank clerk in Ireland scarcely making $5,000 a year, he had been a passionate and skilled member of an Irish hurling team. (Hurling is a ball-and-stick game, somewhat akin to lacrosse.) Hearing of his talent, an agent approached him with a compelling offer: play on weekends for a Boston team, and the owner would pay his round-trip airfare plus $350 per game!

This win-win arrangement went on all season until the finals, which the Boston team lost in a squeaker. Deeply disappointed, the Irish player-bank clerk apologized to the team's owner after the game, who tried to cheer him up. "Yes, we did lose this year," the owner said, "but we did much better than before. You were a phenomenal help to my team. And it can't have been that bad for you—picking up $700 per game, plus airfare!"

The agent, of course, was nowhere to be found.

The "wrong agent" comes in many forms. Put yourself in the very uncomfortable shoes of Nicholas Kristof, a *New York Times* columnist, who had written an article from Saddam Hussein's Iraq, detailing how (among many other abuses) the Iraqi government had tortured a Muslim leader. Kristof and his official Iraqi government "minder/translator" were summoned to account. Kristof describes being called to the ministry, where he was

> *menacingly denounced by two of Saddam's henchmen. But neither man could speak English and they hadn't actually read the offending column . . . [so] my government minder took my column and translated it for them. I saw my life flash before my eyes. But my minder's job was to spy on me, and he worried that my tough column would reflect badly on his spying. Plus, he was charging me $100 a day, and he would lose a fortune if I was expelled, or worse. So he translated my column very selectively. There was no mention of burning beards or nails in heads. He left out whole paragraphs. When he finished, the two senior officials shrugged and let me off scot-free.*[6]

Kristof was fortunate indeed that this "representative" of the Iraqi government—like many agents in more routine settings—had dramatically misaligned incentives from his superiors, and also had the capacity to control and shape the "information" he passed upward.[7]

In contrast, if the person on the other side of the table is a powerless representative of an autocratic boss who doesn't delegate—think of ITT's Harold Geneen, or the Navy's Admiral Hyman Rickover—the real trick lies in figuring out how to connect, if only indirectly, with the real decision maker. That should be your central focus in dealing with autocrats. Your real job is not to persuade the powerless—by formulating endless proposals, giving away information, and making concessions—but to extend your party map.

Ideally, you will have skilled and informed agents faithfully representing you, and they will make negotiating choices that are exactly aligned with your interests. (Indeed, you yourself may act as an agent, representing your organization in deal making with others who are agents of their firms.) But as the previous examples indicate, the reality of agency often departs from the ideal.

We'll have much more to say in later chapters about the potential tensions between principals and agents.[8] For now, as you construct your all-party map, pay special attention to the agents who are there—as well as those that should or should not be there. In particular, try to understand their relationships, their interests, and their ability to filter information and shape decisions away from your direct scrutiny.

Have You Anticipated Negotiations with Those Who Must Approve the Deal?

Most of us are keenly aware of how seemingly bilateral dealings—for example, to buy a cooperative apartment or renovate a house in a historical district—can quickly expand to include neighbors, co-op boards, historical commissions, and zoning authorities. Depending on the situation, vetting the proposed deal in advance with those who ultimately must approve it—before anyone is irrevocably committed to the transaction—can be a wise move. Which brings us to our fifth question: *Does your all-party map anticipate potential negotiations with those who must approve the deal and those who might block it?*

In the United States, for example, certain transactions require the participation of the Securities and Exchange Commission (SEC), the Federal Trade Commission (FTC), and Justice Department before they can be consummated. So when Travelers Group and Citicorp first began *contemplating* a merger—a huge transaction, and one that surely would trigger every federal tripwire—the heads of the two firms together visited Federal Reserve Chairman Alan Greenspan to get a reading on the Fed's likely attitude.[9]

What those two CEOs understood is that regulatory participation implies a prior active negotiation over acceptable terms of the deal, not merely an arm's-length thumbs-up or thumbs-down at the end of the process. Even for smaller deals without regulatory oversight, the broader point holds: you should build the approval stage into your initial party map and strategy.

Have You Considered Those Who Must Implement the Deal?

A close cousin of the "wrong agent" problem discussed above often shows up on the back end of the deal. Be cautious when one team—such as the business development unit—negotiates an alliance or acquisition by means of a process driven chiefly by the numbers, or by legal considerations, or by any other single dominant factor. Why? Because when the deal is done, that team is likely to "throw it over the fence" to operational management, which then has the unenviable job of making it work after the fact. Thus we ask the sixth of our seven questions: *Does your all-party map take account of those who must implement the agreement?*

In almost every negotiation, prior involvement by those responsible for implementing the deal is preferable. Jerry Kaplan, founder of GO Technologies—an early pen-computing firm—was especially critical of the process his firm was subjected to by IBM while Big Blue was negotiating a complex investment in GO. As he later recalled: "Rather than empowering the responsible party to make the deal, IBM assigns a professional negotiator, who knows or cares little for the substance of the agreement but has absolute authority . . . The negotiator begins by assembling a list of all the interested internal constituents, all of whom are free to add new requirement . . . or block some minor concession . . ."[10] With such a negotiating process in place, there's very little chance that the right minds will meet. And when it comes to implementation, the results are almost certain to be disappointing.

In some cases, investment bankers or other deal makers with a powerful interest in making a transaction happen can divert the principals' attention from possibly fatal conflicts in the underlying "social contract"—briefly, the spirit, rather than the letter, of the deal (to be discussed in depth in chapter 11). For example, when Matsushita Electric paid $6.59 billion for MCA—owner of Universal Pictures, record companies, and theme parks—the Japanese consumer electronics firm was mainly interested in ensuring a steady flow of creative "software" for its global hardware businesses. Senior MCA management, meanwhile, agreed to the acquisition largely in the expectation that its cash-rich Japanese parent could provide capital for acquiring the additional properties—a record company, a TV network, and so on—that MCA felt it needed to compete with rivals like Disney and Cap Cities/ABC.

These were two *very different* perspectives, to put it mildly. In order to get the deal done, Michael Ovitz, the unorthodox corporate matchmaker, successfully contrived to keep the parties mostly *apart* during the process—managing expectations separately on each side and building momentum until the deal was virtually closed. In retrospect, it became clear that neither side performed a determined, independent due diligence on the underlying social contract. Yes, this was in part the result of the cultural chasms that divided old-line industrial Japan, creative Hollywood, and the New York financial community—but it was also heavily due to the role of a third party. Because each side had a distorted idea of the other's expectations, there was considerable postdeal friction. A few short years later, Matsushita sold MCA to Seagram, incurring both a substantial financial drubbing (to the tune of ¥165 billion) and a considerable loss of face. Had those ultimately responsible for implementing the merger had more direct involvement, it is unlikely that this unworkable deal would ever have been done.

Are There Too Many Parties?

You might assume from our discussions so far that in 3-D Negotiations more is always merrier. Not so. Ask yourself our seventh question: *Are too many parties unnecessarily complicating the negotiation?* It's true that in our practice, we most often find potentially useful—or even vital—parties that somehow have been left out of the process. But it is also easy to err in the other direction. Sometimes, when you make a sincere effort to include all potential stakeholders, however minor, the process simply gets out of hand.

Many setups become more tractable when they are simplified. This may happen in advance—as, for example, when the two dominant industry players in a technical standards negotiation agree between themselves first, and then sequentially bring the smaller players on board, rather than engaging in a full-blown, unwieldy, multiparty process up front. Or it may happen when the process is under way. If it becomes clear, for example, that negotiating agents with their own agendas are unnecessarily prolonging the process, the principals may decide to get rid of those agents and attempt to dispose of the issue via a direct negotiation.

Perhaps less obviously, the scope of a deal design chosen for a particular transaction can be shrunk to serve a specific purpose. When Bell Atlantic and NYNEX planned a "merger of equals" involving ownership changes on each side, they discovered that this structure would require separate negotiations with regulatory authorities in each of the *thirteen* states served by the two companies! To minimize these kinds of negotiations—which (at the risk of understatement) promised to be intensely political—a functionally equivalent deal design was developed, under the terms of which Bell Atlantic was the nominal acquirer.[11]

From Parties to Interests

We began this chapter with a rhetorical question: aren't the parties to a deal simply you and the person on the other side of the table? By now, it should be clear that except in the simplest of negotiating contexts, this is only rarely so. In this chapter, you've seen a number of cases in which the would-be negotiators got the parties wrong—and paid a price for that failure. The wrong map took them to the wrong place.

And yet, most 1-D books on negotiation persist in taking the parties as a given and focus mainly on improving tactics and interpersonal process at the table. We hope we've persuaded you that this isn't good enough—that you have to use your imagination in a disciplined way to craft the right all-party map, and thereby to ensure that the right parties really are involved.

As we consider many more cases in subsequent chapters, and as we further develop 3-D strategies and tactics, we will return regularly to the parties as a critical setup variable for reasons beyond those we've developed in this chapter. For example: as we look at interests and deals, we'll want to have the right set of parties in place to facilitate maximum value-creation (e.g., weaving the value-net or adding the U.S. to an Egyptian-Israeli deal). And later, we will talk about building up your own no-deal options—or worsening the other side's—which often requires adding hitherto uninvolved parties (i.e., the PMA-Longshoremen case). Finally, as we flesh out the logic of sequencing, you will notice parties will come in and out of the deal for a variety of reasons (e.g., the first Gulf War coalition). Remember, when it comes to parties, it all boils down to one central principle: without the right deal makers, it is hard to get the right deal.

- A vital part of getting the setup right is getting the parties right.

- Think expansively to get the right all-party map.

- To get the right all-party map, take a disciplined look beyond the usual suspects to figure out who might really matter: potential and actual parties, internal and external players, principals and agents, decision makers and influencers, allies and blockers, and high- and low-value parties, as well those who must approve and implement the deal.

- Map the relationships among those on your all-party map by assessing the informal as well as the formal decision and governance processes.

Chapter Five

Get All the Interests Right

G ETTING THE SETUP RIGHT means getting the interests right. Let's simply define *interest* as *whatever you care about that is potentially at stake in the negotiation.* Your interests are why you're involved in this negotiation in the first place. The same holds true for those people on the other side of the table. Without a clear and accurate assessment of interests, you will fly blind in your deal making.

In chapter 2, we described the concept of a "3-D audit" of existing barriers to agreement and gave several examples of cases where one side's inability to figure out the full set of the other side's interests got in the way of a successful deal. Recall the story about Fluffy's grave holding up the construction of a large regional hospital on the outskirts of London. In that case, the property development firm's CEO assumed that the last holdout property owner must be engaging in a classic real estate "holdup." In fact, it wasn't about money at all. Fluffy's former owner simply wanted to do right by her departed and beloved pet. Getting a single interest wrong, in that circumstance, held up (and threatened to block) the construction of a major medical center. The LockStore Systems story highlighted how a company and its sales force failed to put themselves in the shoes of potential buyers, and failed to make the sale. Success for LockStore would have meant approaching a new set of parties whose very different interests could have set up a more favorable situation. When you reset the table with new parties, you're often thinking of the new interests they would bring that would enhance the setup for your purposes; recall the fuller sets of parties and interests in the longshoremen-shipper deal or the biotech-agribusiness acquisition.

In this chapter, we'll review the key do's and don'ts of getting all the interests right. Let's start with an overriding principle, and then move on to some common mistakes—and the best practices that can head off or correct those mistakes.

The Prime Directive: Make Mapping Interests a Central Priority, Early and Often

To be an effective negotiator in most cases, you have to commit to making the interest-mapping process a serious, *ongoing* priority. If you don't take more than a passing look at interests, you're very likely to stay at a superficial level, and possibly leave good options and sources of leverage undiscovered. Sophisticated negotiators are virtually unanimous on this point: you have to know the starting point of your negotiations before you can get to a better point.

Your Interests

Understanding interests has two parts: understanding *your* interests, and understanding *their* interests. Maybe the first part of that prescription surprises you. Don't we always know our own interests?

According to former U.S. Trade Representative Charlene Barshefsky, the answer may well be "no"—especially when it comes to *articulating* that position:

> *You have to know what you want, and be able to articulate [it] in your own mind with precision. This sounds self-evident, but you'd be surprised how many people don't actually know what they want with the kind of precision that a negotiation demands. Then, you have to think of the 2,000 ways to get where you want to go: what the trades might be, what the arguments might be, what the moves might be on the other side. And you watch carefully, and listen carefully, talk less, and remain persistent.[1]*

This is consistent with our experience. Negotiators often fail to sort out the truly "must-have" from the "important" and from the "desirable but not critical." If your main purpose in job negotiations with three potential new employers is to broaden your experience and learn new skills, take care that the talks don't end up focused on near-term compensation.

For a cosmetics and fragrance supplier, some of the most important negotiations with department stores deal with the amount of space allocated to the line, the desirability of the location on the sales floor, the margin, as well as character—the media they use, their themes, their look, etc.—and cost-sharing on special promotions. Important as these issues are, the real success measure is how well they drive the basic (nonpromotional) business over the longer term. This deeper interest should be the compass, consulted time and time again, that guides the process. The best negotiators are very clear on their ultimate interests but know their trade-offs among lesser interests and are remarkably flexible and creative on the means of advancing these ultimate interests.

Their Interests

The other side of understanding interests—equally important, and probably more challenging—lies in understanding *their* interests. What do you need to understand about your counterparts' organization, their hierarchies, their competitive challenges, before you can strike the best possible deal with them? Since your counterparts will say yes for their reasons, not yours, you need the maximum insight possible into how well their interests would be met by a deal versus their best no-deal option.

"We spend a lot of time thinking about how the poor guy or woman on the other side of the table is going to have to go sell this deal to his or her boss," says Millennium Pharmaceuticals' then Chief Business Officer Steve Holtzman. "We spend a lot of time trying to understand how they are modeling it."[2] Holtzman understands the negotiating game intimately: through a series of deals and alliances, he helped build Millennium from a start-up in 1993 to a major industry player (with a $10.6 billion market capitalization) less than a decade later.

Financial modeling and scenario-building—both of your side and theirs—can be critical to understanding interests in a wide variety of negotiating contexts. We've each spent a good amount of time on Wall Street at one point or another in our careers, and in that setting we frequently ran across people who prepared for all-important negotiations mainly by "running the numbers." But this is rarely good enough for important negotiations. You need to push constantly to refine your understanding of both the corporate and the personal interests represented on the other side of the table. What are these people really trying to accomplish with this deal? What is their current strategy, and how would this deal fit in? Who is taking the lead? What is this person (and her team) like, and what's their negotiating history? How will this deal affect their status, compensation, and future prospects? Who else is paying special attention to the deal? Who will have to approve it?

Some negotiators see a focus on the other side's situation as a sign of weakness on their own part, or even as a first step toward capitulation. Determined not to give an inch, they try their hardest to project an image of overwhelming self-confidence. Early in his deal-making career at Cisco Systems, for example,

Mike Volpi—later that company's chief strategy officer—had trouble completing proposed deals. The consensus among his coworkers was that his self-confident attitude was frequently mistaken for arrogance, which hurt him at the table. Many acquisitions later, a senior colleague observed that "the most important part of [Volpi's] development is that he learned power doesn't come from telling people you are powerful. He went from being a guy driving the deal from his side of the table to the guy who understood the deal from the other side."[3]

We've added the idea of "early and often enough" to this section. If the question is, "How soon should I start assessing the other side's interests?" the answer is, "Sooner." If you wait until the critical moments in the negotiation to start investigating interests seriously, protective walls will often be up. Yet with rare exceptions, we have found that, *given interest-focused preparation before and careful attention during the process*, you can develop a very good working understanding, especially since you often negotiate with the same people and companies over time. As Lakhdar Brahimi, UN envoy extraordinaire, once said, "As an old British diplomat once told me, the secret of negotiation is this: every time you visit a country, you talk to as many people there as you can and learn as much as you can about its history and culture, since you never know when you'll have to negotiate with them."[4]

We've already emphasized the central role played by the all-party map. We reiterate that point here. Use that map as a frame for the interest-related do's and don'ts that follow. Your map is the best tool for staying out of trouble—and for getting where you want to go.

Two More Directives: Big Mistakes to Avoid

In addition to neglecting to fully understand both parties' interests, negotiators often make two more interest-related mistakes:

- Letting price "bulldoze" a potentially richer set of interests
- Mistaking bargaining positions for a fuller set of real interests

Let's look at these problems in turn.

Don't Let Price "Bulldoze" a Potentially Richer Set of Interests

The mythical King Midas had a special gift: the ability to turn things into gold simply by touching them. Great negotiators have the same gift. They can take seemingly mundane materials and—by working "magic" both at and away from the table—can produce value for all the parties to the negotiations.

Bad negotiators possess what might be called the Reverse Midas Touch; that is, they turn potential gold into lead. A common way to do so is to pay attention exclusively to price or to short-term economic issues, thereby turning potentially cooperative deals into adversarial ones. By adopting hard-bargaining, price-focused tactics, they leave potential value uncreated. Yes, price is an important factor in most deals. But it's rarely the *only* factor. As Felix Rohatyn, former managing partner of the investment banking firm Lazard Frères, observes, "Most deals are 50 percent emotion and 50 percent economics."[5]

Rohatyn—a veteran of countless business and public-sector deals—knows whereof he speaks. But there's also a large body of research to support his viewpoint.[6] Consider, for example, a simplified, one-shot negotiation—extensively studied in laboratory settings—involving real money. One party is given, say, $100 to divide with another party as she likes; the second party can either agree to or disagree with the arrangement. If he agrees, the $100 is divided according to the first party's proposal; if he doesn't, neither party gets anything.

Pure price logic implies that the first party should propose something like "$99 for me, and $1 for you." She gets as much as possible, but still gives the other party more than he would have gotten otherwise (a buck, rather than zero). Pure price negotiators confidently predict that the other side will agree to this unequal split. After all—they point out—the second party is getting "free money." It's like finding a dollar on the street, right? Who wouldn't stop to pick it up?

But an interesting pattern emerges from these experiments. Most of the people playing the role of the second party turn down proposals that don't let them share in at least a third of the bounty (and some reject 40 percent, or more). This turns out to hold even when much larger stakes are involved and the amount that the parties will forfeit in the name of perceived fairness is significant.

Further, these results recur across widely divergent cultures, suggesting that there may be something cross-cutting in human beings' perception of fairness. When a proposed split feels too unequal to us, we are *offended* on some fundamental level. We not only reject the buck (or its equivalent); we also set out to teach our greedy counterparts a lesson.

The larger lesson, therefore, is that people tend to care about much more than the absolute level of their own economic outcome. They tend to care about—among other things—relative results, perceived fairness, self-image, and reputation. Taking these as a point of departure, here are four nonprice interests that are often neglected in negotiations, despite their demonstrated importance.

RELATIONSHIPS.   In chapter 2, we referred to Wayne Huizenga, who—through literally thousands of negotiations, large and small—personally built the Waste Management, Inc., AutoNation, and Blockbuster business empires. A deal, says Huizenga, in the context of repeated dealings, "has to be a win-win situation for both sides. The other players can't feel they've lost. This is especially critical if the two parties are going to continue to work together."[7]

The cost of neglecting relationship interests becomes painfully obvious in the "great divide" that emerges in many cross-cultural negotiations.[8] Simply put, the world can be said to consist of two very different kinds of cultures: *deal-focused* cultures, in which dominant interests involve substance; and *relationship-focused* cultures, in which the depth of the relationship is the driving interest. In deal-focused cultures (including much of North America, Northern Europe, and Australia), the form and structure of the deal tend to predominate. In relationship-focused societies (e.g., much of Latin America, Southern Europe, and South and Southeast Asia), the spirit of the relationship tends to take precedence over the specifics of the deal. Results-oriented North Americans, Northern Europeans, and Australians often come to grief by underestimating the strength of the relationship interest. When they insist prematurely that the negotiators "get down to business," they are undercutting a dynamic that at least one party at the table thinks is key.

THE SOCIAL CONTRACT.   In the same vein, some negotiators tend to focus on the economic contract (equity splits, cost-sharing, governance, and so on), or the "letter of the deal," at the expense of the "social contract," which might be defined as the "spirit of the deal." The social contract of a deal goes far beyond a good working relationship. It governs people's expectations about the nature, extent, and duration of the venture, about the process that will be followed, and about the way that unforeseen events will be handled. (We'll have much more to say about the social contract and the psychology behind it in chapter 11.)

Especially in the case of new ventures and strategic alliances—where goodwill and strong shared expectations are extremely important—negotiating a positive social contract is critical to reinforcing the *economic* contract(s). If well into the life of a joint venture, the parties scurry off to consult the founding documents when a conflict arises, that's a bad sign. When a well-negotiated social contract is in place, the approach to resolving conflicts is clear to both sides (even if the specifics of the resolution may not be so clear!).

THE NEGOTIATION PROCESS ITSELF. Process counts. It may sound like the realm of bureaucrats and functionaries, but in fact, the negotiation process itself can be critically important as an interest. The story is told of the young Tip O'Neill, who later became Speaker of the House, meeting an elderly constituent on the streets of his North Cambridge, Massachusetts, congressional district. Surprised to learn that she was not planning to vote for him, O'Neill probed, "Haven't you known me and my family all my life?" "Yes." "Haven't I cut your grass in summer and shoveled your walk in winter?" "Yes." "Don't you agree with all my policies and positions?" "Yes." "Then why aren't you going to vote for me?" "Because you didn't ask me to."

Considerable academic research confirms what O'Neill took to heart from this episode: process counts. Desirable and sustainable results are more often reached when all parties perceive the process as personal, respectful, straightforward, and fair.[9]

ETHICS. The potential for self-interested behavior in negotiation raises ethical issues, and this is cause for attention and concern.[10] Ethical issues include questionable tactics such as lying and coercion, as well as issues of distributional fairness and representation in negotiation. For example what are the obligations of an agent negotiating for a principal? Of an agent carrying out an "external" negotiation on behalf of an internally divided organization?

Ethical interests in negotiation have at least two dimensions, both of which can be shaped by context and culture. First, there is the dimension of what is *intrinsically* right or wrong about an action, regardless of its effect on outcomes. (Lying and coercion, most would agree, are intrinsically wrong, even if they're ultimately unsuccessful or irrelevant.) Second, there are the *instrumental* dimensions of different ethical or unethical behaviors. For instance: does full disclosure of my bottom line invite the other party to squeeze me right up to that point? Are the consequences of unethical behavior—which may in fact be advantageous in the short run—disadvantageous in the longer term, if enemies are made or reputations are damaged?

Mistaking Bargaining Positions for a Fuller Set of Real Interests

The wisdom at the heart of *Getting to Yes*, the 1991 version of the negotiating classic by our colleagues Roger Fisher, Bill Ury, and Bruce Patton, can be summarized in the following quote: "Focus on interests, not positions."[11]

Let's agree on some definitions. *Issues* are the things that are on the table and up for direct discussion. *Positions* are the negotiating parties' stands on those issues. Interests, as we've noted earlier, are *whatever you or your counterparts care about that is at stake in the process.*

Positions on issues can reflect underlying interests, but they need not be identical. If you're negotiating a job offer, for example, the base salary is almost sure to be an *issue*. Perhaps your *position* on that issue is that you need to earn $100,000. The *interests* underlying that position certainly include your need for a good income. But they may also include issues like status, security, getting the tools needed to succeed in the position, new opportunities, flexibility to accommodate family-related issues, and a range of other needs that might be met in ways other than salary. So rather than insisting on the full $100,000, you may better serve your real interests by negotiating (for example) for a more direct reporting relationship, a wider set of responsibilities, an expedited compensation review, and a later start date that allows you to take that long-deferred vacation with your family.

The main point here is that *compatible interests often underlie incompatible positions.* True, "positional bargaining"—negotiations based mainly or even exclusively on the assertion of positions—has its place. (We will return to this topic later, when we look at pure value-claiming situations.) And yes, it feels pretty natural to open a negotiation by stating your own position, and asking the other guy to state his. But for the most part, this is unwise. It tends to drive the process into a value-claiming mode, locking people into the positions they've publicly embraced.

Instead, having thought hard about what *you* are trying to achieve, you need to get to the same understanding about the other party. OK, you've heard your counterpart's position; now, what's *behind* that position? We're not suggesting that they are being devious or manipulative; we just want to figure out what's motivating all the parties to the negotiation. Effective negotiation really depends on that level of understanding. So don't stop at positions; dig deeper and uncover *interests.*

Four Practices That Help You Get Interests Right

Now let's look at the other side of the coin: the kinds of practices that can increase your chances of succeeding at the table. We'll list four:

- Ask, listen, and probe.

- Use public sources to map interests.

- Tap internal sources.

- Tap knowledgeable advisers.

Ask, Listen, and Probe

Perhaps the simplest, and most often neglected, technique to set up an effective negotiation is to simply *ask* the other side a series of interest-related questions and then *listen actively* to the responses. Based on those responses, *probe* for an ever fuller understanding of their position. Then repeat the cycle: ask, listen, and probe.

We were once brought in as advisers to a firm that had been diligently preparing—over the course of six months—to negotiate a joint venture with another company. The extent of the preparations was formidable, indeed—many file drawers' worth of information. But our client still felt frustrated at not being able to get a handle on its counterpart's underlying interests. The negotiating team felt that there were still huge gaps in their understanding of the other side's motivations.

In the middle of watching a comprehensive PowerPoint presentation, we were suddenly struck by a realization: *in all of their preparations, they had never had a direct conversation with the senior executives on the other side.* "Great prep work," we told them, "but now it's time to stop talking to yourselves. Set up an exploratory meeting with your presumed counterparts. If the conversation gets off on the right foot, float the concept you have in mind, and listen to their reactions. If they don't like the concept, *probe.* Ask why? Why not X instead? What if Y? Then, listen actively."

In that case—as in many others—direct communication worked wonders. The ultimate result was a very solid joint venture, although we should note that the enterprise, in its final form, was significantly different from the one that our client had imagined in isolation.

We know a buyer who was turned down when he attempted to renew a materials-supply contract. In a written communication, the vendor gave some unconvincing rationales about the increasing cost of raw materials, the difficulty in finding skilled labor, and other factors. The buyer was puzzled: he knew the contract was valuable to the vendor, that he had proposed economic terms that were at least as favorable as those in the previous contract, and that there seemed to be no reason for the vendor to end the relationship.

Our buyer friend was persistent (mainly because there was no good alternative to this particular vendor). He took the vendor's representative out to dinner, and followed our commonsense prescription: *ask, listen, probe.* Gradually, it emerged that the rep's bonus was based on *new* contracts rather than renewals. Armed with this understanding of the rep's underlying position, the buyer was able to cosmetically restructure the deal in such a way that it qualified as "new business"—and at the same time, secured a modest price break for his company.

Use Public Sources to Map Interests

Another friend of ours had a strange business: buying or fabricating expensive gifts for the "person who has everything." The point was to come up with something that would have deep personal significance for the recipient. She explained to us that, assuming the recipient was known at all, even locally, she could almost always find a great "hook"—the necessary insight into that person—simply by surfing the Net.

The same holds true in negotiations, only more so. Especially in the case of public companies, research sources are plentiful—and all too often go unconsulted. As our friend points out, Internet searches often give you a good, even nuanced, understanding of people, companies, and industry contexts. Most major newspapers have digital archives dating back at least a decade. (The *New York Times* archive, available online, goes back to 1851!) Annual reports, 10-Ks, and other statutory filings can be invaluable. Analysts' reports, taken with an appropriate grain of salt, can provide a useful outsider/insider perspective.

Tap Internal Sources

Having stressed the importance of consulting public sources of information, we want to emphasize that nothing compares to having sources who have personal experience in dealing with your prospective counterparts. Frequently, you can find sources like these within your own organization—or not too far away from it. Whom do you know who has already negotiated with these people? What do they know about the other party's concerns, preferences, and hot buttons? A friendly lunch can yield enormous insights.

We were called upon to advise a large firm that was planning a major outsourcing deal with a major IT vendor and systems integration firm. Yet the most attractive vendor largely remained an unknown quantity as the parties moved into more detailed negotiations. "Beyond the obvious and what the friendly vendor's rep was guardedly telling us," our client's team leader remarked to us, "we simply don't know what the other side's vital interests are, or how they are thinking about this deal. Without that knowledge, we might miss the most advantageous deal and leave money on the table."

Our advice, among other things, was that he have a conversation with his own HR director. Based on our experience in similar situations, it seemed likely to us that there was someone on our client's payroll who had worked for the IT giant in the past. In fact, it turned out that there were something like *twenty* such people, some of whom were able to provide very valuable insights into the inner workings of the proposed vendor—without violating confidentiality. Others inside our client's firm had actually negotiated prior deals with the IT firm; it proved quite easy to draw on their direct experience as well.

Tap Knowledgeable Advisers

Most negotiations above a certain level of complexity involve a number of outside advisers: lawyers, accountants, investment bankers, or industry consultants. When you set out to engage these advisers, apart from their technical qualifications, you should ask in detail about their relevant industry experience and familiarity with your potential negotiating counterparts.

Don't be shy about this. Of course, it's improper for you to seek—or for the prospective advisers to disclose—any confidential or proprietary information. But it's fair to expect these advisers to provide you with general insight into how the other side is "wired," and how it is likely to view a possible deal that you have in mind. Who and what organizational units likely will be involved? How will they evaluate a deal like this? What are their special concerns and hot buttons likely to be? What is their history with similar deals? Who on the other side is likely to be reasonable, and who is likely to be unreasonable? To what kinds of arguments are they receptive? Unreceptive?

Staying Out of Psychological Traps

Let's end this interests-oriented chapter with a quick look at the kinds of psychological traps that often get in the way of effective negotiations. Our rationale for including it here is that someone who is viewing the process through a distorted psychological lens will have a very hard time getting the interests right.

Three of the most dangerous traps are:

- The mythical "fixed pie"

- Self-serving role biases

- Partisan perceptions

The Mythical "Fixed Pie"

You're probably familiar with the concept of "win-lose" or "zero-sum" negotiations, in which one side's gain is the other's loss, and vice versa. When we divide a pie of a given size, more for me means less for you.

Yes, there are many situations in which the pie *is* fixed. But there are many more in which that's not the case, although one or more parties perceive it to be the case. Leading psychologists of negotiation Max Bazerman, Margaret Neale, and Leigh Thompson have presented the overwhelming laboratory evidence in support of this claim.[12] Through experiments in which subjects can earn good money for an accurate assessment of interests, these psychologists and others have demonstrated how stubbornly people cling to the perception of underlying conflict, even where their real interests are compatible.

Self-Serving Role Biases

In addition to perceiving fixed pies where there aren't any, negotiators seem almost hardwired to interpret information in strongly self-serving ways. For example: in a senior executive program at Harvard, we gave a large group of senior-level participants financial and industry information about one company negotiating to acquire another. The executives in the room were randomly assigned to the roles of "buyer" or "seller"; the information provided to each side was *identical.*

After being given plenty of time for analysis, all subjects were asked for their *true* private assessment of the target company's fair value—as distinct from how they might tactically portray that value in the bargaining process. Those assigned the role of sellers gave median valuations more than *twice* as high as those given by the buyers. These valuation chasms had no basis in fact; they were driven entirely by the roles that individuals had been randomly assigned. This turns out to be a widespread phenomenon in negotiation, extending beyond just valuations to assessing your chances in court, your chances of prevailing in a conflict, and so on.[13]

Partisan Perceptions

So the evidence suggests that we humans systematically err in processing facts. We are even worse at assessing the other side, especially in adversarial situations. As viewed by an outsider, those caught up in disintegrating partnerships or marriages often appear to hold exaggerated, negative views of each other. Extensive research has documented an unconscious mechanism in our human psychology that leads us to see our own side as "more talented, honest, and morally upright," while at the same time disparaging or even vilifying the opposition.[14] This often leads to inflated perceptions of the other side's position and overestimates of the actual conflict.

Partisan perceptions can easily become self-fulfilling prophecies. Experiments testing the effects of teachers' expectations of students, or psychiatrists' diagnoses of patients, or platoon leaders' expectations of their inductees confirm the notion that expectations shape behavior. (My teacher thinks I'm stupid, therefore I must be stupid, therefore I won't try very hard.) If you're seated at the negotiating table in the absolute, unshakable conviction that your counterpart is a stubborn and difficult character, *you are likely to act in ways that will trigger and worsen those very behaviors.*

Remedies

So what's to be done about these biases? We'll return to the mythical fixed pie problem in the next chapter. As for self-serving role biases and partisan perceptions, sophisticated negotiators should *expect* biased perceptions, both on their own side and the other side. Such views are just the normal order of things in charged situations. Less seasoned players tend to be shocked and outraged by perceived extremism and are wholly unaware that their own views are likely colored by their roles.

How to counteract these powerful biases? While lab studies on "debiasing" mechanisms are not promising in general, just knowing that such mechanisms exist can help in specific situations.[15] Keep in mind the useful admonition from *Getting to Yes*: "don't deduce their intentions from your fears."[16] Or, in a more cold-blooded vein, recall the advice from *The Godfather, Part III*: "Don't hate your enemies. It only clouds your judgment." To avoid these biases, it can be very useful to seek the views of outside, uninvolved parties who are not caught up in the dynamic—and whom you can count on to give you their straight perceptions, rather than what they think you want to hear.

Here's one of our favorite stories about getting a clearer view of interests: A senior partner in a major law firm once called a gifted young associate into his office, late on a Friday afternoon, and asked the younger lawyer to represent the plaintiff in upcoming settlement negotiations, and—if the negotiations failed—in a possible trial. The young lawyer worked nonstop all weekend, and on Monday morning, presented a brilliant plaintiff's brief to his senior colleague.

The older lawyer praised his colleague fulsomely for a job well done. Then he revealed that the firm would actually be representing the *defendant*, rather than the plaintiff, in the impending negotiations. *Now that you completely understand the other side's viewpoint*, he told the young associate, *we need you to prepare our side.*

We've run a version of this exercise ourselves. A few years back, while helping a client get ready for a tough deal, we suggested that the client create a detailed "brief" for each side, and assign its best negotiators to "bargain" for the other side in a role-playing exercise. What happened? Well, not surprisingly, the brief that was prepared for our client's side was lengthy, eloquent, and persuasive. The brief that our client prepared for the other side consisted mainly of reasons why that side should fold up its tent in the face of superior arguments from across the table. It became painfully clear that our client—despite our instructions to the contrary, and despite its eagerness to follow those instructions—hadn't *begun* to fathom the full set of the other side's interests. We suggested that our client bring in an outside firm to lay out negotiating strategy as if it were representing the other side. This preparation became very important in our client's ultimate strategy, as our client was prepared to preempt and effectively counter several well-thought-out moves by the other side.

Advancing our interests is why we come to a negotiation in the first place—and why the other side is there as well. So the most successful negotiations are those that satisfy the parties' real interests. That requires understanding of both their interests and your own. And without that understanding, your negotiations are unlikely to start in a good place, or end in a good place.

- To get the setup right, get the interests right.

  - Whatever each party cares about that is at stake is an interest.

  - Make mapping interests—yours and theirs—a central priority, well before the formal negotiations begin and throughout the process.

  - Avoid the Reverse Midas Touch; don't let price bulldoze a potentially richer set of interests including perceived fairness, self-image, reputation, relationships, the social contract, the negotiation process itself, and ethics.

- Don't mistake bargaining positions for the richer set of underlying interests.

- Don't forget to ask your counterparts directly and indirectly about interests, actively listen to the responses, and probe what you hear.

- Use standard public sources to map interests.

- Tap internal sources as well as others who have negotiated with your prospective counterparts.

- Tap knowledgeable advisers appropriately.

- Be aware of unconsciously skewed perceptions: the mythical fixed pie, self-serving role biases, and partisan perceptions.

- Take deliberate steps to counteract the psychological mechanisms that can powerfully but unconsciously skew interest perceptions.

Chapter Six

Get the No-Deal
Options Right

M ANY INEXPERIENCED NEGOTIATORS think that they must hang on at all costs until a deal is done. But they'd be wise to listen to the words of Robert Rubin, former U.S. Secretary of the Treasury and cochairman of Goldman Sachs: "When others sense your willingness to walk away, your hand is strengthened . . . Sometimes you are better off not getting to yes."[1] Both the perception and reality of no-deal options play a key role in most negotiations. Let's get *really* basic for a moment: contrast two distinct situations in which you might negotiate with a new car salesperson.

- **Situation 1:** The salesperson has the strong impression that you have firmly decided on the car of your dreams—call it car A—and it is right there on his lot. You are obviously a serious buyer. As you settle into the chairs in front of the salesperson's desk, your spouse tells you firmly, "Honey, we've looked for a long time and we've seen absolutely *nothing*. Our old clunker may not even make it off this lot. This car is perfect!" Now you sit down to talk price.

- **Situation 2:** The salesperson sees you debating with yourself whether you really prefer car A (same as previous) that's right there on his lot, or a car (car B) that's at a different dealership. This time your spouse exudes ambivalence: "Honey, I think I prefer car B." Yes, you like car A a lot, but car B has a few features that you clearly prefer, and it is also priced below car A. In this scenario, you are negotiating the price of car A in order to help you decide whether to choose it over

that other nice car, which you also like a lot, but, conveniently, is elsewhere, but not too far away. Now you sit down to talk price.

It won't surprise you to read that you are likely to strike a far better price in
Situation 2—in which you appear to have an excellent no-deal option and the
willingness to choose it—compared with the price you work out in Situation 1, in which you appear to have no good alternative to car A. Much more
broadly than this simple situation, getting the setup right means getting each
side's no-deal options right. And getting no-deal options right is fundamental
to each side's choice of "yes" or "no."

Should you ultimately say "yes" to a proposed deal? The answer to that
question depends on more than simply the value of that deal. It also depends
on a *comparison* of your options in which you determine whether, to you, the
value of saying yes exceeds the value of saying no. Sometimes, going back to
Rubin's words, you are better off *not* getting to yes. And the same logic, of
course, holds true for your counterparts across the table.

The particulars of a proposed deal define the value of "yes." But how is the
value of "no" determined? It depends on how well your interests are served by
choosing your best "no-deal" option—the most promising course of action you
would take if you decided to say no to the proposed deal. Along with getting
all the parties right and mapping their interests accurately, understanding—
and often shaping—everybody's best no-deal option is the third fundamental
element of a negotiation's setup.[2]

Your best no-deal option may involve simply walking away and doing without any agreement. (What will the consequences of that course of action be?)
It may involve going to another dealer, supplier, or buyer, making something
in-house rather than procuring it externally, going to court rather than settling, forming a different coalition or alliance, or taking a strike. In the case of
multinational peace talks, one nation's best no-deal option may involve anything ranging from the imposition of economic sanctions all the way up to the
unilateral use of force—blockading, bombing, or invading. And, in the course
of negotiating, your best no-deal option may be to continue the process, perhaps in the hope of a better offer. In all cases, assessing your no-deal option
helps establish the critical relevant threshold: *as compared to what?* Meanwhile, of course, the other side is (at least informally) making its own assessment of its best no-deal option.

When we work with our clients, we frequently talk in terms of the "deal/no-
deal balance." Picture an old-fashioned scale with two pans. On one of the
pans you stack up the value of your best no-deal option, and on the other pan,

you stack up the value of saying yes to the proposed deal. As the negotiations proceed, you regularly "check the scale," metaphorically speaking, to see how your deal/no-deal balance looks. Although the negotiations often focus on the "yes pan," your actions as well as outside-world factors may be affecting the "no pan," as well. Plus, the other side may have its finger on the scale too: busily improving its no-deal options—and, perhaps, trying to worsen yours. Whatever is going on in the negotiation, your best no-deal option sets the hurdle—in terms of the full set of your interests—that any agreement must clear to be acceptable. Ditto for them.

All too often, negotiators get caught up in intense tactical interplay at the table. It feels like that's where the action is, and where your attention should be focused. Many negotiators, even experienced ones, pay insufficient attention to (1) their best no-deal option, and (2) the deal/no-deal balance. In too many cases, they treat their no-deal options mainly as afterthoughts, rather than as primary elements of the setup. *This can be a fatal mistake.* Like parties and interests—as described in the previous two chapters—no-deal options are foundational to favorably shaping the setup: defining necessary conditions for any deal, strongly influencing outcomes, and often suggesting actions away from the table to set up more promising situations.

In the balance of this chapter, we'll present five prescriptions for using the power of no-deal options to drive great deals.

1. Use your best no-deal option, and those of the other negotiating parties, to determine whether and, if so, where a zone of possible agreement exists.

2. Make sure the other side sees you as ultimately able and willing to walk away. When your counterpart(s) perceives a credible increase in your willingness to walk away—especially in the direction of an attractive no-deal option—your at-the-table outcomes often improve. Therefore, take steps to improve your best no-deal option and consider actions to worsen that of your counterpart.

3. Take care to protect—and do not inadvertently weaken—your no-deal options.

4. Consider worsening your own no-deal option in certain very carefully selected circumstances.

5. When diagnosing a potential negotiation, use your understanding of no-deal options to distinguish between those situations in which negotiation can play a major role and those in which it must play a lesser role.

Determine If a Zone of Possible Agreement Exists

One simplified way to view negotiations is to see them as a sort of tug of war—a battle that takes place along an adversarial line segment (the "rope"), with the seller tugging toward "high" and the buyer tugging toward "low." The buyer's closely guarded true maximum determines the one end of the line segment (i.e., the maximum acceptable price if there is to be a deal), and the seller's equally well-guarded true minimum bounds the other end (i.e., the minimum acceptable price if there is to be a deal). It doesn't much matter whether the tug of war concerns the price of a car or a house, an insurance settlement, or the sale price of a company. In all cases, you should keep the mental image of the "price line segment" in mind; it has a very tight relationship to each side's best no-deal option.

Your best no-deal option, again, is the most attractive course of action you could take in the event of no agreement in the current negotiation. The value you place on your best no-deal option sets the bar—in terms of the full set of your interests—that any agreement must exceed to be acceptable; this is also true for the other side. As such, no-deal options imply the existence or absence of a *Zone of Possible Agreement (ZOPA)*, a bit of jargon we find useful. The ZOPA simply means the set of possible agreements that is better for each side, given its interests, than its best no-deal option.

Suppose that the seller's true minimum falls below the buyer's true maximum, as depicted in figure 6-1. In this case, a potentially profitable ZOPA exists; that is, agreement can be better for each side than the value of its best no-deal option.

To be more concrete, let's say that Joe is selling his condo and has an acceptable offer (to him) for $450,000. Betty, meanwhile, would pay up to $500,000 for Joe's condo, rather than (a) buying another condo or (b) doing without a condo. The Joe-Betty ZOPA, therefore, obviously exists and is the set of prices between $450,000 and $500,000.

Of course, it's easy to imagine a scenario with no ZOPA. For example: if Joe already had a $500,000 offer while Betty could buy exactly what she wanted elsewhere for $450,000, there'd be no ZOPA for Joe and Betty.

Each side typically knows its own limits, which it must continually assess and reassess as new information unfolds. The problem is that many negotiators have only a hazy sense of their own no-deal options, or how to value them—especially when it comes to more complex no-deal options than the simple buy-sell price deal we've been using to illustrate our points so far. If Joe

FIGURE 6-1

The ZOPA (Zone of Possible Agreement) as a Battle Line

Seller's minimum ⊢————————————————————⊣ Buyer's maximum

and Betty were involved in trying to settle a major class-action lawsuit, rather than selling and buying a condo, the no-deal options would be considerably more difficult to calculate.

Let's see how accurately assessing the true ZOPA—trivial in theory, but tricky in practice—can be immensely profitable when done well. Sometimes the most important attributes of the other side's no-deal options can be invisible—unless you actively look for them.

We once advised an American firm during a lengthy negotiation with a major Japanese company. The stated goal of the talks was to create a large-scale joint venture under Japanese control. In fact, creating this joint venture would represent a sale of about two-thirds of the U.S. firm, permitting it to concentrate on what it felt to be another business line with higher potential. During an excruciatingly detailed, two-year process, the negotiations were suspended several times, due to what the Japanese negotiators described as a "breakdown of its internal consensus process." Each time, however, the Japanese managed to resume negotiations, after painstaking internal efforts to rebuild and strengthen consensus within their company on the central role of the deal to their long-term global strategy.

When a European firm unexpectedly made a tender offer for the entire American business, the Japanese firm suddenly had to fish or cut bait. When the Japanese signaled their intention to intensify the negotiations—in part to head off the Europeans—negotiators for the U.S. firm reassessed the ZOPA on price: that is, the least that the U.S. firm would accept and the most the Japanese company would pay for majority control of the part of the U.S. business to be contributed to the JV.

Obviously, the price ZOPA depended on financial valuations, including the strategic benefits and costs to each side of completing the transaction. Yet, at the very last moment before the U.S. board was about to authorize its negotiators to proceed in the final deal process, we pressed our client to think once again about the reality of the Japanese no-deal option. We quickly reviewed the other strategic options open to the Japanese firm and confirmed their undesirability.

This last-minute, deeper look at the Japanese situation, moreover, began to focus our collective attention on the *internal* consequences of no deal to our Japanese counterparts. Having worked through a grueling consensus process, virtually everyone at the Japanese company—from the major owners, to the board to senior managers, to all those subunits that had required that massive persuasion effort—was deeply committed to doing this deal. The company was cash-rich, so minimizing the price of the deal was important, but not central.

Armed with this understanding, the U.S. negotiators were able to leverage the Japanese company's nearly irresistible organizational momentum—the firm had spent over two years mentally integrating the U.S. operations into its long-term strategy. Now, rather than face the extreme internal organizational costs of "losing," the Japanese firm agreed to pay an extraordinarily high amount for the U.S. firm, far more than would have been the case absent the frustratingly lengthy consensus process. (In fact, it was almost *triple* its share price at the outset of the process.) One American negotiator described how, in effect, the Japanese entity had "fallen in love" over time with its target—and paid the price.

This exceedingly profitable outcome (from the American point of view) probably would not have been possible had the U.S. negotiators thought of the transaction in conventional valuation terms and focused on external no-deal options. Instead, the other side's consensus process—when recognized by the U.S. side as affecting the Japanese no-deal option—was used to recognize that the true ZOPA extended well beyond what would otherwise have been justifiable.

Make Sure They Believe You Can Walk Away

Although many people associate "bargaining power" with the ability to inflict or absorb damage, the other party's perception that you have a good no-deal option can be just as important—or even more important. Recall the car-buying story above, or the case in chapter 1 of Tom Stemberg's successful cultivation of outside financing to give himself better no-deal options in his ongoing negotiations with the venture capitalists. Or how in chapter 3, Joseph Miniace's Pacific Coast shippers—who at first felt completely at the mercy of the long-shoremen's union's ability to shut down the ports—acted internally and externally to boost their no-deal possibilities and worsen those of the union.

Echoing Robert Rubin (and a host of other first-class deal makers), WebTV founder and entrepreneur Steve Perlman bluntly asserts: "If you can't walk away, you can't negotiate . . . He who cares least, wins."[3] There are circumstances from which you can't always walk away easily, especially those involving long-term partnerships and important relationships. But your apparent willingness to walk—a quiet confidence about doing so rather than a bald threat—can confer real advantage. The other side's observation of your calm readiness to walk away—the psychological opposite of visibly craving a deal—normally serves as a major advantage. Of course, this willingness should not preclude a genuine joint search for a still-better agreement. But your apparent readiness and ability to walk offers a tactically invaluable backdrop for the process.

In two-party negotiations out there in the real world—where the stakes generally are far higher than simply car A versus car B above—most top negotiators insist on taking steps to build up some level of competition, thereby improving their no-deal options in the initial negotiation. A senior AOL executive commented on the importance of such moves to favorably change the setup and tilt the deal/no-deal balance as follows: "You would never do a deal without talking to anyone else. Never."[4]

Martin Lipton, de facto "dean" of New York's community of takeover-oriented legal specialists, has contrasted the effects of adding another interested party at the front end of corporate acquisition negotiations with the effects of simply negotiating more effectively with your initial counterpart at the back end of the process. Lipton even roughly quantified the added value of adding a competing negotiator relative to greater negotiating skill in the initial two-party deal: "The ability to bring somebody into a situation is far more important than the extra dollar a share at the back end. At the front end, you're probably talking about 50 percent. At the back end, you're talking about 1 or 2 percent."[5]

Converting a two-party setup into more of an auction can change the psychology of a negotiation, as well as the inherent competitive pressures. In chapter 5, we referred to the string of negotiations that transformed Millennium Pharmaceuticals from a start-up into a multibillion-dollar firm in less than a decade. Then-Chief Business Officer Steve Holtzman is a firm believer in the power of adding parties:

Whenever we feel there's a possibility of a deal with someone, we immediately call six other people. It drives you nuts, trying to juggle them all, but it will change the perception on the other side of the table, number one. Number two, it will change your self-perception. If you believe that there are other people who are interested, your bluff is no longer a bluff, it's real. It will come across with a whole other level of conviction.[6]

Indeed, transforming your two-party negotiation into an active auction, with many bidders vying for your deal, can be a potent strategy.[7] Even partial steps in that direction can improve the appearance and reality of your no-deal options. But use this strategy wisely—if you publicly announce an auction and no other bidders show up, this will underscore the weakness of your no-deal options and hurt your position at the table.

Some actions simultaneously boost your best no-deal option while worsening that of the other side. You should be alert to these situations that involve what we call "*interdependent no-deal options.*" Obviously, to spot and take advantage of such situations, you need not only to assess your own no-deal options, but also to think very carefully about those of the other side.

Here's an illustration of one such defensive move. In the midst of a rancorous negotiation to settle a business dispute over intellectual property, Party A preemptively filed a lawsuit against Party B in a jurisdiction known to be favorable to Party A's point of view. Not only did this protect (and even enhance) Party A's walk-away position in the talks, it worsened that of Party B, which—if terms could not be negotiated—would have been compelled to fight the suit in a less favorable legal venue. By the same token, had Party B filed first in its preferred jurisdiction, Party A's no-deal situation would have been worse.

Similarly, imagine that BigCo and its larger rival, BiggestCo, coexist in a scale-driven industry that is ripe for consolidation. BigCo, as the second-largest firm in the sector, must decide which of two viable potential merger partners it wants to approach: SmallCo or SmallerCo. Who should BigCo talk to, how quickly should it do so, and how generous should it be in trying to close a merger quickly?

BigCo chose to act very quickly and offer unexpectedly generous terms to SmallCo, the larger of the two merger candidates. Why? Suppose that BiggestCo, the industry's dominant firm, acted first to tie up SmallCo. BigCo would have been left with a less potentially valuable negotiating partner (SmallerCo). And if BiggestCo had already absorbed SmallCo, then BigCo would have faced a dismal no-deal option in its negotiations with SmallerCo— failure to come to terms with SmallerCo would have meant no consolidation deal at all, since there would be no more viable potential partners left. In other words, by acting quickly to tie up SmallCo, BigCo was both substantially improving its deal prospects and protecting its no-deal option. A really proactive BigCo might negotiate simultaneously with SmallCo and SmallerCo so that it might try to conclude both acquisitions before BiggestCo even had a chance to enter into negotiations (assuming the antitrust authorities would not have a problem and that the two smaller firms didn't open up talks with BiggestCo to boost their leverage).

Here's another example in which one side felt acutely the weakness of its bargaining position at the outset of negotiations and took steps to find and exploit interdependent no-deal options. In the three decades following World War II, efforts to persuade Swiss banks to compensate Holocaust survivors—who claimed that these banks had unjustly held their families' assets since the war—had been notably unsuccessful and had been become largely inactive. When former Seagram's head Edgar Bronfman sought to revive these negotiations, he felt that top Swiss banking executives in Zurich were simply stonewalling him. Evidently, they believed that the relevant restitution issues had been settled years earlier and that they were on strong legal ground. As a result, Bronfman found the bankers not at all forthcoming. Simply put, the bankers felt they had a very strong no-deal option, whereas Bronfman's appeared poor.

A scant eight months later, entrepreneurial actions away from the table by Bronfman, the World Jewish Conference, and others had dramatically expanded the negotiations to the detriment of the Swiss banks. Now the bankers faced a de facto coalition of interests that credibly threatened the lucrative Swiss share of the public finance business in states such as California and New York, and also put in jeopardy a major merger between Swiss Bank Corporation and UBS over a "character fitness" license vital to doing business in New York. This potentially hostile coalition also threatened to work for the divestiture by huge U.S. pension funds of stock not only in Swiss banks, but in *all* Swiss-based companies, and made noises about retaining some of the most formidable U.S. class-action lawyers to launch intrusive (and expensive) class-action suits. And finally, the very visible lack of progress threatened to incur the displeasure of the U.S. government, which had become an active party in attempting to broker a settlement.

In other words, the coalition simultaneously improved its no-deal option and greatly diminished the appeal of the Swiss bankers' no-deal option. The result? An agreement by the bankers to pay $1.25 billion to the survivors. This was an almost unimaginable outcome at the outset of the initially small, initially private negotiations. But it became possible—even unavoidable—in the context of a radically reshaped game that came to include a large coalition of parties, all with distinct kinds of leverage, and all pressing the bankers to cut a deal.[8]

There are important exceptions to the rule that better no-deal options for you (and worse ones for your counterpart) tend to improve your chances of good outcomes. They mainly arise in circumstances where your very willingness to seriously consider no-deal options puts you in a negative light in the eyes of your counterpart. For example, if you're in negotiations with an employer who prizes loyalty, invoking the specter of all the alternative jobs you've lined up may signal to him or her that you are little better than a mercenary. Or your expressed willingness to, say, go to court or act to break a union can easily come across as a threat, stimulate countermeasures, and inadvertently lead to escalation that is bad for everyone. In most circumstances, though, developing attractive outside options and calmly signaling your willingness to choose them improves your negotiated outcomes.

Protect Your No-Deal Options

A no-deal option is like a dike: you can't afford to have it spring leaks. Protecting your no-deal options—and avoiding actions that inadvertently worsen them—requires close attention to the options of each side, in part because those options may be inadvertently affected by your bargaining moves. For example, to raise urgently needed cash, the chief executive of a Canadian chemical manufacturer decided to sell a large but nonstrategic division and assigned his second-in-command to negotiate the sale at the best possible price. A logical buyer was an Australian firm, the canny chairman of which knew the Canadian company's chairman from days together in a British prep school. During a chief-to-chief conversation setting up the overall negotiations, the Australian said that his firm was indeed potentially interested, though it was utterly consumed at that moment with other strategic priorities. But if the Canadian firm would grant him a nine-month period of exclusive negotiating rights to "confirm its seriousness" about the sale, the Australian said, he would "divert the necessary management resources" to make it happen. His Canadian counterpart agreed to this deal.

Now put yourself in the shoes of the poor second-in-command charged with disposing of the division for a high price on an urgent basis. As he jetted off to Sydney, he knew he had no credible alternative to whatever the Australians offered for the next nine months. Not surprisingly, the Australians were *not* generous, the "old school tie" notwithstanding. As you decide on moves in negotiation, keep a hawklike eye on how they may be affecting your no-deal options.

Under Very Special Circumstances, Consider Strategically Worsening Your No-Deal Option

There are cases in which you may wish to consciously *worsen* your no-deal option. As you can well imagine, this should be done with great care. Ancient armies sometimes burned their bridges or torched their fleets so that escape would be impossible, and a battle to the death the only option. In theory, at least, this would deter potential foes, who could well imagine how desperately the cornered soldiers would fight, given death as their only no-deal option. The risk, of course, was that the encircling forces would *not* be deterred, and the cornered army would have no bridges or boats to fall back on.

People sometimes worsen their own no-deal situations to bind themselves to staying with a deal. This was the case when AT&T and British Telecom formed Concert, a massive 50-50 joint venture of pooled assets to provide international telephone and Internet service. AT&T and BT sought to force themselves to make Concert work, in part by ensuring that the venture contained *no* exit provisions—not even provisions for routine arbitration.[9] In the name of closing the deal, the bridges were burned and the boats were scuttled.

It didn't work. Three years into the joint venture, the enterprise was losing £150 million per quarter, and AT&T and BT decided to throw in the towel. But the total lack of exit procedures led to nightmarish negotiations to unwind 21 subsidiary ventures in 230 countries, 47,000 miles of fiber optic cable, at least $1 billion in new technology investments, as well as a headquarters staff of over 400—all in an soured atmosphere of failure and the keen knowledge that each party would need these international assets for its post-Concert strategy.

So yes, sometimes there are strategic reasons to consider worsening your no-deal options, but they should be weighed warily. You may wind up wishing you had a bridge, or a boat, at your back.

Analyze Each Side's Best No-Deal Option to Determine the Potential Role for Negotiation

Imagine a situation in which one utterly dominant player can achieve all of its objectives vis-à-vis another player without much effort or cost. For example, picture an 18-wheeler barreling down the highway engaging in a "negotiation" with a bug over which party will get out of the way. In such a situation, negotiations have virtually no meaningful role, since the dominant player has a terrific no-deal option and the other player has a most unattractive one.

Moving on to another circumstance in which negotiation plays an unimportant role at best, imagine an economist's perfectly competitive market, which includes a large number of buyers, a large number of sellers, and a pure commodity product. If one party tries to negotiate a better price with another, the second party's no-deal option is simply a deal at the market price.

In short, the closer the situation becomes to costless dominance or a perfect market, the less important the role of negotiation becomes. Conversely, the potential for negotiation increases in cases where (1) a player can't fully achieve its objectives by unilateral action and at an acceptable price, or (2) an imperfect market (meaning smaller numbers and different kinds of buyers and sellers, more avenues for product differentiation, and so on) predominates. In either case, your no-deal assessment can suggest the extent of negotiation's potential role in a given situation, which can range all the way from negligible to nearly limitless.

The Power of No-Deal Options—and Your Understanding of Them

For many people, the poker game over perceptions of no-deal options—and the implied ZOPA as a line segment or "Battle Line"—represents the essence of negotiation, the whole point of sitting down at the table in the first place. In later chapters, we will challenge this conception as a general view of negotiation; there are better mental models to adopt before you sit down at the table. In this chapter, though, we wanted to give you a better feel for some of the critical functions of no-deal options as part of the negotiation's setup.

No-deal options can indeed be *powerful*, at every stage of the negotiating process. At the outset, an analysis of no-deal options can provide an important guide to the potential role for negotiation in the first place and what the ZOPA might look like. Improving your no-deal options, or worsening those of the other side, can greatly influence the outcome of the negotiation. And, as we will later see, once a deal is struck, each side's incentive to comply is heavily influenced by the continuing balance between "yes" and "no."

But the important truth is that you continually face a *choice* in negotiation over how you want to affect the deal/no-deal balance: whether to concentrate on interpersonal moves that will improve prospects at the table, or to spend your limited time, energy, and resources on improving your no-deal options (or worsening theirs). The naive negotiator often draws the analytic circle too narrowly, focusing mainly on interpersonal tactics at the table. The sophisticated negotiator, by contrast, always weighs the value of moves at the table against the value of those away from the table to shape the no-deal part of the setup.

- Use your best no-deal options, and those of the other negotiating parties, to determine whether and, if so, where a zone of possible agreement (ZOPA) exists. (Don't neglect "internal" no-deal options in your assessment!)

- Make sure the other side sees you as ultimately able and willing to walk away. When your counterpart(s) perceives a credible increase in your willingness to walk away—especially in the direction of an attractive no-deal option—your at-the-table outcomes often improve. Therefore, take steps to improve your best no-deal option and consider actions to worsen that of your counterpart.

- Take care to protect—and do not inadvertently weaken—your no-deal options.

- Consider worsening your own no-deal option, in certain very carefully selected circumstances.

- When diagnosing a potential negotiation, use your understanding of no-deal options to distinguish between those situations in which negotiation can play a major role and those in which it must play a lesser role.

Chapter Seven

Get the Sequence and Basic Process Choices Right

U P T O T H I S P O I N T, we've concentrated on defining the right *scope* for your negotiations—in other words, defining the parties, issues, inter-ests, and best no-deal options correctly. The last two items in this "setup" sec-tion of *3-D Negotiation* are *sequence* and *basic process choices*. Getting these right also helps set the table for favorable negotiations.

An example from our own experience illustrates the importance of these factors. Not long ago, a U.S. auto parts manufacturing firm called us for urgent help with its faltering joint-venture negotiations in Mexico. Having determined that setting up a Mexican JV was a strategic priority, the U.S. firm had researched the industry and ranked its three potential partners according to the competencies they found most desirable. One Mexican firm appeared to be the superior potential partner; a second firm looked like a pretty good fit. Another firm seemed acceptable but was clearly the third choice.

The U.S. team had opened negotiations with the most attractive of the potential partners. After reaching a truly unpleasant deadlock—characterized by high tempers, name-calling, and long silences when trying to set up meetings—the U.S. team abandoned the talks. The U.S. executives in charge suspected that their own firm's dominant engineering culture had been a prime contributor to the impasse, so—on a crash basis—the U.S. firm tried to pin down the nuances of "Mexican culture."

It soon found several possible "cultural" guidelines that its negotiators had violated at least once, and sometimes repeatedly. For example: at the start of the talks, send suitably senior people, not just techies. Don't launch right into business, but work first to build a relationship with your counterpart. Take your time during the negotiation process. Pay attention to Mexican national history; it means a lot to a proud people. And so on, and so on.

To the chastened U.S. executives, it seemed possible, even likely, that violating these cultural norms had doomed the first set of talks (the ones with the most desirable partner). So now, having adopted a more culturally sensitive approach, the U.S. firm was deep into negotiations with the second most desirable candidate. Once again, though, things were going badly. This was when we were called in.

We listened hard as our clients described their *tactical* moves up to that point. Quickly, though, we refocused our discussions on the *setup* of the negotiations. We pointed out that they had set up the negotiations in *series*, starting with the most desirable potential partner, and—if necessary—moving on to the next firm. We encouraged them to play out the implications of this seemingly routine setup choice. Suppose that second set of talks also fell apart. In an industry where all players would quickly hear about it, what effect would that have on the *next* negotiations, with the third and barely acceptable partner? As each set of negotiations failed, we pointed out, the U.S. firm's best no-deal alternative—a deal with another Mexican company, or no joint venture at all—became progressively worse.

Yes, the path they had chosen embodied a certain straightforward engineering logic: start negotiating with the most promising partner, and if that doesn't work, move on to the next most promising partner, and so on. But negotiations, we pointed out, often follow a different logic.

Our clients revised their approach, opening exploratory discussions with the third firm *in parallel with* the second. This helped them learn which potential partner actually made the most business sense. It helped them avoid closing down options prematurely. It helped them stimulate competition between the two Mexican companies still in the running. And when these parallel talks began, the first and most desirable partner—facing the prospect of one of its rivals becoming part of a potent combination—made moves to come back to the table.

But let's back up all the way to the beginning and think in 3-D terms, focusing on the setup itself. The U.S. company should have initially set up the process so that the prospect of a deal with the most desirable Mexican partner would function as its best no-deal alternative in talks with the second most desirable partner, and so on. This alternative setup would have created the equivalent of a *simultaneous four-party negotiation*—structured as one U.S. firm negotiating in *parallel* with each of the three Mexican firms—rather than *three sequential two-party negotiations*. And of course, this far more promising setup would have drawn upon whatever cultural insight and tactical ingenuity the U.S. firm could have brought to bear on the negotiations.

Here's an even more promising setup: suppose that the technically well-regarded U.S. firm had let it be known—through influential Mexican sources (or through a U.S. economic attaché)—that it was considering a joint venture in that country. Suppose that this move had induced potential Mexican partners to approach the U.S. firm. Setting up a parallel process in which the other side *comes to you* generally trumps a serial process in which you go to them.

This simple case illustrates the importance of setup moves to get the sequence and basic process choices right. In this chapter, we generalize on these points, starting with the right *sequencing* of the negotiation—the right order of approach to the parties, and the most productive staging of the negotiation. Then we move to making the right *basic process choices*—the right "rules of engagement" and expectations within which each party will negotiate.

Get the Sequence Right

Whether picking the most likely path to "yes" from the most desirable Mexican joint venture partner, building support for a product initiative, putting a high-profile meeting together, or negotiating a new wireless industry standard, sequencing matters. In chapter 2, we recounted the case of how the United States carefully sequenced its approach to building political and military coalitions when Saddam Hussein invaded Kuwait. While important, we saw that getting the sequence right could be tricky; rules of thumb like "get your allies on board first," or "negotiate internally first, then externally," were not always right. In our example from chapter 3, the biotech firm's efforts to acquire a desirable division of an agribusiness concern entailed fairly complex sequencing, both within the biotech firm itself and with different groups in the target entity.

Through effective sequencing moves away from the table, negotiators act to bring about a more promising "target" setup whose scope usually entails improved no-deal alternatives and enhanced possibilities for joint gains. Sequencing to come up with a better setup calls for a number of related steps:

1. Scanning widely to map the range of potential parties as well as the relationships among them.

2. "Mapping backward" from the target (more promising) game to the current (less promising) situation.

3. Carefully orchestrating the stages of reaching the target setup, which calls for:

- Decisions on which parts of the process should be separated or combined, public or private.

- Decisions on how the stages should be framed and their informational aspects managed.

Let's look at each of these aspects of effective sequencing by way of a few examples.

Scanning Widely and Mapping Backward

If you want to "think outside the box," you must first *look* outside the box, using a process that we call *scanning*. Although this is more art than science, the negotiator can be guided by several key principles.

It's helpful to think in terms of a "value net," which may extend beyond the immediate confines of the negotiation.[1] Who outside those confines might value an aspect of a deal the most? Who might minimize the costs of production, distribution, risk-bearing, finance, and so on? Who might supply a piece that's missing from the current process? What devices might bring these potential value-creating parties and issues into the deal?

Scanning works in the other direction, as well. When does the complexity of the negotiation, or the presence of potential deal breakers, argue for scanning the involved players to develop a set of candidates who can be carefully pruned to "shrink" the negotiation? The simpler and/or less contentious remaining players may be able to realize a beneficial deal more easily.

Scanning extends beyond value-*creating* to value-*claiming* as well. Are there potential additional parties who, individually or in combination, could improve your best no-deal option? Worsen your counterpart's? Do other parties bring issues that could be linked for leverage? As answers to these questions become clearer, issues of sequence tend to increase in importance. For example, entrepreneurs generally try to construct the most promising sequence of deals that will lead to a self-sustaining company. Consider WebTV founder Steve Perlman's situation after he had obtained seed funding, developed the technology to bring the Web to ordinary television sets, created a prototype, and hired the core technical and management team members.[2] Running dangerously low on cash, he faced the "cloud" of potential deal partners depicted in figure 7-1: having identified this cloud, the essence of Perlman's setup problem was how to draw on the elements of this cloud, sequencing and designing negotiations in a way that would yield an interlocking set of deals to build his company.

Sometimes the answer to "who first?" is perfectly obvious. But in more complex situations, it often helps to focus on an interim "target" negotiation, and *map backward* from that target to the current situation. Again, take the WebTV example: with Perlman's promising new venture running on fumes, venture capital firms might have seemed an obvious next focus of negotiations. Unfortunately for the nascent WebTV, though, VCs were quite skeptical of consumer electronics investments at that time. So instead of taking a direct approach to venture firms, which Perlman believed would be his ultimate targets, he mapped backward from these targets. He reasoned that the value of WebTV would be greatly enhanced by first getting a prominent consumer electronics firm on board, and then seeking venture funding. In other words, he embarked upon a sequential strategy.

FIGURE 7-1

"Cloud" of possible deals to be pursued by WebTV

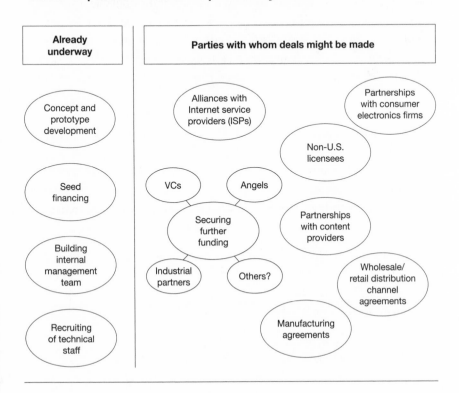

After a lengthy negotiation, Sony—the optimal choice—turned him down. Perlman kept reasoning backward, moving from Sony to Philips. Finally, he was able to get Philips on board, and then use the Philips deal to reopen and forge a complementary deal with a jealous Sony. Then he negotiated fresh capital from VCs, at a far higher valuation than would have been possible before Sony and Philips signed up. With new money in the tank, Perlman then hammered out supporting agreements with manufacturers, wholesale and retail distribution channels, content providers, ISPs, and alliance partners abroad.

The final chapter, of course, came with the sale of WebTV to Microsoft, at a huge profit. Brilliant scanning and sequencing pays!

As you scan for sequencing purposes, pay attention to the relationships among the players you'll be dealing with. A common problem for a would-be sequencer is that the most critical party can be the most difficult to approach. One way to improve the odds of an ultimate "yes" is to figure out who influences whom, or tends to defer to whom. We've already seen cases in which an initially negative party (like the biotech CEO in chapter 3) became motivated to support an initiative because a carefully sequenced process had ensured that the "right" players were already on board; this both strengthened his belief in the value of the idea and meant that implementation would be easier.

More generally, consider the successful sequencing logic of Bill Daley, President Clinton's key strategist for securing congressional approval of the then-controversial North American Free Trade Agreement. As the critical and hotly contested vote neared, news would arrive in Daley's office that a member of Congress who had been leaning toward "yes" had come out as a "no." Daley's response: *make more calls*, and in specific directions. "Can we find the guy who can deliver the guy?" he'd ask his aides. "We have to call the guy who calls the guy who calls the guy."[3]

These examples suggest some of the elements of effective sequencing in negotiations, a vital one of which we have referred to as *backward mapping*.[4] Backward mapping logic is similar to the logic of project management. In deciding how to undertake a complex "negotiation project":

1. You start with the endpoint and work back to the present to develop a timeline and critical path. With a good sense of the parties and their relationships, you can estimate the difficulty and cost of gaining agreement with each party as well as the value of having it on board.

2. Next, you focus on the most-difficult-to-persuade player, who is either the ultimate target or is otherwise critical to the deal. You ask "which

prior agreement or agreements among which set of the other players would maximize the chances of the target saying yes?" Phrased differently, whom would you ideally like to have on board when you initiate negotiations with the target? As the answer to this question becomes clear, you have identified the next target.

3. Now that you have identified the next-to-last target, ask the same question. How will you get that party on board? What would make it easier for him or her to say yes? Whom would you ideally like to have already on board to maximize the chances of this next-to-last player saying "yes?"

4. Finally, continue mapping backward in this fashion until you have found the most promising path through the cloud of possibilities.

Effectively Orchestrating the Stages of the Process for Achieving the Target Setup: Separate? Together? Public? Private? Framed How? Revealing What Information?

Some negotiations are best approached by gathering all affected parties together, sharing all information, and brainstorming a solution to the shared problem. In other cases, though, it may be far more promising—for the purposes of at least one player—to carefully separate and sequence the stages of the process, while actively managing and framing the information flow. Some stages may be *private*, by which we mean that the negotiations or their results are known only to the direct participants. Other stages may be *public*, by which we mean that the negotiations or their results are known to a wider set of players.

Carefully deploying these choices can help to build support for an ultimate deal; it can also be used to outflank potential opponents. For example, consider how Percy Barnevik brought about the merger of Asea and Brown Boveri, the Swedish and Swiss predecessors of global engineering giant ABB. According to Barnevik:

We had no choice but to do it secretly and to do it quickly . . . There were no lawyers, no auditors, no environmental investigations, and no due diligence. Sure, we tried to value assets as best we could. But . . . we were absolutely convinced of the strategic merits . . . Why the secrecy? Think of Sweden. Its industrial jewel, Asea—a 100-year-old company that had built much of the country's infrastructure—was moving its headquarters out of Sweden . . . I remember when we called the press conference in Stockholm on August 10. The news came as a complete surprise . . . Then came the shock, the fait accompli. [Then] we had to win over shareholders, the public, governments, and unions.[5]

By choosing to secretly negotiate with a tiny group of each side's executives first, Barnevik generated an irreversible commitment to a preferred deal. This high-risk sequence was designed to prevent factions such as unions and the Swedish government from blocking the deal. In two-level cases like this, an "internal" faction often can block the initiative favored by the protagonist.[6] Try the following thought-experiment involving a different and public sequence: had Barnevik openly tried first for agreements with unions, the government, or shareholders, the process would have been thwarted, and ABB would not exist.

Along with illuminating the sequence of moves needed to set up or change the game, the ABB case underscores the importance of whether stages of the process are public or private, as well as how information from one stage spills into, or is framed at, other stages.

Take another example. We once heard a story about how a prominent nineteenth-century U.S. statesman decided to help a capable young man of very modest background from an Eastern European country.[7] Approaching the chairman of the state bank in that country, the statesman indicated that a very gifted and ambitious young man, soon to be the son-in-law of Baron Rothschild, was seeking a fast-track position in banking. Shortly thereafter, in a conversation with the baron—who was known to be searching for a suitable match for his daughter—the statesman enthusiastically described a very capable young man who was making a stellar ascent at the state bank. The baron's daughter found him charming. When she and her father both said "yes," the three-way "deal" went through—to all parties' ultimate satisfaction.

Notice how the statesman's actions set up the most promising negotiation for his purposes. By separating and sequencing the stages of the process, as well as opportunistically framing his message at each juncture, the statesman created a setup that supported his hoped-for outcome. Had the chairman, the baron, the daughter, and the young man been initially thrown together in a face-to-face meeting—an alternative setup—no amount of diplomacy could have closed the deal.

Business and financial negotiations often include a version of this staging, including the manipulation of information. For example, when a private equity firm approaches an institutional investor, that potential investor may make its capital commitment conditional on the commitments of others who have reputations for toughness and savvy. Some investment firms use an unscrupulous work-around when raising money: they get investor A to commit funds *conditional on* the supposed commitment of B when in truth, B has committed *only* on the informal (and wrong) understanding that A has unconditionally agreed to do so. Because the two deals are kept separate, both go through.

Most parents encounter the teenager's version of this gambit: getting Dad to say yes ("since Mom said OK" [untrue]) and then scurrying to Mom in the *other* room asking for permission ("since it's OK with Dad" [also untrue: Dad's OK depended on Mom's]). By the time the parents get around to comparing stories, Junior has already left with the car.

Influencing whether a related negotiation happens before or after one's own negotiation—as well as whether its results become public—can greatly affect outcomes. For example, while the United States was in separate talks with Japan, Hong Kong, and Korea over textiles (the "multifiber agreements"), a Korean negotiator announced that Korea would wait for the other Asian negotiators to go first. "After waiting for Hong Kong and Japan to go first," one observer reported, "Seoul asked for the features they had secured and then also held out for a bit more."[8]

Before moving on to process choices, let's summarize our key advice on sequencing to build winning coalitions or deal with blocking ones. By this stage, it should be obvious that standard rules of thumb—"get your allies on board first," "negotiate internally first, then externally"—need deeper scrutiny to decide whether they offer the best guidance.

- To sequence effectively, start by scanning widely among internal, external, actual, and potential parties that you have mapped.

- Be sure your map includes a sense of the key relationships among the parties, especially who defers to whom and who influences whom, positively or negatively. Estimate the costs and benefits of gaining each party's agreement.

- Focus on the most difficult-to-persuade player who is either the ultimate target or is otherwise critical to the deal. With respect to the target player—and using your assessments of relationships and interests—ask which prior agreements among which of the other players might help persuade the target to say "yes." Do the same for the penultimate player. Keep working backward in this fashion until you have found the most promising path through the cloud of possibilities.

- Refine your sequencing decisions by asking whether the parties should mainly meet together or separately at each stage of the process. Similarly, decide whether it would it be more productive for the stages of the negotiation to be public or private.

- Manage the flow of information carefully and think through how you will frame it at each stage.

Get the Basic Process Choices Right

Beyond scope and decisions related to sequencing are a series of *basic process choices*—the rules of engagement and overall negotiation characteristics, subject to which each party will negotiate. Wise process choices can help set up productive negotiations almost anywhere along the complexity spectrum.[9]

Negotiators often just fall into a set of process choices without thinking through their implications. We will not attempt to present an exhaustive list of such possibilities here; rather, we will highlight some important ones— beginning with some of the most familiar design choices—and show how 3-D Negotiators can effectively use them.

Some Basic Process Elements: Third Parties, Special Procedures, and Negotiation Systems

As we've seen, face-to-face negotiations sometimes run up against show-stopping barriers: communication problems, interpersonal friction, emotional escalation, ego clashes. Being too close to the problem may blind the parties to potential solutions. A party may overoptimistically assess its best no-deal alternative (e.g., its chances in court, or how well it would fare in a strike) and stubbornly hold out for more than is possible. Or the right agreement may be evident, but the two sides may have painted themselves into a positional impasse, with no face-saving way to make the necessary concessions to get there.

A standard at-the-table response to such barriers is redoubled efforts at more effective negotiation techniques and better interpersonal process. Often, however, basic process changing moves, such as the decision to bring in a skilled third-party mediator, can offer a value-creating alternative. For example, deep-frozen negotiations between Microsoft and the Department of Justice finally thawed with the help of two intensive mediation efforts by outside parties.[10] Mediators can help negotiators in a number of ways: lowering the emotional temperature, fostering more effective communications, helping uncover less obvious interests, offering face-saving possibilities for movement, suggesting solutions that the parties might have overlooked, structuring the process more efficiently, reducing the risk of sharing information, and proposing new fairness principles.[11]

While the parties may not be able to reach an agreement on the substance of their dispute, they may agree on a different kind of game-changing process move, such as binding arbitration, to render a decision if the parties deadlock. Arbitration has many variants. For example, in more complex cases, two sides may each choose an arbitrator, with the arbitrators themselves choosing a third arbitrator.[12] In the "shadow" of arbitration—which, of course, shifts perceptions of no-deal alternatives—negotiations may be radically transformed.

Beyond mediation and arbitration, there are a variety of more specialized alternative dispute resolution (ADR) procedures that can offer advantages over traditional litigation in both cost and time. While the specifics are beyond this book's scope, various innovative ADR mechanisms can be matched productively to different kinds of disputes.[13]

Even without third-party involvement, a number of process mechanisms can help resolve impasses. For example, two sides seeking to wind up a partnership may be unable to negotiate a specific deal as to who gets what. They may, however, be able to agree to a "Texas shootout," in which one side names a price at which it would either buy the other's shares or sell its own—and the other side must respond.[14]

Closely related to mechanisms designed for single disputes is the design problem of influencing a *stream* of negotiated outcomes, when ad hoc negotiation doesn't seem to work. Examples include the design of organizational dispute resolution systems.[15] Similarly, the institutional and regulatory context may be consciously shaped to influence the frequency and quality of negotiations carried out within that setting. For example, our colleague Mike Wheeler has offered advice on the best design characteristics of policies to stimulate productive negotiations in Massachusetts over hazardous waste treatment facilities, as well as a New Jersey system designed to foster socially desirable intermunicipal trading of affordable housing obligations.[16]

Setup choices for the most productive possible negotiations also take place at a global level; for example, we have actively contributed to the debate over the best process design choices for international negotiations such as those over CFCs and global warming.[17]

Two Broad Design Approaches

Two very different approaches exist for designing the negotiations that are often required to develop complex entities like mines, oilfields, power plants, or dams. These can be summarized as "decide-announce-defend" (DAD) and "full consensus" (FC).[18] By contrasting two cases utilizing these polar approaches to large project negotiations, we can highlight underlying design choices that have much wider application to deal making.

DECIDE, ANNOUNCE, DEFEND (DAD). The DAD approach treats a large project mainly as a contractual matter between those parties who will sign the relevant documents. A decision is made on the project, and its characteristics and private terms are negotiated with those who must formally approve the deal. Then it is announced. If opposition arises, the contracting parties defend what they have done.

For example, Stone Container Corporation, then one of the world's largest paperboard entities, used a DAD approach on a forestry initiative in the La Mosquitia region of Honduras.[19] La Mosquitia was a desperately poor area of the country that suffered from pirate logging and accelerating deforestation. After years of rule by its military and wealthy elite families, Honduras had recently democratized. Stone executives negotiated quietly with the new president and his ministers, arriving at an agreement that, at the president's request, was kept secret until the implementing regulations could be finalized.

In the interim, however, the Honduran Congress became alarmed. Leaked versions of the supposed agreement identified a huge tract that had been earmarked for logging by Stone (over a very long time frame). International activists from the Rainforest Action Network (RAN), along with other environmental and indigenous peoples' advocates, rose in protest. A broad coalition of Honduran labor, business, and political players soon became energized in opposition. On the eve of major protests in the capital city, the president unexpectedly withdrew his support. Despite a three-month process of reformulation, Stone withdrew from the effort to negotiate project approval.

The irony of Stone's withdrawal is that its plan probably would have benefited most major interest groups in Honduras, and certainly would have been vastly better for the country than the no-agreement alternative of massive unemployment in the region, pirate logging, and accelerating deforestation and desertification. But the DAD process called forth a nearly unstoppable adverse coalition of domestic and international interests which sunk the idea. Many other examples of DAD processes exist; in general, as in the Honduras example, it is a high-risk strategy when potentially influential stakeholders are likely to take an interest.

FULL CONSENSUS (FC). In sharp contrast to DAD is FC, which seeks agreement among the full set of stakeholders. And yet a straight FC approach is equally vulnerable to failure. As an illustration, let's look at Conoco's effort to build consensus for its environmental management plan (EMP) for oil extraction in Block 16 of Ecuador's Oriente region.[20] Conoco— then a subsidiary of the DuPont Corporation, which had embraced a "beyond compliance" environmental strategy—saw an opportunity to become the oil-field developer of choice in environmentally sensitive areas. Believing that the major oil finds of the future would be located in socially and ecologically fragile regions, Conoco sought to draw together a diverse set of stakeholders and build consensus around its EMP for its Ecuador project, nicknamed "Block 16."

But this was a daunting task, since the oil find—representing some 20 percent of Ecuador's known reserves—was located not only in the Amazonian rainforest, but also on the lands of threatened indigenous peoples (and in a national park, to boot!). Domestic and international advocacy groups became energized. Meanwhile, factions within the Ecuadorian government battled each other and behaved erratically, adopting a variety of internally inconsistent arguments: revenue potential, environmental protection, and national security imperatives.

Conoco sought to generate a consensus for its EMP among the affected groups during a four-day meeting on a floating hotel on the Rio Napo. Not surprisingly, these groups voiced deep skepticism about Conoco's real motives, and that consensus-building effort rapidly degenerated into suspicions and recriminations. Conoco then launched an effort to negotiate an agreement with the Natural Resources Defense Council (NRDC) and other "moderate" environmental groups. Leaked minutes of these Conoco-NRDC meetings generated even greater controversy among stakeholders.

The upshot? Conoco eventually sold its shares to the Maxus Energy Corporation and a Taiwanese company. Development of Block 16 was later carried out by YPF, the Argentine oil company, in a way that many observers argue was more destructive of native cultures and the environment than Conoco's plan would have been.

TYPICAL OBJECTIVES: DAD VERSUS FC.   The Stone and Conoco cases point up number of starkly different basic process choices:

- In the DAD approach, the negotiation process usually focuses on "getting the deal done." By contrast, the objective of the FC approach typically is to achieve consensus among a set of stakeholders. Getting the deal done is part of the objective, but only in the context of building ongoing relationships.

- Typically, the DAD approach aims at generating a comprehensive, detailed, legally binding, and permanent deal. This agreement, with recourse to the courts or binding arbitration, is expected to govern the details of the relationship. The FC approach, in contrast, seeks a framework document with the key terms fixed, but often with a built-in expectation of continuing adaptation and possible renegotiation in the face of specified (or even unanticipated) events.

- The contractually oriented DAD approach emphasizes gaining the support of the legally required parties who must sign the document. The consensus-oriented FC approach generally emphasizes a more expansive set of stakeholders, with the formal contracting parties at the center, but seeks explicit or informal support from a wider group.

Of course these choices are applicable in situations well beyond the forestry or pipeline projects described above, nor are they doomed to failure, as they were in those examples. But negotiators should make the choice carefully, or better yet, create a judicious hybrid. The design chosen should depend on the context, the range and profile of likely stakeholders, as well as the long- or short-term outcomes your side desires.

BEYOND DAD AND FC.   Hybrids and variants of DAD and FC abound, and they can be located on a spectrum of possible process choices. Most big players resort to more than one set of process choices as they operate in a variety of contexts. For example, Stone Container undertook another forestry project in Costa Rica using a stakeholder process but this time it was hosted by the government.[21] Unlike Stone's Honduran adventure, its Costa Rican talks included stakeholder groups, but only as advisers to the ultimate decision makers in government. While this project also attracted protesters, the process generated enough support that Stone could move forward with a version of the project, which was widely hailed.

In another example, Exxon Mobil led a consortium to build an oil pipeline in Chad and Cameroon that generated immense controversy.[22] But the company solicited heavy involvement from the World Bank to help create an innovative mechanism—largely outside the control of the two (very corrupt) host governments—for channeling project revenues to agreed-upon social projects within the two countries; under this favorable arrangement, and the pipeline was approved, though long-term compliance was anything but certain.

Basic Process Choices: A Checklist

Let's look at some of the process choice implications suggested by these case studies.[23] We'll start with two cross-cutting considerations: (1) whether process choice questions should be dealt with explicitly, and (2) whether you should simply seek to impose them, or treat them as negotiable issues.

- First, you can either be explicit about the range of basic process choices for a negotiation, or you can treat these choices in a much more implicit, ad hoc way. In general, clarity is preferable—to promote efficiency and commitment to the process, and to avoid potentially costly misunderstandings and conflict—*but not always*. That's because in contentious situations, you may face endless haggling about the "shape of the table." Process choices may become proxies for other issues, and pointlessly consume valuable time. Before launching into a "negotiation about the negotiation," therefore, you should have a good sense of whom you're dealing with, and how reasonable they're likely to be.

- Second, consider how decisions about process choices are reached. Does one party decide, or are process choices open to negotiation by the group? Stipulating such choices unilaterally presents advantages of control and efficiency, but may generate resentment from other parties and a willingness to subvert or reopen the choice.

We list several of the most important design choices below. You should think of the process choice categories that follow as a kind of checklist for key setup moves.

AUSPICES. Without even thinking very hard about it, Conoco, in its Rio Napo meeting, decided that the negotiation process should be under its own auspices. This was a disastrous call, since to some of the more skeptical participants, this looked like unilateral power grabbing. In other cases, such as that of Stone Container in Costa Rica, it would make good sense for government entities to host the forum. When the principal parties are at odds, you may want to seek a more neutral third party to provide the auspices.

MANDATE. Clarity on the intended output of the forum is important. Is there a commitment, explicit or implicit, that any agreements arising from the forum will bind the group of participants and the constituents they represent? Or are its agreements advisory to another body, such as a government agency, that must later make the formal decision? Stone in Costa Rica, for example, used a process hosted by the government whose output was only advisory to the final decision makers, but was understood to carry considerable weight in that choice. Ambiguity of mandate can be a killer.

PARTICIPATION. The choice of who issues the invitations and who participates in the process can be all-important. The status of participation may range from full principal to nonvoting observer. Participation choices may be directly negotiated, or groups may be invited to select representatives who may or may not have the power to bind the constituent group. The breadth and basis of participation bears a clear relationship to the underlying vision of the process—that is, a DAD process, an FC process, or some sort of hybrid.

DECISION RULES AND PROCEDURES. An important process characteristic is how the group will make choices. At one extreme, there may be *ad hoc* deliberation without formal decision by a set of unspecified procedures. Alternatively, decisions may be made by majority vote, by specified majority procedures (such as "sufficient consensus"), or by full-blown consensus. The procedures by which the forum operates can include the following: the powers of a chair, who is to be recognized, whether the group will break into subgroups or operate in a plenary fashion, how documents will be adopted, and how they will be revised and accepted.

AGENDA. Beyond whether the agenda is prespecified or is to be negotiated—and, if so, how—there are several related questions. For example: once agreed upon, is the agenda fixed, or open-ended? If it needs to be changed, how will that happen? Are the issues tightly focused—for example, specifically related to a contract—or are they broader and related to a wider set of stakeholders? Once the agenda is determined, you face the related choice of who deals with what issues. For example, participants may be separated into specialized groups to deal with specific issues, or all participants may deal with all issues.

STAGING OF PROCESS. Beyond pure sequencing, the evolution of deliberation and negotiations can either be ad hoc or consciously staged. Staging may begin, for example, with efforts at a joint problem definition, and can continue through fact finding, negotiation of agreed issues, and a decision and commitment phase. Alternatively, these stages may be blended, or left to the group.

EXTERNAL COMMUNICATION. Negotiating groups often have conflicting views about what information can be legitimately shared with those outside the negotiation, including representatives of the press as well as their constituencies. The group may decide to have no rules on this issue, may agree to highly restrictive condition, or something in between.

PROCESS SUPPORT. For more elaborate negotiations, the parties may seek support from a "secretariat" that can range from informal to elaborate. Third parties, either as substantive experts or in the roles of mediator or facilitator, may be included. In some cases, especially where the parties have divergent technical expertise and limited resources, you may want to bring in outside technical resources.

POSTDEAL ARRANGEMENTS. The forum may or may not have a life beyond the agreement. A process may be agreed upon in advance to deal with implementation, as well as any proposal for adaptation or renegotiation.

Good Basic Process Choices Make for Good Negotiations

As we've tried to make clear in the preceding pages, basic process choices can significantly affect negotiated outcomes. Such choices can drive the negotiation either toward cooperative, joint problem solving, or toward hardball, distributive battles. They can make salient interests narrow, tangible, and tractable—or, alternatively, they can make those interests broad, general, ideological, and intractable. They can leave the no-agreement alternative vague, or they can shine a bright light on a worse alternative that's lurking in the wings.

And most important, these process design choices ultimately can contribute to the quality of the outcome, by generating (or not generating) options, and by enhancing or damaging key relationships.[24]

- To sequence effectively:

  - Scan widely to map the range of potential parties as well as the relationships among them, including the costs and benefits of gaining each party's agreement.

  - Map backward from the key players who are critical to the deal. With respect to a target player, ask which prior agreements among which of the other players might help persuade the target to say "yes." Do the same for the penultimate player. Keep working backward in this fashion until you have found the most promising path through the cloud of possibilities.

  - Ask whether the parties should mainly meet together or separately at each stage of the process. Similarly, decide whether it would be more productive for the stages of the negotiation to be public or private.

  - Manage the flow of information carefully and think through how to frame each stage.

- Beyond setup moves, negotiators should make basic process choices, including:

  - Classic process choices include whether to involve mediation, arbitration, other various alternative dispute resolution devices, and special procedures such as "Texas shootouts."

  - Though a wide range of options is available, two polar sets of basic process choices can be captured in very different overall approaches to the negotiation process: a contractually oriented decide/announce/defend (DAD) method, and a stakeholder-relationship-focused full consensus (FC) option.

  - A useful checklist of basic process characteristics includes the auspices of the process, its mandate, participation rules, decision and procedural expectations, agenda considerations, staging, external communication norms, process support (from technical advice to third parties such as mediators or facilitators), and postdeal arrangements.

  - When considering the process elements on this checklist, think hard about whether it is better to deal with them explicitly, or leave them on a more ad hoc and implicit basis. You should also decide whether these elements should be put up for negotiation, or whether you should try to stipulate, or even impose, your basic process preferences.

Part Three

Design Value-Creating Deals

"On the Drawing Board"

Chapter Eight

Move "Northeast"

L ET'S BRIEFLY REVIEW where we are, in the larger 3-D Negotiation landscape.

In part 1, we gave you an overview of our three dimensions and explained how those dimensions come together to inform and direct more effective negotiations. In part 2, we looked in depth at what we call the *setup*, or third dimension, which comprises most of the work that you do away from the table to get the parties, interests, no-deal options, sequence, and basic process choices right. In part 3, beginning with this chapter, we're going to dig deeper into our second dimension: *deal design*. Some of the most important work in negotiation takes place "on the drawing board." It involves one or more parties trying to *create value*—not only for themselves, but for the other parties as well.

In our work, we often encounter experienced negotiators who are openly skeptical about the idea of creating value for parties other than themselves. *It's all about claiming the value that's already on the table*, they tell us. *It's all about hard-nosed tactics.* As we've explained earlier, there *are* some negotiations that really are truly zero-sum discussions: my gain is your loss, and vice versa. (In fact, we'll spend all of chapter 12 developing detailed "value-claiming" tactics for just such cases.) But we've also pointed out that in many cases, negotiators are too quick to perceive a fixed pie. They give up far too quickly on the possibility of expanding the pie for the benefit of all concerned.

So we need to move beyond zero-sums and fixed pies, and develop a different fundamental picture—a different metaphor—that can serve as a guide for better deal designing, and for more productive negotiating. In our work with experienced executives, we tend to talk about *moving northeast*—a kind of chart-based, landscape-based image that often resonates powerfully once it becomes clear. If north is the direction that I want to go, and east is the direction you want to go, then moving northeast may be a very attractive option. In fact, it may be the best option for all parties—better than any of them could do on their own.

"Moving Northeast" to Create Value

Sometimes, negotiations go nowhere. Remember our discussion of zones of possible agreement, or ZOPAs, in chapter 6; if there's no ZOPA, there's no space for a deal. Sometimes, negotiations get to a solution that nobody loves, but everybody can live with. And sometimes, negotiations lead to a solution that is the bargaining equivalent of the perfect trade between two sports franchises, or two stamp collectors: *it's the deal that's better than any other deal either side could imagine as possible.* It's the deal that makes everybody far better off than they would have been without it, or than they would have been if they had focused only on value-claiming at the table.

A Good Beginning

To explore the idea of moving northeast, let's look at the case of a struggling radio station. Let's assign to it the call letters "WORN."[1] Let's say that it broadcasts out of Worntown, Massachusetts (our home state).

WORN is cash-poor and technically shaky, and it consistently fails to sell all of its advertising time. Its poorly maintained transmission equipment puts out an uneven broadcast signal that annoys listeners and has even drifted dangerously from its assigned frequency (which can get you shut down by the FCC). The station has recently invested in some new computerized systems but is having trouble finding enough cash to configure those systems to maximize their value to the station. In short, WORN's future looks bleak.

Meanwhile, Worntown also has another underutilized resource: the recently established Worntown Engineering Services, Inc. (WESI), which has a book of business that is only partly full. The partners at WESI have discussed ways to get more publicity for their firm, including increased advertising. But a recent conversation with the ad-sales manager at WORN has underscored the fact that the engineers simply don't have the budget for an expanded radio ad campaign.

A cash transaction is a nonstarter. But you can easily spot a potential deal in the making, right? Couldn't WORN trade some free (or deeply discounted) advertising airtime to WESI in return for some much-needed technical support? By embracing a move like this, both sides would improve their circumstances dramatically relative to their best no-deal alternatives.

But What If Both Sides Could Do Still Better?

Let's say that representatives from WORN and WESI continue to talk and develop a more sophisticated understanding of each other's situations. In the course of these conversations, the engineers learn that the radio station has some surplus electronic equipment left over from a recent technical upgrade. To most companies, this surplus equipment would have no value. It turns out, though, that WESI has an important client that needs hard-to-obtain parts nearly identical to those that are gathering dust at WORN. The engineers make an informal proposal: *what would you think about accepting help from us in configuring your new computer-based systems in return for that surplus gear?*

A quick diversion: think about pure price haggling at an auto dealership, where a better deal for one side is by definition a setback for the other. Recall the Battle Line from chapter 6, along which both sides must fight to gain advantage, is price—pure and simple. Now think about the kind of discussions being described above. Where's the Battle Line? There isn't one. If they play their cards right, both sides can do better, at no cost to either. This idea is illustrated in figure 8-1. The point where the two axes intersect—the "Southwesternmost Point" (or "(0, 0)" in graphing terminology)—represents the initial no-trade circumstance of WORN and WESI. The further to the right, or "east," one goes along the horizontal axis, the more valuable the deal becomes for the engineering firm. The further up (or "north") one goes along the vertical axis, the more valuable the outcome for the radio station.

If the two sides agree to trade engineering services for ad time, you get movement to the north *and* movement to the east. Let's call this "Northeast Point A." Clearly, Northeast Point A is better for both sides than was the Southwesternmost Point. And, as we'll keep stressing, unlike any price concessions in a haggle, *it comes at no cost to either side.*

Northeast Point B, still further to the northeast, combines the surplus-gear-for-configuration-help trade with the ads-for-services swap. What's happening? The deal is getting better. No one is making concessions; no one is getting hurt. It's a "win-win," to employ standard negotiator's terminology.

Obviously, this is a simplified example. And just as obviously, competitive value-claiming moves can still be taking place alongside the cooperative,

FIGURE 8-1

Two joint value-creating moves "northeast"

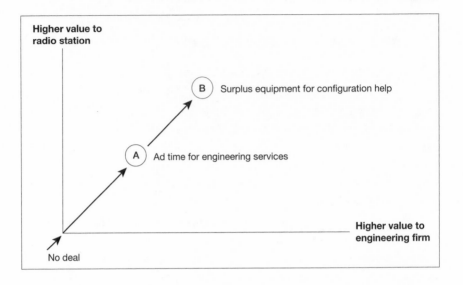

value-creating moves just described. For example, the engineers will certainly demand more ad time for fewer services, and the radio station will bargain for the opposite outcome. We'll have more on this shortly, but we wanted to open this discussion with a readily accessible example because—in our experience—so many people are using, and *misusing*, standard negotiator's terminology. They talk "win-win," but their mental image of win-win is a midway point along an established Battle Line: a price that both sides can live with that is better than no deal. Because they're focused on potential points of friction, they're *not* focused on creative deal design. It's as if you put a thumbtack at (0, 0) on our chart above, looped a string around the tack, and tied one party to each end of the string. They would tug each other at right angles around that tack, until one or both parties were exhausted. They would never venture out onto the vast unknown territory of mutual gain: the turf between the two axes.

The point, of course, is to lose the thumbtack, and start exploring that unknown territory. Take, for example, the story of two sisters quarreling bitterly over dividing an orange. Their positions were incompatible: each demanded at least two-thirds of it, but there was only one orange. Tense impasse. Yet when their battle of positions gave way to an exploration of deeper interests, it turned out that one sister was hungry while the other wanted citrus flavoring for a gourmet recipe. The no-compromise, jointly beneficial, "northeast" move was now obvious: give the peel to the sister who needs flavoring and give the edible fruit to the hungry one. Or think back to the dam versus no-dam debate described in chapter 3; the bargaining moved northeast, relative to an inconclusive and protracted legal battle, when the negotiators started talking about a smaller dam built on a fast track, stream flow guarantees for farmers, and an environmental trust fund to preserve whooping crane habitats.

All too often, especially in public disputes, negotiators are driven to extreme positions. Because of their own strong feelings, or those of their constituents, they are *not* inclined to think win-win. They are inclined to think of compromise or meeting someone halfway as a form of surrender. "The only thing in the middle of the road," as progressive Texas commentator Jim Hightower once famously put it, "is a yellow stripe and a dead armadillo."

Well, it's a good one-liner. But our experience tells us that in most cases, there are many, many choices other than compromising your way into the middle of the road. Two central deal-design principles, described in the following sections, point the way toward moving northeast.

Deal-Design Principle #1: Dovetail Differences to Create Value

Here's the first principle: to set the stage for moving northeast, all parties need to relentlessly probe for different interests that are relatively easy for them to give, and relatively valuable for the other side to get, in short, for high-benefit, low-cost moves.

We've already made the case that to succeed at negotiations, you have to focus on learning about the interests that lie behind the positions being articulated at the table. But what does that mean, exactly? And why is that important? Conventional wisdom says that we negotiate to overcome the differences that divide us; thus, we're advised to shape win-win agreements by searching out common ground. And yes, finding common ground is generally a good thing, if we're talking about building trust and fostering communication. It's also a good thing in the relatively unusual case in which there's an *exact overlap of interests* among the negotiating parties. But the fact is that the most frequently overlooked sources of value in an agreement arise from *differences*—or complementarities—of interest among the parties.

It's not usually very helpful to ask, "What's something that both of us value highly?" It's usually far more helpful to ask, "What's something that they need badly, and which I don't value anywhere near as much?" Where are the high benefit–low cost possibilities?

Think back to the story of WORN and Worntown Engineering Services. The two parties could have hung up on their opening positions: *Our drivetime spots cost $X* (WORN). *We can't and won't pay $X for drivetime spots* (WESI). But what about the interests behind those opening positions? To the station, unsold airtime and surplus equipment weren't worth much—but engineering expertise was critically important. To the not-very-busy engineers, the cost of giving technical support to the station was low, while the value of getting low-cost advertising and acquiring surplus equipment for a key client was extremely high. It was the complementary differences in their respective interests that resulted in the potential for a value-creating agreement.

In chapter 2, we related the story of the London developer whose proposed medical center was being blocked by a single holdout landowner in the middle of the development site. It was only after the developer figured out the *interest* behind the *position*—the landowner's strong sense that her deceased pet needed an appropriate resting place—differed from his own interest that value could be created for both parties.

We've also talked earlier about the Egyptian/Israeli negotiations over the Sinai in the wake of the 1973 war. As those negotiations opened, the two countries' positions on where to draw the new boundary were incompatible. Despite great diplomatic ingenuity and creative mapmaking, no proposed map worked for both sides. Each attempted map gave up too much hard-won territory either to the Egyptians (in the eyes of the Israelis) or to the Israelis (in the eyes of the Egyptians), or—in the worst cases—both. It appeared to be a hopeless impasse.

But when negotiators probed the territory beyond their opposing positions, they uncovered a vital difference of underlying interests. The Israelis cared far more about security, and the Egyptians cared far more about sovereignty. Rather than focusing on a forever-elusive compromise over where to draw a line in the sand, the parties looked at interests behind positions and hit upon a value-creating solution based on the creation a demilitarized zone (security) under the Egyptian flag (sovereignty). This is just a high-politics version of the two sisters and their one orange. To restate our opening principle in slightly different language: differences of interest or priority can open the door to an unbundling of interests, which in turn can give each party what it values the most at relatively low cost to the other side.

Even when an issue seems purely economic, finding differences can unlock deadlocked deals. For example, a small technology company with which we worked was stuck in a tough negotiation with a large strategic acquirer. The technology company's investors were demanding a high price; the acquirer appeared to be dead set on paying a much lower price.

Upon further investigation, it turned out that the acquirer was actually willing to pay the asking price, or close to it—but was deeply concerned about raising price expectations in a fast-moving sector in which it intended to make additional acquisitions. The solution that the two sides ultimately agreed on had two major components: (1) a modest, well-publicized, initial cash purchase price; and (2) a set of less-well-publicized (and purposefully obscure) contingencies that virtually guaranteed substantially greater profits to the seller over time, but that avoided setting a highly visible precedent that would be costly to the acquirer in future deals.

In other words, the seller's interest in a higher selling price (although not necessarily all up front) fit together neatly with the buyer's interest in avoiding adverse precedents. Borrowing an old carpenter's term, we refer to this circumstance as *dovetailing*. As we'll make clear in subsequent chapters, dovetailing extends well beyond simple differences of interest or priority. It also comprises differences in forecasts about the future, differences in attitudes toward risk and time, and a wide range of other differences that can be profitably dovetailed for mutual benefit.

Deal-Design Principle #2: Maximize the Total Net Pie

Dovetailing can be considered to be a critical subset of a larger principle: maximize the total net "value pie" that is available to the negotiators.[2]

By *net*, we just mean the remaining value after costs have been accounted for. In other words, you compare the overall value that's in the system after your northeast moves with the value that was available beforehand, or the value that would have been available as a result of simple "meet-you-halfway" compromises. In both cases, you should see higher overall value relative to such compromises, and certainly relative to the no-deal alternatives.

To get there, you and your counterparts have to brainstorm together (and separately) to get good answers to the following questions:

- Thinking creatively, and perhaps outside the confines of this specific deal, what can we possibly do to create the most value together?

- What specific steps can we take to maximize the net value of the total pie?

Scrutinize each issue on the table, and—based on what you've been able to learn about interests, costs, and values—ask where the aggregate gain is largest. Where can you find the highest net value? Where can you find the lowest net cost? If it turns out that one side is a loser in terms of net value creation, both parties need to go looking for efficient and legitimate compensation mechanisms to adjust the value balance. The goal, of course, is to find linkable issues that don't destroy value, but rather transfer it efficiently to make possible the deal that creates the most value.

Remember that with a bigger pie overall, each party's ultimate share can be larger than *whatever* it would have been in the case of simply dividing up the fixed (and smaller) pie. For example: let's say that as a standard value-claimer, you bargained very hard and ended up with $600,000 of the value in a $1 million–sized pie, while the other side took home $400,000. But if you had both focused instead on increasing the pie by 50 percent—to $1.5 million—and split the gain, results for both of you would have been better: $850,000 for you, and $650,000 for them. *We're not talking about moving northeast for altruistic reasons; we're talking about creating value and getting to better results for all parties.*

Maybe that example sounded a little abstract. If so, consider a real-life story that captures a shift away from a complete emphasis on "my share" to an emphasis on the "total pie." Stone Container (which we encountered in chapters 4 and 7) had a standard vendor-purchaser relationship with Baxter Healthcare in North Carolina. In other words, based on the give-and-take of fairly routine purchase-order negotiations, Stone would sell its corrugated packaging to Baxter. For years, Stone's trucks ran fully loaded from Stone's warehouse in Charlotte to Baxter's facility in North Cove, and then made the return trip empty.

Then one day, an alert manager in Stone's shipping department noticed that Baxter also had a Charlotte facility not too far from the Stone warehouse. Stone's negotiators realized that this was an issue that ought to be on the table during the next round of negotiations: why couldn't Stone's trucks make the return run from North Cove full of Baxter products? Wouldn't that be a better deal for both Stone *and* Baxter? Wouldn't the total pie get bigger? As it turned out, the answer was "yes"—and the negotiated agreement for round-trip shipping was only the first of something like two hundred negotiated cost-saving, value-creating agreements between the two companies.[3]

Don't assume that these kinds of pie-growing activities can only arise in an environment of reasonably cooperative relations, such as existed between Stone and Baxter. They can also result from a more "hardball" tradition. For example: Sweetheart Cup Company sold standard cups to McDonald's, which at one point issued an edict to many of its suppliers: *cut prices 10 percent, or else!*[4] In other words, a standard value-claiming demand from an important customer. In an attempt to deal with the McDonald's demand, Sweetheart turned to its major paper supplier, Georgia-Pacific, for help. Unfortunately for Sweetheart, however, Georgia-Pacific was then preparing to impose an across-the-board increase in paperboard prices, citing increases in its own raw materials costs.

Typically, in negotiating along two hostile fronts at once, a company tries to push back the price demands as much as possible without damaging critical relationships. But when the dust clears, the company in Sweetheart's position is simply living with a smaller slice of a fixed pie. "Victory," then, means keeping the slice from getting *too much* smaller.

But rather than mounting a standard, value-claiming defense, Sweetheart asked for and got the opportunity to negotiate intensively with both Georgia-Pacific and McDonald's—and to expand the scope of those parallel discussions beyond pure pricing issues. In those separate (but linked) discussions, Sweetheart scrambled to find ways whereby the total three-way pie could be expanded. The answer that eventually emerged was a much fuller integration of the three firms' operations, characterized by a far more intensive electronic data interchange. This integration enabled significant cuts in administrative and inventory-related costs. When combined with three-way negotiations over improved (and joint) production planning, the results were a more consistent product and higher volumes for all three players.

And—not incidentally—Sweetheart strengthened its position vis-à-vis would-be competitors for the McDonald's business. The tight operational coordination between the fast-food giant and Sweetheart helped entrench Sweetheart's position as McDonald's paper-products supplier of choice.

One lesson to take away from these real-world stories is that the first step toward growing the pie and moving northeast is *believing that it's possible*. What was the Little Engine That Could's refrain? *I think I can; I think I can.* After that, you (and your counterparts on the other side) have to suspend your natural impulse to look for your best individual outcome on each issue and focus on making the pie bigger. Imagine—at least during this inventing stage—that instead of being "face-to-face against each other," you are "side-by-side against the problem."[5] Instead of playing winner-take-all, imagine (for the moment) that you are working for the same company and trying to enhance total value for the firm as a whole.

Take the following case: G&F Industries, a major plastics supplier to Bose Corporation, long ago realized the importance of "moving northeast" in its negotiations and other interactions with Bose—abandoning the traditional Battle Lines of supplier-customer bargaining, and looking for bigger pies. As one G&F executive put it: "When you look for opportunities and solutions, you don't play by the rules, you make the rules. You invent new ways to add value together. You see things in a different light."[6] In negotiations between two companies, for example, we often ask our clients (to their initial amazement) what they could do to make the other parties in the negotiation more profitable. Then, we ask what the *others* could do to make them more profitable. As they think this through, possibilities for creating value seem to emerge.

In summary, moving northeast involves three concurrent activities, which together add up to creating value in a negotiation:

- Probing behind bargaining positions to understand interests, and to discover differences

- Dovetailing these differences into joint gains

- Relentlessly focusing on how you and your counterparts might jointly maximize the total net pie

Some Words for the Skeptics

At the opening of this chapter, we made reference to the people who are skeptical about our emphasis on value creation and moving northeast. In our work with practitioners, both in executive education programs and in our real-world advisory role, this skepticism often takes the form of questions: *Is this pie-growing stuff realistic? How widespread is it today, and how significant is its potential? What if the other side isn't interested in creating value, only claiming it? When do we start* claiming *value?*

These are fair questions. We're not naive. Some individuals are ill-suited to moving northeast, even when the specifics of the deal at hand argue strongly for giving it a try. Some situations are mainly about value claiming, not value creating. (We'll have much more to say about these situations in the next part of the book.) So in the remaining pages of this chapter, let's look a little more closely at two topics that address the concerns of our skeptics: (1) the psychological reasons that sometimes undercut value creation in negotiations, and (2) the time and place for value *claiming*, as well as value creating.

Acknowledging Our Psychological Inheritance

If you sit down to a conversation with an evolutionary biologist, you're likely to hear a great deal about the brutal lives of our prehistoric forebears. Our genetic legacy from those hunter-gatherers, you'll hear, has hardwired us to see the world as a clash of value claimers—a vision of nature "red in tooth and claw."[7] The Battle Line ZOPA that we've referred to earlier is therefore an inevitable outcome of our psychological predispositions. (If it weren't there, we would have to invent it.) Phrases like *dog-eat-dog, looking out for number one,* and *only the strong survive* capture the essence of this mind-set. The strong emphasis on sports in our culture reinforces the battle-line mentality: you don't look to athletic competitions for examples of win-win thinking. For better or worse, in many aspects of our lives, we revel in adversarialism.

As noted in earlier chapters, experimental psychologists who have studied negotiating behavior have confirmed that adversarialism is a pervasive and deep-rooted human tendency. And even though both the laboratory and real-world experience offer countless examples of "expanding the pie" and moving northeast, our hardwired preconceptions still lead us to believe, on some level, that *your gain is my loss.* Indeed, in one striking survey of more than five thousand people in thirty-two negotiating studies—most of which offered the participants cash rewards for conducting successful negotiations—participants failed to spot and take advantage of value-creating issues about 50 percent of the time.[8] Free money left on the table for both sides was the norm, not the exception. And the real world incidence of poor deals, soured relationships, impasses, and downward conflict spirals suggests that these lab studies are (sadly) on target.

So we should draw three related lessons from this psychological backdrop. One is that learning how to negotiate effectively takes time and effort. The second is that *it can be done.* Half of the people in those studies *did* find the value-creating issues. The examples cited previously also point to the practicality of growing the pie. The third is that to the extent that psychological biases get in the way of our negotiating success, we have to recognize and work to overcome them.

We humans undertake all kinds of things—ranging from monogamy to sky-diving—that run counter to some of our basic instincts. A few of us step out of the open door of that airplane—and are glad of it—because someone has persuaded us that it is (1) safe, and (2) worthwhile. Moving northeast in negotiations is *far* safer, and much more worthwhile.

Claiming Value Has Its Place

Expanding the pie in the ways we've talked about in this chapter doesn't do away with the need to *divide* that pie. In fact, a bigger pie tends to concentrate the mind wonderfully on the dividing process. The challenge is to keep these two somewhat contradictory processes in the proper balance.

Think back to the negotiations between the radio station and the engineering firm. Their first value-creating move involved a swap of unsold advertising time for uncommitted engineering services (point A in figure 8-2, below). Of course, as noted earlier, that swap could have been made on a variety of terms—some favoring the radio station (e.g., point C), and others favoring the engineering firm (e.g., point D). Note that while all the terms on segment CAD were better for both sides than no deal, there was a clear Battle Line being drawn. At that point, both sides could have focused less on creating value, and far more on claiming it.

Instead, as you'll recall, they probed further and found another way to make both parties better off: trading surplus equipment for configuration

FIGURE 8-2

Creating *and* claiming value

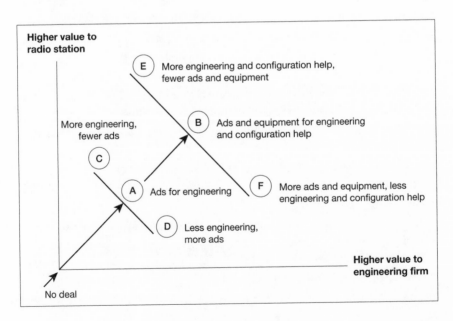

help. This moved them northeast to Point B, where both sides were clearly better off than they were at Point A. Once again, though, a new Battle Line emerged: line segment EBF. The new deal could have tilted toward the station's preferred Point E (more configuration and engineering help; fewer ads and less equipment) or toward the engineers' preferred Point F. In other words, even as the pie got larger, the allocation problem remained, and even intensified: the added value still had to be claimed.

We think this example illustrates why it's wrong—conceptually and practically—to cast win-win and win-lose approaches as *alternatives* to each other. The Battle Line doesn't go away when the parties create value; it simply moves northeast.

The "Negotiator's Dilemma": Productively Managing the Creating/Claiming Tension

Unfortunately, the implications of this analysis aren't just to "expand first, then divide," though that advice would be a big step up from the misleading views of the pure win-winners or the pure win-losers. No, it turns out that the *way* you expand the pie normally affects *how* it gets divided. And the battle over shares often affects the extent to which it is expanded—if at all. As we will later see in greater depth, competitive moves to claim value individually, or protect yourself from being exploited, often drive out the cooperative moves needed to create value jointly. This "Negotiator's Dilemma" can powerfully work against realizing the potential for value creation.[9]

For example, in setting itself up to achieve a better outcome, each side may stake out a very aggressive position. Each side may strenuously resist any movement from its position, hoping the *other* side will end up making most of the concessions. Even though in reality a significant, mutually beneficial zone of agreement may exist, such incompatibly aggressive positions may prevent the two sides from finding a deal at all. In such a case, each would leave money on the table, or value uncreated. Even if a compromise of some sort is finally reached, these determined individual efforts to claim value may block the two sides from even realizing the additional potential for cooperation to create value.

Such incompatible efforts to claim value are one version of the Negotiator's Dilemma, but there is a much more subtle and pervasive version. Each side may (reasonably) fear that being too forthcoming can open it to exploitation. For example, if I know your bottom line, I can squeeze you right down to it, so there is a bare minimum of value left in the deal for you. This risk may quite reasonably lead you to hold back from putting your other cards on the table. Facing similar risks, I may also hold back from being too open. Result? Too little information may be shared for us to figure out what value might actually be created. In the radio station–engineering firm negotiation—even with substantial underlying potential for value creation—this competitive dynamic may mean no deal at all or a limited deal along CAD (figure 8-2), when, if the truth were known, both sides would prefer a deal on EBF.

In our emphasis on joint actions to create value, we don't want to lose sight of the importance of individual efforts to claim it. Yet, in our experience, the world does not suffer from excessive cooperation and an overabundance of value creation in negotiation. We think that the more common risk comes from an excessive focus on claiming "my share" of the pie. Many otherwise experienced deal makers forget that they can advance their interests in three ways: to claim a bigger share of a small pie, a somewhat smaller share of a much bigger pie, or, best of all, a full share of a very large pie.

We want this chapter to leave you with the conviction that creating value is a real, important, and an attainable counterweight to value-claiming incentives. As you negotiate, consciously seek to do so in a manner than moves northeast from the familiar line of battle (see figure 8-3).

So when assessing the potential of deal, instead of thinking Battle Line, as illustrated in figure 8-3, your actions should be guided by a "northeast" conception more like that shown in figure 8-4.

Figure 8-4 reminds us that the inventing process is strongly affected by the claiming process, and vice versa. The two parties work their way toward a certain endpoint through a whole series of decisions, large and small, that comprise the entire negotiating process. Negotiating is not a process where you suddenly go from being an idealist to a realist; in fact, you are *always* a realist.

FIGURE 8-3

Claiming value on the Battle Line

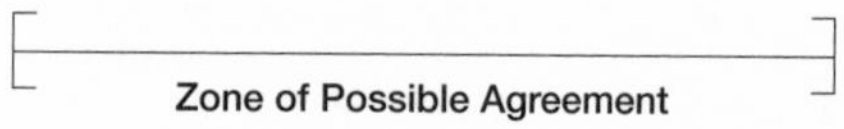

Zone of Possible Agreement

FIGURE 8-4

Move "northeast" to create (and claim) value

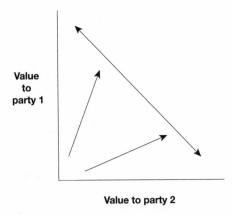

Value to party 2

You *always* have your best no-deal alternative in mind, along with the proper role of value claiming, as does your counterpart across the table.

Let us conclude by emphasizing that it's valuable for both parties to *try* to find ways to create value and move northeast. This isn't always possible, of course. You won't know it isn't true for you until you try to make it true for you. But what if the other side isn't interested in creating value, only claiming it? What if he scoffs when you mention this expanding-the-pie, value-creation business? What if he is named Igor, has huge muscles and tiny red eyes, carries a nail-studded club, and relishes eating idealistic, would-be value-creators for lunch?

Fair enough. We're not advocates for a naive version of the potential for creating value. We will dig much deeper into process of envisioning value-creating deals in the next chapters of this book when we more systematically discuss the art and science of deal design. There we will describe a number of real situations in which the parties were deeply convinced that they were stuck in fixed pie, pure value-claiming deals. Yet, these negotiators were able to reconceptualize the situations to open up value-creating possibilities. They did so, consciously or unconsciously, in line with the powerful deal-design principles we'll make explicit. And we'll give you considerable guidance for dealing with hard bargainers.

- Many people see the zone of possible agreement as a Battle Line, in which one side's gain necessarily implies another side's loss.

- Negotiation also involves "northeasterly," value-creating moves that simultaneously benefit all sides, at no cost to anyone. Such moves are fundamentally different than mutually acceptable compromises along a Battle Line.

- While common ground and shared interests are important, value is often created by dovetailing differences of interest or priority.

- Relentlessly probe for different interests that are relatively easy for one side to give—yet highly valuable for the other side to get. Such differences can be profitably unbundled or form the basis for mutually beneficial trades. Search for high benefit–low cost moves.

- Thinking creatively and perhaps well beyond this specific deal, ask what could the two sides possibly do jointly to create the most value together? What specific steps could be taken to maximize the net value of the total pie?

- If you encounter skepticism—or feel skeptical yourself—remember that there are good psychological reasons why people think that value-creation can't be for real. At the same time, remember that these psychological blind spots sometimes prevent negotiators from spotting immense cooperative potential.

- Don't forget that creating value is only half the story; it must also be claimed. This tends to happen concurrently, rather than sequentially. The real challenge in negotiation is to productively manage the Negotiator's Dilemma: the tension between the cooperative moves that are necessary to create value and the competitive moves needed to claim it.

Chapter Nine

Dovetail Differences

W E ' V E S U G G E S T E D T H R E E W A Y S to design deals that create value: (1) probing behind apparently incompatible bargaining *positions* to understand the full set of *interests* at stake for all sides, (2) *dovetailing differences*, and (3) thinking imaginatively, perhaps beyond the deal at hand, about how you and your counterpart(s) could maximize the *net value of the total pie*. Uncovering new value can often overcome impasses, hardball tactics, or refusal to negotiate. Think back to the holdout blocking a major hospital construction project (the "Fluffy" problem) and the farmer–environmentalist–power company impasse over building a dam (both in chapter 3), or the Sweetheart–McDonald's–Georgia Pacific price battle over cup and raw material prices (chapter 8).

In this chapter, we will dig much deeper into the second of these principles, dovetailing differences, which we have described as a way to take advantage of the complementary interests, priorities, and capabilities of the parties. Sometimes differences lead to a *trade*—recall the barter deal between a cash-poor radio station needing tech help and a publicity-short engineering services firm.

Sometimes "unbundling" different underlying interests leads to a dovetailing breakthrough; recall the last chapter's discussion of dividing the orange, and the Israel-Egypt negotiations. In setting up a new venture, one partner may crave control while the other is focused on return. Instead of just allocating shares of stock—which ordinarily combine votes with claims on earnings—it may be wiser to unbundle voting from profit sharing and assign these rights separately. Across these cases, one side values one thing highly that the other side can provide at relatively low cost, and vice versa. Such complementary differences—pairs of high benefit–low cost items—fit together in ways that aid, and even define, the deal design.

Beyond trades and unbundling possibilities, we now look at how differences in many other categories—forecasts of the future, attitudes toward risk, attitudes toward time, tax status, accounting or regulatory treatment, constituencies, and so on—can also drive joint gains. We'll do this by looking at cases with an eye toward answering three key questions:

- What are the key categories of differences?

- What kind of deal design can take advantage of this difference?

- What's the general design principle that grows out of these illustrations?

These examples are useful in and of themselves—in negotiation, the devil is often in the details, and these stories provide plenty of details. They should also have a cumulative impact, nudging you toward a general orientation for successful deal design: to develop an inventory of all the ways you differ from your negotiating counterparts, and then to use those differences as the ingredients for joint gains.

Dovetailing Differences in Forecasts (or Beliefs About the Future)

Mark Twain once observed that it is differences of opinions that make horse races. Twain's comment has a lot of relevance to the field of negotiation. Differences in beliefs about how future events will unfold—for example, what a certain price will be at a certain point in time, whether a technology will actually work, whether a permit will be granted or a lawsuit settled favorably—can be the basis of mutually beneficial *contingent* agreements, in which one thing only happens if another thing has happened before it.

When an entrepreneur seeks to sell his or her company, there is usually a gap between the highest price that the buyer will pay and the lowest price that the seller will accept. The entrepreneur often sees much brighter prospects for the company, thinking that only a lack of capital and scale stands between today's reality and glory. The buyer—although clearly interested in the target company—is more skeptical.

In other words, we have a difference in forecasts about what the future is likely to look like. A solution, in many cases like this (and which we mentioned in chapter 1), is a contingent agreement—an earn-out—in which the seller pays a fixed amount today and then pays additional sums subsequently based on the future performance of the firm. And often, the contingent component of the deal is much larger than the noncontingent component.[1] The optimistic seller signs up because he or she *knows* the company will perform. The skeptical buyer gets a good deal today and will only have to pay more in the future if the acquired property meets its performance goals. Their different worldviews can be dovetailed quite successfully.

So earn-outs have become quite common in acquisition-related negotiations. But they are not without their inherent problems. For example, they can create incentives for perverse behavior. To cite one obvious scenario, if the entrepreneur stays on to run the company for a specified period—and if he or she will receive substantial payments based (for example) on the profits of the company generated during that period—there may be a conflict-of-interest problem between the new owners and the entrepreneur. The entrepreneur may well optimize against whatever performance measure is used to compute the earn-out. This could mean emphasizing initiatives that generate short-run profits even if this weakens the firm's long-term competitive strength.

Contingent agreements can be structured to serve as a "truth serum" of sorts. Imagine a transaction in which an acquired company will only retain its high value if key customers stay with the company. The acquiring company should consider proposing a deal whereby a payment is made *only* if those customers stick with the company. Confronted with such a proposed deal, the seller will either accept it outright (a good sign), reject it outright (a bad sign), or engage in some useful truth-telling about the future prospects of the client base—or offer a "creative" reason why the customers will surely stay but why it is not a good idea to include this term in the deal (probably a bad sign).

Before designing a contingent agreement based on differences in forecasts, you should *probe deeply* into the source of those forecast differences. Do you have different beliefs because the other side is better informed about something? If so, crafting a contingent deal based on this kind of "information asymmetry" may not be advisable. Uninformed players should not generally bet against well-informed insiders or experts. But in many cases, different forecasts are based on different interpretations of shared data or simply on different worldviews.[2] (You are bullish on oil prices; I'm bearish.) Then contingent deals may make good sense, permitting otherwise desirable—but stuck—deals to happen.

Now let's look at a case in point. In the 1980s, an engineering firm wanted to build a series of plants that would burn solid waste to generate electricity. The firm would be paid both for disposing of the waste and providing power to its customers, in one form or another. In its first deal, the firm found a city that was willing to supply waste and would be able to use steam generated by such a plant to augment its other power sources. But the two sides couldn't come to an agreement on a fixed price for the steam. Yes, the city needed new power sources, but only at an affordable price. Meanwhile, the cogeneration company planned to finance the construction costs of the plant based on this contract with the city, including its steam purchase price, and could not borrow sufficient funds if that price that was too low.

Fortunately, the two parties agreed to probe behind their incompatible price positions. What they discovered was not a significant difference in *interests* that lay behind their seemingly incompatible positions, but in *forecasts*. The city planning department expected an oil glut and resulting lower energy prices over the next few years, while the cogenerators expected oil prices to rise. The solution? The two parties structured a contingent agreement in which the steam price would vary in relation to oil prices.

Contingent agreements should be structured in such a way that they are *sustainable*. In the example just cited, for example, it would have been foolish either to (1) let the price of steam fall below the level needed for the firm's debt service and plant maintenance, or (2) let steam prices rise to levels that would be politically disastrous. This could be avoided by partially indexing the price of steam to the price of oil and/or setting floor and ceiling prices for steam. Or, by resorting to a setup shift by involving outside parties, the two parties might hedge future oil prices by using sufficiently long-dated futures, or options, written by third parties or markets with different effective future expectations and risk attitudes.

Dovetailing Differences in Attitudes Toward Risk

The next extension of our dovetailing differences principle involves differences in the parties' attitudes toward risk—and specifically, differences in the ability to bear, influence, or assess specific risks. Let's look at four examples.

Selling a Restaurant

First, let's look at a case in which a restaurant owner was selling his highly successful restaurant to his head chef, in a friendly transaction. Both agreed that a sale price of $2 million, more or less, was fair—absent any complicating factors. But there *was* a complicating factor: the owner and chef had to consider how to reflect in the sales price an ongoing dispute with a contractor who had recently done major renovations to the restaurant. Pending the resolution of this dispute, the owner had withheld $1 million—money that the contractor felt she was owed, and was determined to collect. Because the dispute had not been settled through negotiation, it had gone into arbitration, and that process was likely to be completed soon. Both the owner and the chef agreed that there was no way of telling which way the arbitration would come out, and that the safest bet was that the contractor would be awarded about $500,000.

So there was no difference in forecasts about the future outcome of the lawsuit. But the chef—who was putting the bulk of his assets into the restaurant purchase—was very concerned about the risk of having to pay additional money to the contractor at some point in the future. As a result, the chef valued the restaurant at $2 million if he *didn't* have to bear the arbitration risk, but only $1.3 million if he had to bear that risk. In other words, the chef's aversion to risk caused his valuation of the restaurant to drop by $700,000, even though the expected cost of resolving the dispute was likely to be only $500,000.

The restaurateur, by contrast, was already wealthy, and this sale would only add to his substantial assets. He was much less averse to the arbitration risk and didn't want to pay a premium to avoid it. Being much less averse to the arbitration risk, he assessed it at its expected value and didn't want to pay more than $500,000 to avoid it.

What did the two negotiating parties do? They decided that the chef should pay the owner $1.6 million for the restaurant, with the current owner bearing the construction-dispute risk. Under this arrangement, both sides would benefit. Relative to his $2 million valuation for the restaurant, the chef would have been willing to pay up to $700,000 to avoid the arbitration risk. The purchase offer of $1.6 million shifted the risk to the seller—that is, the chef would effectively pay only $400,000 to avoid the risk; so he would be $300,000 better off. The restaurateur-owner was willing take on the risk for $500,000 or less, implying a minimum acceptable sale price of $1.5 million to him. However, he would be getting paid $1.6 million (with the obligation to accept the risk), and thus be $100,000 better off. Both parties thus gained by shifting the risk from the more risk averse to the less risk averse—and compensating the less risk-averse party so that the gain was shared.

A Joint Venture of Opposites

In our second example, a marginally profitable, publicly traded, risk-averse steel company was discussing a joint venture with a highly profitable, privately held scrap-metal company. The proposal on the table was to jointly build and operate a modern specialty steel facility, to be operated by the steel company, that would use scrap metal as an input. The proposed deal called for an even split of the investment costs, operating costs, future funding obligations, and returns. Even though this seemed "fair" to both sides, and even though both sides had nearly identical financial forecasts for the entity, this proposed deal structure soon led to an impasse. What was the problem? The publicly traded company was highly averse to the risk of any losses that could hurt its earnings, reduce its share price, or increase its cost of capital, and therefore was reluctant to go forward. The scrap company, by contrast, was far more aggressive in terms of its attitude toward risk.

How did the two firms dovetail their differences and convert the prior impasse into a happy deal for all? By structuring an agreement whereby the scrap company accepted more than a pro rata share of the losses in return for a larger share of the profits. Both parties, it turned out, strongly preferred capping the steel company's downside in return for a higher share of the upside going to the scrap company. In this case, value was created by allocating more risk to the less risk-averse party, and compensating that party by means of a higher prospective return.

A Public-Private Real Estate Deal

Our third example concerns a public-private real estate development negotiation. A city with a blighted downtown area was seeking a developer for a major mixed-use project, with office, retail, and residential components. The city was prepared to commit significant resources to assist in the development of this public-private project, but the mayor made it clear that getting approval from the zoning board could be a significant hurdle. Although its members had been appointed by the current mayor and his predecessors, the board was structured—and acted—as a quasi-independent body.

In addition to the zoning board, another wild card loomed: market risk. Would the project generate acceptable occupancy rates and rents within a reasonable time frame? The stakes were raised by the significant costs inherent in preparing a proposal for the zoning board. Dramatically higher costs would be incurred if and when the project went into the construction phase.

In early negotiations, the city's attorney proposed that the city and the developer split the project costs evenly, even if the proposal was turned down by the zoning board. The developer rejected this trial balloon. He believed that the mayor could and should exert significant influence on the zoning board's review process, and therefore should bear most of the costs of failure in that area. Following the same logic, however, he made a linked proposal of his own. Since the project would either succeed or fail in the marketplace based on his experience as a developer, *he* should bear the bulk of the risk at that later stage.

The final agreement reflected this central concept: that the party who had the greatest influence over the outcome of a particular risk would bear the largest share of that risk. And, significantly, the agreement also included appropriate incentives to minimize the respective risks. *Both* parties preferred this deal to the city attorney's initial "equal split" proposal.

Assessment Ambiguities

So far we've looked at cases in which the ability to *bear* risk (restaurant, steel company) was critical. We've looked at a case in which the ability to *influence* risk (public-private development) was the most important determinant. For our last example in this section, let's look at a case in which the ability to *assess* risk proved most important. The small developer of a waste disposal facility was deadlocked in his negotiation to sell the environmental permits he had obtained for a particular site to a large player in the waste-management industry. The problem grew out of an ambiguity in the relevant state law; under the regulations, the permits would automatically transfer to a buyer in the case of an existing facility, but it was not clear whether the permits would transfer (or *could* transfer) if no facility had yet been built.

Understandably, the buyer's attorney demanded a representation that the permits were indeed transferable. Just as understandably, the seller was reluctant to make such a representation. Was this an indication that he knew more than he was telling?

In this case, the answer was "no." The seller was an entrepreneur who had started out, years before, driving garbage trucks. By experience and training, he was far less capable of assessing the transferability risk than was the large waste-management company, which had full-time staffers devoted to legal and regulatory compliance issues. The solution? A deal whose ultimate structure included provisions whereby (1) the seller split the premium he was willing to pay to avoid the risk in the form of a reduced sale price, and (2) the risk was transferred to the buyer, who now had a very strong incentive to draw upon its specialized in-house assessment capabilities before completing the deal.

Dovetailing Differences in Attitudes Toward Time

In addition to differences in forecasts and attitudes toward risk, differences in parties' attitudes toward time can often be dovetailed to produce joint gains. The simplest version of this involves one very patient side negotiating with a very impatient counterpart.

Suppose that these two parties want to invest equally in a safe, predictable business that offered a steady income stream. A natural division of the profits would be 50/50, from start to finish. But it's very possible that, faced with this proposed division, *neither* party would want to move forward. The impatient party might greatly value relatively high early returns, and the more patient player might want much more money down the road. The value-creating answer, obviously, is to weight the returns to reflect this difference in time preference: more, early on, to the impatient player, and the mirror image of these returns at a later date to the patient player. Stating the same issue in slightly more technical terms, *patience or impatience can be captured in what economists call a discount rate.* A higher discount rate means that future costs and benefits count less in one's evaluations than do early ones; a lower discount rate means the reverse.

Let's look at a practical example of an impasse that was broken through the dovetailing of time-preference differences. A venture capital group had provided early-round financing to a promising biotechnology firm, which was now seeking additional financing. The biotech firm had contacted a large European pharmaceutical company that was impressed with the smaller firm's technology and expressed interest in making a later-stage investment.

The European company placed a high value on this investment as a window into a new area of biotechnology. Using its own *hurdle* (or minimum discount) rate for evaluating investments of this kind, it negotiated the terms of an investment that provided a 10 percent projected rate of return. But the European pharmaceutical wanted the comfort of seeing others investing in the biotech firm at the same time, and requested that the original VCs also go in on this next round equally. To the surprise of both the biotech firm and the pharmaceutical, however, the VCs declined to participate. What was wrong? Had the original investors lost faith in their biotech venture?

Eventually, through long discussions, it became clear that the VCs' hurdle rate for an investment at this stage in a company's life was a 35 percent rate of return. So a huge gap—between a required ROI of 10 percent and one of 35 percent—had opened up, and that gap was preventing the deal from moving northeast. To break the deadlock, the biotech firm's managers moved from equal returns to a structure that provided the VCs with a larger share of the early profits, and the pharmaceutical company with a higher share of the later profits. Although both sets of owners obviously valued today's returns more than tomorrow's, this was a far higher priority for the VCs, who would discount later returns so much more highly than the pharmaceutical company would. By building this kind of time-based dovetailing into the deal, greater value for both parties was created.

Think about all the ways that one party's attitude toward time may vary from another's; such differences may also lend themselves to effective dovetailing. Officials in grant-making agencies (both in government and the philanthropic sector) may have a strong interest in allocating certain funds before the end of a fiscal year. Conversely, companies that have annual budgets for consulting or for certain kinds of supplies may be more amenable to negotiating a large deal early in the budget cycle, when the necessary funds are more likely to be on hand. And those who deal with sales organizations with quarterly goals know that it is often possible to get better prices and terms at the end of a quarter—when the sales reps are stretching to reach their goals—than at the beginning. A manager who will be taking a new job overseas at year's end may care much more about the near-term effects of a current negotiation than its potential effects several years out.

Each of these differences in attitudes toward time offers the potential for joint gain among the negotiating parties. Once you have understood that your attitude toward time differs from that of the person across the table, you may be able to dovetail those differences and create a deal that both of you will find more attractive than you could have come up with if you looked at time the same way.

To summarize the overriding principle for this section: *Match payments and benefits received to relative time preferences.* The relatively impatient party should get greater returns earlier, and the patient party should be compensated more generously later. Treat the timing of cost sharing similarly and—as noted—keep an eye on the longer term.

Dovetailing Differences in Other Arenas

There are a host of other types of differences that lend themselves to dovetailing. Once you get in the habit of looking for them, they may show up often and unexpectedly.

Take, for example, a difference in *tax status*. An individual in the United States can't deduct interest on a loan used to purchase a car. But if a corporation borrows money to purchase the same car, it can deduct that interest. The corporation can then lease the car to the individual, resulting in a joint gain. How? Compare the after-tax cost of the corporation borrowing to buy the car with the cost to the individual who borrows to buy the same car. Since the corporate buying cost is much lower than the individual cost—by the amount of the tax savings from the interest deduction—lease terms can be worked out that leave both parties better off. In effect, this arrangement "shares" the tax savings resulting from tax-status differences between the two parties.

Dovetailable differences may also be found in *liquidity*. If one firm has cash on hand and another firm is in desperate need of capital to exploit a new technology, the liquid firm can provide capital in return for an attractive percentage of the profits generated by that new technology.

You may also come across valuable differences in *attitudes toward relationships and precedents*. One player may place great value on the deal at hand, while another may focus primarily on the relationship. In some organizations, decision makers are very much concerned with the precedents (or appearance of precedents) that may be established by a particular agreement, while other decision makers care much less about precedents (and the relationships they may affect) and care more strongly about the substance of the deal at hand.

Bringing It All Together: The Example of Structured Settlements

Many deals create value by dovetailing multiple differences simultaneously. For an example (our last in this chapter!), let's look at the interesting arena of *structured settlements*.

In attempting to settle personal injury-claim litigation, insurers and plaintiffs may cast themselves primarily as value-claiming combatants along a Battle Line. But in some cases, these negotiators could dramatically improve the value of an agreement to each side, relative to a straight cash settlement by offering settlements geared to the specific circumstances of the injured party and the skills and expertise of the insurer. These so-called structured settlements create value by dovetailing several of the kinds of differences we have described above, including:

- **Attitudes toward time.** Injured plaintiffs often exhibit lower effective discount rates than those of the insurers. There may a symbolic gain for the plaintiff, as well; plaintiffs often focus on maximizing the undiscounted sum of a settlement amount—the total payout—while insurers evaluate the stream of payments by calculating the discounted cash flow (bringing the stream back to its much smaller present value). As a result, insurers and plaintiffs sometimes can gain by settling upon higher aggregate amounts spread over longer time periods.

- **Tax status.** Income to a plaintiff generated by investing a cash settlement is taxable to the plaintiff. By contrast, annuity payments are *not* taxable to the plaintiff, as long as the plaintiff doesn't control the principal amount. By dovetailing this difference in tax status, the insurer and plaintiff can both gain from structuring the settlement as an annuity, and implicitly splitting the tax savings, which can be considerable.

- **Investment expertise, opportunities, and costs.** In insurance-related litigation, there is usually an asymmetry in investment capabilities: the insurance company usually has far greater skill and more resources than the plaintiff. Having the insurance company invest the settlement amount on behalf of the plaintiff, therefore, can be advantageous to the plaintiff's investing personally. In addition to getting (and spotting) better investment opportunities, the insurer generally pays lower commissions and other fees. This means for any level of benefit, it will cost the insurer less to provide the benefits than it would the plaintiff. They can in effect split that expected lower cost and higher returns.

- **Forecasts.** Insurers and plaintiffs are likely to have different forecasts about the plaintiff's life expectancy. Plaintiffs often overoptimistically believe that their life expectancy is equivalent to that of noninjured persons of their age. The truth is, however, that injuries often shorten life expectancy. As a result of these dynamics, plaintiffs may value the payment stream based on a longer forecasted life expectancy than that predicted by the insurer's actuarial tables. This may lead to a higher perceived benefit (by the plaintiff) and lower cost (as seen by the insurer).

- **Differences in attitudes toward risk.** Some plaintiffs are concerned that their resources may not last for their entire lifetimes. As a result, they may value highly the peace of mind that comes from knowing that they have an assured income in the form of an annuity. Again looking at the actuarial tables, insurers know that they can provide this peace of mind at a relatively low cost.

To reiterate the main lessons of this example: a structured settlement provides the opportunity to bundle groups of dovetailed differences together. When a plaintiff and an insurer settle a litigation by agreeing on an annuity, they may bundle joint gains based on differential forecasts, time and risk profiles, tax status, investment options and expertise, and so on. And this, in turn, points at a broader lesson of this chapter: when a variety of differences exists among the parties to a negotiation, substantial value can be created by devising agreements that dovetail, and thereby take full advantage of, those differences.

Imagine a World . . .

Imagine a world in which everybody is exactly the same—a world populated by identical twins, times millions or billions. In this world of clones, everybody has the same interests and capabilities. They look at the future the same way. Their attitudes toward time and risk are identical. They have the same amount of money in the bank. They're all equally good at investing.

To the negotiator eager to create value, this world is hellish.

Why? Because with the possible exception of banding together to achieve economies of scale, there is absolutely no opportunity to design mutually beneficial deals. There are no differences to dovetail.

Fortunately, our world—the real world—is full of differences, waiting to be discovered. And it is in the ways that we *differ* from one another—not in the ways that we're the same—that we can make the pie bigger, unlock joint gains, and move northeast.

- A deal-design approach complements an interpersonal process view of negotiation with an understanding of the principles behind value creation. Knowing what you are looking for can counteract powerful psychological biases toward seeing the world in "fixed-pie" terms.

- Rather than looking mainly for common ground and shared interests, deal designers probe for differences of many kinds to create value.

- The basic "differences" principle counsels a search for high-benefit, low-cost items, or those that are relatively cheap for one side to give, but that the other side finds relatively valuable to get.

- Develop a differences inventory, with clear knowledge of how characteristic deal designs can unlock joint gains from distinct classes of differences:

  - ➤ Differences of interest or priority can lead to mutually beneficial trades or creative solutions that unbundle underlying interests.

  - ➤ Differences in cost and revenue structure suggest crafting arrangements of highest net value.

  - ➤ Complementary differences in capability can be profitably combined.

  - ➤ Differences in beliefs about the future can lead to joint gains from carefully crafted contingent agreements, paying careful attention to incentives and the informational underpinning of the difference.

  - ➤ Differences in attitudes toward risk—assessing, bearing, or influencing it—can lead to mutually preferable mechanisms.

  - ➤ Differences in attitudes toward time, whether simple discount rate differences or more complex manifestations—can suggest collectively shifting benefits and costs to match differing time preferences.

  - ➤ Many other differences—in tax status, accounting or regulatory treatment, sensitivity to constituencies, etc.—can profitably be arbitraged, singly or in combination, by sophisticated deal designers to create value on a sustainable basis.

- By looking beyond the immediately involved parties and issues, a differences orientation can often suggest moves to profitably change the setup for all sides—by adding or subtracting parties and issues that manifest complementary differences.

Chapter Ten

Make Lasting Deals

L ET'S THINK FOR A MOMENT about the origins of a common expression: "a deal's a deal" or, in more formal settings, "we need to insist upon the sanctity of contracts." The expression is usually heard when one party to a deal has grown unhappy with the bargain that he or she has struck, and is now trying to get out of it, or at least get better terms.

Given that parties will sometimes try to get out of deals that all parties were reasonably happy to sign—the question is: *what can you do to make your deal stick?* And better: *can you craft deals that adapt well to changing circumstances, especially reasonably predictable ones?* Fortunately, the answer to both of these questions is often "yes."

In previous chapters, we have offered you a fair amount of commonsense advice on how to make agreements more sustainable. For example:

- Emphasize a positive and productive *process* as part of the negotiation itself.

- Don't neglect the importance of perceptions of *fairness*; deals that seem unbalanced can trigger renegotiation pressures or halfhearted compliance.

- Pay attention to building a positive *relationship* during and after the negotiation process, and expanding that working relationship into a constructive *social contract* over the life of the deal (in the next chapter we will focus on negotiating a positive social contract).

In this chapter, we look at the sustainability of agreements in greater depth, especially in the face of external and internal change. Some negotiators craft their agreements to take advantage of the reality that change is bound to occur; others are blindsided by it. Obviously, we want your deals to be in the former group.

Change Happens—and That's Often a Good Thing

When you sell off a pair of football tickets or negotiate the sale of your house through an unconditional cash transaction, you want the deal done, over, and put to bed. Under normal circumstances, you don't want any further interactions with the other party. In other kinds of deals, however, you may not want that kind of closure. You may want to keep some options open, to allow the deal to grow into a new and better form. Two very different agreements—one between Ford and Mazda, the other between Timberland and City Year—illustrate how a "done deal," carefully structured, can actually evolve for the better.

In 1969, Ford, Mazda, and Nissan signed a 50-25-25 agreement to manufacture automatic transmissions and offer U.S. market access to the Japanese partners.[1] As shared experience and trust grew—the result of regular meetings of U.S. and Japanese alliance teams—that agreement became the platform for developing a host of subsequent worldwide opportunities. For example, Ford purchased 15 percent of Kia Motors, matching Mazda's share of that Korean firm, and both used this entity as a base to source inexpensive small cars. Mazda provided design and manufacturing input to a new Ford plant in Mexico. Senior executives from Ford and Mazda met regularly. In addition to talking about the state of their joint investments, they spent a day talking about the state of their relationships and how to resolve issues that arose; in short, they were making a considerable and explicit investment in a positive social contract. By 1992, the bond grew even closer when Ford acquired 50 percent ownership and management control of Mazda's U.S. plant. By that time, the two companies had worked jointly on ten current models; 25 percent of Ford's models sold in the United States had Mazda input, and 40 percent of all Mazda models had Ford input.[2]

When Mazda fell into crisis in the mid-1990s, the positive social contract built over twenty years enabled a remarkable development. Prodded by Sumitomo Bank, Mazda's principal creditor, Ford purchased a controlling stake in Mazda. A Ford executive, Henry Wallace, was named the president of the $19 billion Japanese company. Hired specifically to engineer a turnaround, Wallace was the first foreigner ever to run a major Japanese corporation—a nearly unthinkable outcome, absent the long shared history and positive social contract.[3] And in 1999, Mark Fields—also a non-Japanese, and at thirty-eight, remarkably young for a senior management post in Japan—took the helm at Mazda to continue the turnaround.[4]

The changing relationship between footwear manufacturer Timberland and the urban youth initiative City Year also illustrates the potential advantages of evolving social and economic contracts. The relationship started as a purely philanthropic arrangement: a one-way, check-writing or in-kind deal (such as the donation of fifty pairs of Timberland boots to City Year). As Timberland's COO, Jeff Schwartz, later remarked, "Our expectation was a thank-you note, and a small sense of self-congratulations, and nothing more."

Our Harvard Business School colleague, Jim Austin, describes how this tightly circumscribed collaboration grew into a more "transactional" relationship—Austin's word—involving the shared expectation that each would seek out mutually beneficial deals, such as cause-related marketing, event sponsorships, and City Year–organized community service projects for Timberland employees.[5]

Finally, the relationship became what Austin calls "integrative," with the expectation of an ever-widening set of personal and organizational connections, and a subsequent meshing of organizational missions and values. Timberland executives joined City Year's board of directors, while City Year has offered diversity and team-building training to the firm. Community service became an integral part of Timberland's strategy and culture, with every employee getting up to forty hours of paid time-off annually for service-oriented activities.

Meanwhile, Timberland has assisted City Year in financing, operations, and recruiting additional corporations to enable it to expand its operations nationally. As with Ford and Mazda, openness to the possibility of a major evolution in the deal—from simple financial or in-kind support, to a transactional search for mutual benefit, to a more fully integrative relationship—created great value for both sides.

The main point: while many negotiated agreements are clearly time- and task-limited, others should not be considered closed, or static. You should be open to monitoring the success of a deal and reevaluating its terms over time. The balance of this chapter tells you how that's done.

Design Your Agreements to Accommodate Predictable Change

Sometimes you can see change coming, and you can build it into your deal structures. To illustrate this point, we like to tell the story of Benetton, the

Italian apparel maker, which has successfully entered a large number of new markets over the years. It does so following a predictable sequence of steps:

1. Establish a local agent to develop licensees for products from Italy.

2. Develop local production capability.

3. Partner with a local firm for further market development.

4. Buy out the local partner, which typically retains a significant role.

5. Integrate this foreign subsidiary into Benetton's global network.[6]

If you *know* that you're likely to follow a five-step process in a staged approach, it makes sense to draw up social and economic contracts with local partners that embody clear expectations of this planned trajectory and that include formal mechanisms to accomplish it. These may include, for example, buyout timetables and criteria, valuation methods, and written mutual expectations of post-buyout roles.

Anticipate Buyout or Exit

Building in buyout or exit provisions may sound like common sense—and yet, it's not unusual for joint ventures between multinationals and local enterprises to go off the rails over just these kinds of issues. In many cases, the local partner feels shocked and betrayed when, after a few years of increasingly successful joint operations, its multinational partner launches an "unexpected" buyout initiative. The local partner may feel entitled to a major ongoing role in the now-successful enterprise. By this time, however, the multinational firm has developed an understanding of the local market and has forged its own customer and channel relationships. From its parochial perspective, the local partner is now a far less useful ally—and may even be a hindrance.

The point is to *anticipate* and *articulate* what you know is coming. No successful private equity or venture capital firm would invest without negotiating clear exit expectations when agreed milestones are met or circumstances require it, because that's how they do business. In general, partnership and joint-venture agreements should include carefully crafted termination and exit provisions that match the contributions and value added of the parties and how these will shift over time.

It is easy enough to incorporate all-or-nothing exit clauses like "Texas shootouts" (see chapter 7), in which one party names a price and the other party is required to be a buyer or seller at that price. Yet such boilerplate clauses may not be at all well tailored to the situation's specific circumstances (which may involve intellectual property held in common, joint customers, etc.). In fact, this kind of mechanism can sometimes encourage opportunistic behavior—for example, when one party is illiquid and another party uses the fact of that cash crunch to put pressure on it. Boilerplate buy-sell agreements, or the standard arbitration clause in a contract, often prove inadequate to real breakup needs. More sophisticated exit provisions should provide procedures and timetables to compensate each party for contributed assets and to allocate shared assets such as customer relationships and intellectual property. They can go beyond valuation procedures and formulas, and comprise things like structured mediation, arbitration, and other alternative dispute resolution mechanisms.

Such mechanisms should be carefully tailored to the objectives of the parties in each case. For example, some joint ventures with up-front options for one party to progressively acquire greater shares over time are often better understood in reality as staged sales—taking effect after the parties have become more familiar with each other and have reached interim goals. Without well-designed provisions and clear mutual expectations, however, these sorts of arrangements can lead to costly stalemates as each party maneuvers to build leverage. In cases where the venture has been very successful, for example, the producing partner may be forced to buy out the marketing partner at a much higher price than would have been necessary had the exit provisions and expectations been negotiated up front.

Will your prospective partner find this off-putting? Maybe. But there's often no better time than the outset of a relationship—when good will and optimism tend to be at high levels—to talk about the other end of the relationship. And it's often helpful to have *different* people negotiating the exit provisions than those who are working out the near-term fate of the exciting new venture.

Anticipate Shifts in Attitudes

While savvy deal makers generally build workable formal exit and buyout mechanisms into their agreements, they may pay less attention to likely changes in one or more parties' *attitudes* toward the deal over time—attitudes that may be sharply at odds with the economic contract and may even erode the deal's value.

For example, the founders and financial backers of new ventures typically anticipate a period of cooperation, during which they will have a shared interest in growing the firm and enhancing its value. Both parties may find common ground in negotiating early capital investments or marketing strategies with longer-term payoffs. Over time, however, the equity investors begin looking forward to an IPO or sale and become much less enthusiastic about investments that do not promise quick, low-risk increases in valuation. The founders, meanwhile, may remain passionately committed to long-term growth and long-term investments.

Experienced investors (and even some founding entrepreneurs) anticipate this likely divergence of interests and seek to ingrain—from the beginning—a social contract that anticipates and detoxifies it. They sometimes remind each other from the outset about how economic interests necessarily diverge over time in cases like this, and about how important it is to understand that these differences are structural, rather than personal. In other words, even where there are good contractual provisions in place to govern investment and exit, a conscientious negotiation of the social contract may prove quite beneficial.[7] To underscore the point, let's look at two cases—negotiated by different investors during the same year—in which subsequent attitudes toward the deal played key roles.

The first involves a group of prominent pediatricians who were looking for financial and other assistance to make a series of innovative interactive CDs on parenting issues. A venture investor provided capital in return for a substantial interest in the new company, which would own all of the doctors' efforts in this business area. The investor then helped the doctors create a demo CD, wrote a business plan and marketing material, and brought the demo CD and the plan to the attention of key people at major software publishing houses.

Shortly after a number of those publishers expressed enthusiasm, the doctors surprised the investor by arguing that he "owned too much of the company," that "their ideas and reputation *were* the company," and that he should voluntarily reduce his stake. Given his hard work to get the venture off the ground and his willingness to invest cash when the business concept was only a concept, he felt stung. When strenuous efforts at resolution ultimately reached impasse, the new company languished and the doctors were blocked from developing their ideas elsewhere.

The root problem? The two sides hadn't envisioned how they would feel if their efforts were successful. They had neglected to work through different scenarios to test what would seem fair to each party after a tentative proof of the concept had been achieved—and indeed it seems relatively likely that after the investor's risk was "sunk" and the company had achieved its first success, the doctors would see the investor as less critical. The investor might have taken time up front to firm up the social contract, clarify the parties' mutual expectations about what would happen if the venture was successful, and alter the economics if necessary.

In sharp contrast to this value-destroying impasse, our second example involves a prospective investor approached by a commercial banker who financed independent filmmakers, normally a risky business. This particular banker, though, had either made money or broken even on every one of the forty-one such loans that he had put together. This success grew out of his web of contacts worldwide, to whom he advantageously presold foreign rights to the films and secured other sources of income.

Now, dissatisfied with his compensation as a bank employee, he was planning to go out on his own and was seeking an $18 million investment in a new film finance company to complement the $2 million he himself would invest. He offered the prospective investor 90 percent of the new company. The prospective investor's own analysis projected a *100 percent* annual rate of return on the investment. What a deal!

But the prospective investor turned this particular offer down. Instead, he counterproposed a new deal—one that was *more* lucrative for the banker and *less* so for himself. What was going on here? The investor reasoned that, within two or three short years, he would have simply taken the place of the bank, providing little more than "commodity capital." At that point, the banker-turned-entrepreneur would be seeking a better deal from new sources of less expensive capital. Therefore, the investor's counteroffer contained a series of results-linked options. For example, the banker was given the right to buy back some of the investor's equity at a relatively low price after the investor had received his first $5 million, an option to buy back more of the equity after the investor had received the next $5 million, and so on. At each point, under this deal structure, it would be in the banker's interest to *stay in the relationship*, rather than to start out on his own again.

The investor's projected rate of return on this offer was now closer to 30 percent. But he preferred a 30 percent return that he would *actually* receive over the long term to a short-term 100 percent return that contained the likely seeds of its own destruction.

The first deal described above—the parenting-CDs venture—did not take into account the likely psychological reaction of the doctors to success. The second accommodated reasonably predictable changes in circumstances and likely attitudes. When human capital is a central contributor to success, matching the economic contract to predictable shifts in power over time is vital. So, too, is an explicit discussion of the nature and duration of the relationship, to establish a strong social contract.

Anticipate External Shocks and Their Effects on Attitudes

Now let's look at some cases in which attitudes were affected by external circumstances, thereby putting agreements at risk.

In the early 1970s, when copper prices skyrocketed on a global basis, the value of the output of Rio Tinto Zinc's (RTZ) huge Bougainville copper mine in Papua New Guinea shot up accordingly. But rather than boosting RTZ's share price, this seemingly welcome turn of events *depressed* the stock.[8]

Why did the stock price *fall* in response to good news? Because investors quickly figured out what was likely to happen next. The contract between RTZ and the host country was relatively inflexible and included no provisions for dealing with windfalls. This meant that RTZ would be doing much better than either party had anticipated when it had negotiated the agreement. As the market correctly anticipated, an unhappy Papua New Guinea soon forced a tough renegotiation on RTZ, in what proved to be the first step toward effective expropriation. A more flexible profit-sharing arrangement—structured in such a way that windfall profits would be shared automatically with the government—would almost certainly have been a better choice for RTZ.

An equally unsustainable set of electricity contracts was signed at the height of the electricity crisis in California in 2001, when energy prices were soaring and the state was desperate. Calpine and several other power companies negotiated some very high-priced deals with the state, prospectively valued at some $15 billion.[9] When the market cooled, these relatively inflexible contracts became a major political issue. Pressure for renegotiation intensified as political figures cast about for ways to invalidate the deals and bring pressure on the companies to renegotiate. As the governor's director of legal affairs put it, "One way or other, we're going after these people."

As part of the contract renegotiation deal, the state Public Utilities Commission voted 5-0 to drop its petition to the federal regulators to declare the contracts illegal on grounds that the companies had manipulated the electricity market. The state's attorney general negotiated a multimillion-dollar settlement to drop his investigation into the companies' pricing practices. When the dust settled, Calpine's contracts were shortened from twenty to ten years, and the estimated value of all the power companies' contracts was reduced by $3.5 billion. Clearly, a more flexible set of contracts could have avoided this painful legal, regulatory, and publicity-intensive exercise, and yielded comparable or better ultimate economic results for the firms.

You could argue that these are extreme cases. But in fact, *all* kinds of contracts can fail to function as originally expected if external circumstances pose unanticipated challenges. Rather than letting such events force an emergency reconsideration, it is useful to have carefully thought through their sustainability across a range of such possibilities. In other words, it's useful to structure the social and economic contracts to anticipate the outcomes that are likely to be unsustainable.

Having said that, we'll also offer a caution: don't incorporate design features that end up triggering the very events you're trying to avoid. For example, some mining companies—rightly concerned about the risk of renegotiation or expropriation—demand larger up-front returns to offset these country risks. This may be precisely the wrong approach—in some cases, that higher return *itself* raises the odds of government renegotiation pressure.

"Multiplex" Agreements to Protect Against Likely Vulnerabilities

Forging an agreement with a single party over a single issue sets up what we refer to as a *simplex* arrangement. This kind of deal often proves quite vulnerable. For example, the implementation of the Camp David accord to fully normalize Egyptian-Israeli relations was dependent on the continued commitment of two specific individuals: Anwar Sadat and Menachem Begin. When Sadat was assassinated, the spirit of the deal was lost, and only the letter of the deal—a "cold peace"—remained.

Similarly, although in a very different realm, when Ben Cohen and Jerry Greenfield negotiated the sale of their social responsibility–oriented ice cream firm, Ben & Jerry's, to Unilever, they were reassured by the sympathy that their Unilever counterpart demonstrated for their unconventional business strategy. But when that executive left the company after the acquisition, the sellers felt that their firm was now hostage to the alien values of the multinational.[10]

To reduce your vulnerability to the whims (and health) of single parties, consider a negotiating strategy that deepens and broadens commitment to the deal. *Multiplexing* the process means adding more parties, more issues, or both. For example, senior partners in strategy consulting firms often depend primarily on their relationships with CEOs or group presidents in client companies; not incidentally, these relationships confer great power on the top consultants. But if the CEO or group executive leaves, the consulting firm is at risk of losing its mandate. It's wiser (although often less efficient) for the consultants to purposefully negotiate an expanding web of involvements and dependencies within the client corporation.

Obviously, this is true for all kinds of businesses. One manufacturing exec-utive whom we've advised not only wines and dines a range of people within one of his customer organizations, but also strives to broaden the types of relationships he fosters. He links this customer business to other businesses owned by his parent company, invests money in a range of joint projects, and makes introductions for them to some of his other key customers—all in the interest of developing multiple and enduring points of contact.

Analogous multiplexing strategies can help protect near-commodity busi-nesses that would otherwise be vulnerable to better prices offered by others. By becoming much more tightly integrated with their customers' operations and providing a web of customized services as Sweetheart did with McDon-ald's and Georgia-Pacific, their deals generate higher value for both sides and are far more sustainable in the face of price-based attack by competitors. Not only are the gains harder for a competitor to match, but for the client, the switching costs are higher.

Make "Insecure Contracts" Secure

In chapter 3, we talked about the importance of continuing to monitor the deal/no-deal balance after an agreement has been signed. Now we'll look at a broad class of agreements in which monitoring, and taking preventive steps, are especially important: what we call *insecure contracts*.[11]

This category of agreements involves irrevocable or costly-to-reverse moves by one side that give the other side an opportunity, and even an incentive, to terminate or favorably renegotiate the deal. The deal is negotiated up front on one set of terms, but when the project is completed and the costs are sunk, these terms become vulnerable. This is especially a problem when legal systems can't be relied on to ensure longer-term compliance.

For a homely example of an insecure contract, let's say your family agrees to get that new puppy that your fourteen-year-old has been begging for, *on condition* that she will take full responsibility for feeding it and taking it on walks. What happens when she fails to keep up her end of the bargain? You're stuck.

Let's say your firm spends a great deal of time and money training a few key employees in skills with a very high market value—without long-term con-tracts or noncompete agreements. What if they walk?

When you're faced with a potentially insecure contract, you need to take active steps to secure it. The Bougainville negotiations described above, as well as other mining deals, suggest some useful moves to secure potentially insecure contracts. These might include:

- **Prevention.** Use more flexible contracts (e.g., with profit-sharing contingencies that are less likely to trigger political pressures for renegotiation).

- **Performance bonds.** Insist that the host country post a bond or equivalent to be forfeited in event of expropriation or forced renegotiation.

- **Linkage.** Multiplex to involve other players with valued future links to the other partner (such as NGOs, insurers, governments, global firms, outside industrial and financial parties, potent local partners).

- **Detection and avoidance.** If the problem looks truly insurmountable in advance, don't invest in the first place, or, at the very least, invest with realistically reduced return expectations.

Let's look at another kind of potentially insecure contract. Suppose that your firm employs high-end professionals who develop key outside relationships. These might include people like asset managers, bankers, lawyers, major salespeople, and management consultants. As these individuals assiduously cultivate important clients, your firm may be at increasing risk of "holdup" on the part of these individuals, who may threaten to leave and take key clients with them.[12]

What to do? If the threat is already on the table, it may be too late to fix the problem. Here are some useful measures:

- *Recognize the structural characteristics of the situation that tend to make such contracts insecure* (e.g., the growth of employee-specific "assets" and relationships, hungry competitors, etc.). Actively monitor both employee disaffection and competitor activity, being especially alert to the possibility of poaching. Be on high alert at times of transitions, promotions, and major organizational changes.

- *Make anticipatory moves to set up a more favorable situation*—one that makes defection and holdup less likely. For example, give more weight to demonstrated loyalty when hiring professionals. Use teams, rather than individuals, in dealing with key clients. Rotate jobs, and set up knowledge-capture processes.

- Within this more promising setup, *design agreements to lessen the chances of such holdup even happening.* For example, negotiate situation-specific noncompete agreements. U.S. courts generally don't like to enforce boilerplate noncompetes; they tend to look more favorably on carefully negotiated contracts that include additional explicit compensation in return for the employee's agreement.

- *Give extra weight to negotiating longer-term contracts,* with significant vesting of benefits over time and even "golden handcuffs." These elements can tip a key employee's deal/no-deal balance in the direction of a continuing agreement.

In short, the best way to head off potentially insecure contracts is to favorably shape both the setup and deal design. After that, the trick is to monitor the deal/no-deal balance continuously and ensure that it remains tilted toward compliance. In this way, you are more likely to prevent holdup—and other forms of defection—and to be in a much stronger negotiating position if it occurs.

- Many of the moves described in earlier chapters do more than create a positive process, build good working relationships, and set the stage for good outcomes. They can also enhance the sustainability of agreements in the face of very significant change, whether internal or external.

- While many negotiated agreements are clearly time- and task-limited, it may be a mistake to treat social and economic contracts as fixed and static. In many cases, the likelihood of new challenges and opportunities calls for the expectation of change—which calls, in turn, for deals designed for profitable evolution.

- Think through the likely future evolution of agreements and accompanying attitudes. Design economic agreements and negotiate expectations that productively anticipate foreseeable changes in circumstances.

- If possible, avoid simplexed negotiations and agreements, because they tend to be fragile. Consider multiplexing both parties and issues of a potentially vulnerable agreement to broaden and deepen its supporting coalition, and to weave an interest web that is harder to dislodge.

- After the deal is done, keep an eye out for likely adverse shifts in the continuing deal/no-deal balance.

- In particular, beware of potentially insecure contracts—agreements in which, when one party makes an irrevocable or costly-to-reverse move, the other side has an incentive to defect from the deal.

- To make insecure contracts more secure, consider:

  ➤ Setup moves to render the situation more sustainable

  ➤ Deal-design moves aimed at prevention; for example, contingent or more flexible contracts, performance bonds, linkages and multiplexing, and various compliance mechanisms

- In some cases, the best prevention is to stay out of the deal altogether.

Chapter Eleven

Negotiate the
Spirit of the Deal

M OST EXPERIENCED NEGOTIATORS are comfortable with working out the terms of an economic contract—bargaining for the best price, haggling over equity splits, ironing out detailed exit clauses, and so on. In other words, when it comes to the letter of the deal, they are experts. In our experience, though, many of these same seasoned professionals give short shrift to the *spirit* of the deal, or what we call the *social contract.* One result is that while the parties can agree to the same terms on paper, they may actually have very different expectations as to how those terms will be met. And because they fail to achieve a true meeting of the minds, the deal they've signed may well fall apart.[1] Getting the deal design right calls for getting *both* the letter and the spirit of the deal right and in sync with each other.

Consider the fate of a joint venture launched by a national hospital organization and a regional health care provider. Executives at these two organizations agreed that at two of their hospitals—geographically very close to each other—the two parties were building redundant facilities and competing for both doctors and patients. In an effort to address this perceived problem, they negotiated a joint venture that would manage the two hospitals and buy or build facilities within the shared market area. The partners created a governance system, appointed managers, and offered management incentives to maximize the venture's profits, which would then be shared between the parties.

Despite compelling economics, however, the arrangement ultimately dissolved—largely because the partners held different but unspoken assumptions about the joint venture's purpose. The contract they negotiated, and signed enthusiastically, did not really reflect either partner's most fundamental objectives.

How can this be? Let's look at this failure from both sides. Because the national chain had only one hospital in the region, it insisted that the joint venture jointly operate—but not own—the two facilities and it resisted economically sensible steps like eliminating redundant departments, even though such actions were consistent with the joint venture's formal contract and management incentives. The national chain was concerned that the joint venture might fail one day. If it did, the chain's hospital—offering only reduced services—would no longer be competitive.

Executives at the regional chain, by contrast, saw the joint venture in another light: as a way to extend their regional network. They consistently sought to optimize the efficiency of their overall network (including the national chain's hospital), but the formal contract and management incentives—to maximize stand-alone JV profits—conflicted with that goal.

Had the parties better understood each other's views of the underlying purpose of the venture, they might have forged a more limited, and more effective, agreement. Such a deal would have ignored possible operating efficiencies, and focused on gains from jointly buying practices and building shared feeder facilities in their common market area. As it happened, a clash of underlying expectations and a contract inconsistent with either set of expectations transformed enthusiasm and potential profits into a swamp of recriminations.

Based on our participation in and study of hundreds of negotiations, along with a growing number of academic studies of contracts, we believe that cultivating a shared understanding of the spirit of the deal—the social contract—can be every bit as important as coming to agreement on the letter of the deal.[2] The term *social contract*, evoking the writings of Locke and Rousseau, has a grand sweep and far-ranging political connotations. We use the concept in a much more limited way, to mean the *expectations held by two or more negotiating parties about their agreement*.

These social contract expectations operate on two levels: The *underlying social contract* answers the question "what?" For instance, are we working out a series of discrete transactions or a real partnership? An acquisition or a merger of equals? What is the real nature and duration of our agreement? The *ongoing social contract*, by contrast, answers the question "how?" How will we make decisions, handle unforeseen events, communicate, resolve disputes?

This chapter examines the two kinds of social contracts. It explores problems that arise when the social and economic contracts are at odds with each other. And finally, it suggests ways to negotiate both so that they are independently strong, as well as mutually reinforcing.

The Underlying Social Contract

Let's look at the *underlying* social contract first. Too many negotiators leave the underlying social contract implicit, which can cause misunderstandings and ultimately poison a relationship. Rather than discuss their expectations during negotiations, the parties sometimes project their own assumptions on the deal, and let it go at that. Some people, for instance, view a contract as a starting point for a problem-solving relationship. Dan Orum, the president of Online Operations at Oxygen Media, is in that camp. He says, "The five words I most hate to hear in my business dealings [are] 'It's not in the contract.'" But what if his negotiating counterpart takes a more legalistic approach—seeing the written contract as an end point? Serious issues are almost certain to arise.

Divergent assumptions about autonomy versus conformity may also scuttle a deal. Consider what happened to an entrepreneur who failed to get clarity on this issue before she sold her boutique enterprise to a very enthusiastic corporate buyer. She agreed to stay on for five years after the sale because she got and believed assurances that she was the essential player who would lead the business to the next level, and because she envisioned her still-autonomous unit being turbocharged by the acquirer's size, reach, and resources.

The responsible corporate executive, meanwhile, passionately shared her goal of taking the boutique concept global. But he was convinced that the hoped-for global rollout would be successful only if the new division followed highly disciplined corporate procedures. Soon after the celebratory dinner, when the seller started receiving thick policy manuals from corporate and hearing patronizing lectures on who bought whom, she began to realize what she was in for. Even though the provisions of the *economic* contract—the letter of the deal on economic terms, governance, and the like—were not in dispute, it was clear that there had been no meeting of the minds on the underlying social contract.

Giant companies can make the same mistake. Take, for example, the proposed mega-merger between Deutschebank and Dresdner, which would have produced the third-largest bank in the world (with $1.25 trillion in assets), leading many to view it as a landmark in the transformation of Europe's financial services industry.[3] The banks planned to merge their retail operations, enabling them to close about seven hundred branches and concentrate on their more profitable corporate businesses.

Throughout the negotiations, Deutschebank chairman Rolf Breuer implied that this was to be a "merger of equals." Although the new bank was to bear Deutschebank's name, the corporate color was to be the green of Dresdner. Dresdner's chairman Bernhard Walter was particularly concerned that Deutschebank would sell off Dresdner Kleinwort Benson (DrKB), the investment banking division that had contributed more than half of Dresdner's 1999 pretax profits. Aware of Dresdner's sensitivities, Breuer uttered words that would soon haunt him: "[DrKB] is a jewel and we want to keep that jewel. It will be neither closed nor sold, and any reports to the contrary are *barer Unsinn* [pure nonsense]." Satisfied, Walter declared, "A merger means you combine both parts into a new whole. I never had the slightest feeling that things would go differently."

Yet within hours of the joint announcement to merge, Deutschebank apparently decided to sell DrKB, believing that its own investment banking arm had greater global reach. And by selling the unit, Breuer apparently concluded, the merged entity wouldn't have to go through the long and expensive process of integrating DrKB's seventy-five hundred employees. When DrKB staff learned of this decision (through a *Financial Times* article from a source who came to be called the "torchman"), they moved to a state of high alert. The report mobilized powerful internal opponents to block the deal. After a month of furious negotiations, protestations of misunderstanding, and failed efforts at compromise, the merger was called off. During this time frame, Deutschebank's share price plunged 19 percent, and Dresdner's fell by almost the same amount. Again, we see how one party's vision of the underlying social contract was at odds with the other's, and those opposing assumptions helped doom the deal.

Divergent views of the underlying social contract are especially likely when the parties differ along basic dimensions: small versus large, entrepreneurial versus bureaucratic, centrally managed versus decentralized, finance-driven versus operations-focused, and so on. For example, serious post-alliance ownership conflict between Northwest Airlines and KLM Royal Dutch Airlines was less a U.S.–Dutch clash than a disagreement over management focus and risk tolerance. Pieter Bouew, Dutch president of KLM, stressed operations and conservative financial management. Gary Wilson and Al Checchi were high-profile, risk-taking financiers who had acquired Northwest in a highly leveraged buyout. Even agreement on the detailed terms of an economic contract could not resolve those fundamentally different expectations about the right way to run an airline. The result, at least in its early years: what *Fortune* called the "alliance from hell." [4]

Discussions about the economic contract tend to eclipse those about the underlying social one, which often remains implicit and unexamined. When designing a deal, therefore, you need to make sure that minds have truly met on the underlying social contract. Is this a short-term or a long-term deal? Is it open-ended, or task focused? Will it be learning- or production-oriented? Do we believe in lifetime or at-will employment?

It's certainly true that some ventures are too fragile to stand up to this kind of scrutiny and explicit discussion. Sometimes events simply move too quickly to allow the establishment of a social contract. In such cases, it sometimes makes sense to think about a pilot program. Imagine, for example, two companies that both want control in a proposed equity joint venture. If pressed to fully resolve the issue from the start, they would probably walk away from the deal, forfeiting potential value. Yet if they could agree to launch a pilot venture with shared formal control—even if each side still believes that it must have final control of the ultimate venture—the pilot might build confidence in their relationship and their ability to work together, help to align their expectations, and minimize the concern over control.

The trick, of course, is to distinguish true confidence-building steps from the papering over of fatal differences. The former are good; the latter can be disastrous. (See "Auditing Perceptions of the Underlying Social Contract.")

Auditing Perceptions of the Underlying Social Contract

To negotiate truly compatible views, consider an explicit and periodic "audit" of all sides' perceptions. Here's a sample checklist:

- *Real nature and purpose.* Do you envision a discrete transaction or partnership? A merger of equals or something different? Building an institution for the long term or making a financial investment? Do you see the driving culture as, for example, operational? Research-oriented? Marketing? Engineering? and so on.

- *Scope and duration.* Are you focused on a discrete task in the short term or is it more open-ended? Is it a likely prelude to a larger or different arrangement? Of what actions, even outside the formal bounds of the deal, do each of us expect to be informed and over which do we expect some say? and so on.

The Ongoing Social Contract

The underlying social contract answers the question of *what* the deal is about. By contrast, the *ongoing* social contract answers the question *how* you and the other side will interact. Part of the "how" is the expectations about the working relationship. Every skilled executive understands the importance of a good working relationship in realizing the potential of agreements. As former GO Technologies' CEO Jerry Kaplan puts it:

> *[Lawyers] tend to confuse "the deal," the working understanding between two parties, with "the contract," the written words that attempt to capture that understanding at a point in time. Words are good for capturing some things, such as the rules of chess, but not for others, such as how to ride a bicycle. What makes deals work are not the written words but . . . personal relationships between the individuals charged with making them work.*[5]

Here's a vital point that's easy to get wrong: the "social contract" is *not* just a synonym for the "working relationship." While the ongoing social contract *includes* the all-important working relationship, it also has many other elements: broader expectations for how the parties will interact, norms for communication, consultation, and decision making, how unforeseen events will be handled, conditions and means for renegotiation, and the like.

Needless to say, aligning expectations about these factors takes management time and focus. Indeed, well before the ink is dry on the deal, these expectations are tacitly being negotiated. Dick Allen, Sun Microsystems' Global Commodity Manager for Memory, oversaw a billion-plus dollars of purchases annually from multiple suppliers. He focused primary attention on the ongoing social contract:

> *[Allen stated that] "both Sun and our suppliers sign a letter of agreement and put it in a drawer." He likes to keep his agreements down to 3 or 4 pages, as opposed to the 30- or 40-page documents the legal staff would prefer in order to cover all contingencies. The Commodity Team feels that the key to a successful ongoing relationship is based on trust that has been built up over many years, rather than in the words of a legal contract.*
>
> *. . . Sun shares a lot of technological and strategic information with its suppliers. This relationship is not based on contracts or monetary exchange during the development phase, but on the common goal of profitably bringing new technology to market.*[6]

Most experienced managers value trust, good working relationships, and shared expectations much more highly than elaborate contracts. Many academic studies validate the advantages that "self-enforcing" understandings and "relational" contracts tend to have over explicit legal contracts. In a fast-changing world, a positive ongoing social contract can foster efficient sharing of information and know-how; lower the costs of complex adaptation; permit rapid exploitation of unexpected opportunities without the cost and delay of trying to write, monitor, and enforce complete contracts; and reduce transactions costs and fears of exploitation more generally.

For example, in his extensive 1997 study of North American and Asia automakers and suppliers, Jeffrey Dyer found that "General Motors procurement (transaction) costs were more than twice those of Chrysler's and six times higher than Toyota's. GM's transactions costs are persistently higher . . . because suppliers view GM as a much less trustworthy organization."[7] Analogous positive performance results have been found in the electrical equipment industry and among Silicon Valley firms.[8]

A productive economic contract can sometimes obscure shortcomings in the social contract. Imagine, for example, a global manufacturer that is in a joint venture with a major local distributor. The relationship runs smoothly until the manufacturer approaches another distributor about selling a different line of products. Since the existing economic contract said nothing about distributing a new product line, the manufacturer thought it was perfectly reasonable to use another distributor. But the existing distributor fully expected to be given the opportunity and concludes that the manufacturer has acted in bad faith. Because their assumptions have never been made clear, their relationship suffers, even though no actual breach of contract has occurred.

Conscious efforts to shape the social contract, including explicit discussions of what and how the parties expect to communicate over time, can help stave off problems of this kind. Straightforward practices—such as creating shared operating principles that govern confidentiality, information exchange, the creation and use of intellectual property, and dispute-resolution systems—can build needed trust and stability and give the partnership the proper launch. To minimize the risk of a debilitating "we-they" split, the parties should also explicitly discuss how decisions will be made when the inevitable conflicts emerge. Similarly, it is wise to negotiate a mutual understanding of the circumstances that could trigger a reconsideration or even renegotiation of the agreement, as well as the means by which such a process would be carried out.

Companies entering into longer-term agreements such as joint ventures or strategic alliances often allocate a massive amount of time to the initial economic contract. After such an exhausting ordeal, it is natural to deploy a much smaller fraction of senior executive time to ensure compatible underlying and ongoing social contracts. This argues for predeal attention to the social contract—before exhaustion sets in—and agreements regarding sustained investments of senior executive attention in the ongoing social contract.

Ford and Mazda, discussed in the last chapter, did an excellent job at managing their ongoing social contract during much of their relationship.[9] In 1969, as noted, the automakers began a remarkable strategic partnership, initially driven by Ford's search for a low-cost production source and Mazda's desire to break into the U.S. market. Serious disputes erupted because of U.S.–Japanese political tensions, efforts to protect proprietary technology, cultural differences, product design, and material selection. To deal with these problems, senior executives—the top three executives from Ford and Mazda, and six other operating heads—held a three-day summit every eight months. The first two days of these summits were devoted to strategy and operations, but the third typically functioned to repair or realign the social contract as needed.

Negotiating the ongoing spirit of the deal requires shaping attitudes and expectations, but tangible business processes can simultaneously enhance productivity and reinforce the ongoing social contract. (See "Auditing Perceptions of the Ongoing Social Contract.") For example, the Bose Corporation has integrated itself very closely with key suppliers—an integration that has become a source of competitive advantage. Many of Bose's suppliers have "in-plants"— that is, supplier employees who work full-time at Bose as all-in-one salespeople, purchasing agents, and planners, and who are empowered to act on behalf of Bose and the supplier.[10] The coordination advantages that result are compelling—but so are the daily opportunities to align and realign mutual expectations, and strengthen the social contract.

The Social Contract: The Risk Factors

The most common risk factors behind social contract problems are (1) lack of awareness and (2) benign neglect. Discussed or not, expectations inevitably form about how the deal will be carried out. Even if initially compatible, those assumptions can silently shift in response to actions taken. Red flags should go up when certain risk factors are present that make a meeting of the minds on the social contract especially challenging: different cultures, the "wrong minds" meeting, and too few initial negotiators to ensure widely compatible expectations.

Auditing Perceptions of the Ongoing Social Contract

Consider an explicit "audit" of all sides' perceptions of the ongoing social contract and continual action to ensure that it is positive. Here's a sample checklist:

- *Consultation.* How fully, about what, with whom, how formally and frequently does each side expect to consult with the other? How about actions nominally outside the agreement? How extensively is information to be shared or protected?

- *Decision making.* Beyond formal governance mechanisms, by what process do you want decisions discussed and made? By consensus? Majority? Informally? Formally? Involving what parties, at what levels, or even outside the agreement?

- *Dispute resolution.* Beyond formal mechanisms specified in the contract, how do you expect to handle conflicts: informal discussion, mediation, binding arbitration, court? What if disagreement persists?

- *Reevaluation and renegotiation.* How do you expect to handle unexpected challenges (e.g., changing competition)? What should trigger reevaluation or renegotiation and what should each side expect from the other in such a case?

When Negotiators Come from Different Cultures

The risk of diverging views of the underlying social contract increases when the parties are from different organizational, professional, or national cultures. Such negotiators often make powerful assumptions that pull in nearly opposite directions. For example, to many from legally oriented cultures, "a deal is a deal" and "a contract is a contract." To others in more relationship-oriented cultures, the signed deal or contract is clearly understood as simply the *starting point* for ongoing negotiation.

Ming-Jer Chen, director of Wharton's Global Chinese Business Initiative, reviewed unhappy experiences of Western firms in China, from Morgan Stanley Dean Witter to the Foxboro Company. Chen's conclusion: "Because relationships evolve and situations shift, the Chinese perceive contracts as too rigid to take new circumstances into account. Hence there is no stigma to changing the terms of an agreement after it has been signed and Western businesspeople can expect to renegotiate or reinterpret points of the contract during their entire working relationship with the Chinese party."[11] A blunter lament came from Jürgen Hubbert of DaimlerChrysler: "We saw that we had a contract, [but] we saw our partner try to change the rules every day."[12]

Executives in some regions of the world (such as North America and Northern Europe) tend to be comfortable with deal making that is accompanied by a comparatively modest relationship, while a more extensive relationship is often required to support negotiated agreements in East Asia, Latin America, and Southern Europe. This implies different levels of emphasis on the underlying social contract, which in turn raises broader questions. Can the joint arrangement be understood primarily as a business relationship, or is it more personal and social? Are relationships with employees, customers, and suppliers primarily understood in economic terms, or are they more complicated? There are many sources that can help you to systematically review potential problem areas in cross-cultural negotiations.[13] The point here, however, is to underscore the fact that divergent national and organizational cultures should raise warning flags about social contract alignment.

Take another case. Although NCR Japan was American-owned, it had a history of stable, lifetime employment and a "company union" that enjoyed close relations with management. When a new U.S. plant manager arrived and instigated downsizing in certain units he saw as overstaffed—although the plant was profitable overall—he provoked massive employee resistance to this perceived violation of the underlying social contract. A second union, which took a far more adversarial approach—driving labor costs up sharply and insisting on job guarantees—was quickly organized. Local suppliers refused to do business with the plant, seeing it as untrustworthy. A full decade after the plant manager was ousted, both the second union and the supplier boycott continued.[14]

This example underscores not only cross-cultural risks, but also how strong the negative reactions can be to perceptions that the social contract has been breached. The good news is that all breaches need not be fatal; how they are handled can strengthen (or further damage) the social contract. If a breach was inadvertent, managers should act to reassure the other side that the breach was unintentional, not exploitive. Sincere efforts to rebuild confidence can have the effect of rebuilding and reinforcing the social contract.[15]

When the Wrong Minds Meet

Sometimes problems arise not because of cultural differences, but because the wrong people are involved in negotiations. Our advice in chapter 4 on how to ensure that the "right parties" are part of the negotiation is particularly relevant to forging a positive social contract. Recall, for example, the case in which two CEOs negotiate a quality-based strategic alliance, but in which evaluation at the buyer-supplier level is mainly on price and quarterly numbers. As a result, the actual relationship is neither strategic nor quality-focused, but an ongoing, bruising price battle.

Similarly, we showed how the risk of the wrong minds meeting on the social contract rises when third parties drive the deal but "throw it over the fence" for others to implement. Examples may include third parties like corporate matchmakers (e.g., Michael Ovitz's role in the ultimately unhappy Matsushita-MCA deal) or business development deal teams (such as the one Jerry Kaplan encountered at IBM).

There are other, less obvious, ways in which key parties may be inadvertently omitted from social contract negotiations. For example, in 1988 Komatsu Ltd., Japan's leader in earthmoving equipment, and the American conglomerate Dresser Industries combined their North American engineering, manufacturing, and marketing efforts in order to attain what they called "a mountain of treasure."[16] Dresser sought Komatsu's design technology and a cash infusion for plant modernization and capital expenditures. Komatsu hoped to become a successful global player, so it wanted better North American market penetration. While preserving parallel brands and distributorships, Komatsu and Dresser created a 50-50 joint venture (Komatsu Dresser Corporation, or KDC), merging manufacturing, engineering, and finance operations. The joint venture maintained equal management representation on the six-person oversight committee and committed to $200 million of new joint investment. Beyond the economic terms of their arrangement, they sought to foster a strong social contract between the two management teams.

Yet the implementation of their arrangement strained the emerging deal, and the separate distributors—who never subscribed to the new expectations—began competing against one another for sales. Tensions escalated: Komatsu saw Dresser as backward and unresponsive; Dresser complained of learning about key Komatsu decisions after the fact. As the situation worsened, executives from both companies clamped down on communications, which prevented dealers from getting vital information about their counterparts' inventory levels and warranty coverage. This, in turn, further exacerbated the conflict.

Despite last-minute efforts to bring in industrial consultants and conduct "employee swaps," the dealer conflicts intensified. KDC market share declined sharply, losses mounted, two thousand jobs were cut, and ultimately the venture was dissolved. The lesson? Yes, KDC was subject to the usual cross-cultural hazards. But it also suffered because it failed to ensure that potentially influential parties bought into the new social contract.

When Too Few Negotiators Are Involved

Even a tightly aligned social and economic contract can be vulnerable if the expectations and agreements are held by only a select few, especially when deal making is separated from implementation. For example, a small business development team representing one side of a proposed alliance may negotiate secretly with a tiny designated group on the other side. Or, as noted in the last chapter, senior partners in consulting firms often depend primarily on their relationships with CEOs in their client companies. But if the CEO leaves, the consulting firm may lose the account.

Dovetailing the Social and Economic Contracts

In ideal circumstances, the social and economic contracts should reinforce each other. Sometimes it's obvious how to accomplish this task. For example, a discrete, project-oriented agreement should have clean, workable exit and termination provisions linked to both sides' understanding of the point at which the objective will be considered to be accomplished. In one such case, Wal-Mart and Procter & Gamble agreed to share data across their mutual supply chains, a deal that grew from $350 million to $1 billion in ten years. To cement their commitment to total discretion as the alliance was forming, the alliance team members signed confidentiality agreements, which became an "insurance policy" for senior management, protecting the nascent working relationship and leading the parties to share closely held information necessary to realizing joint gains.[17]

If a central objective of the agreement is an ongoing transfer of knowledge, an equity position may align incentives better and be more conducive to success than contractual provisions.[18] If an economic contract under negotiation between independent upstream and downstream parties in a value chain proves too laden with conflicts and difficult-to-align interests to achieve mutually desired cooperation, the parties may want to consider a completely different economic contract—for example, an outright acquisition of one by the other—to internalize the conflicts and better achieve the underlying objective. Whatever the goal of the deal, it will be much easier to reach if the economic and social contracts mutually reinforce each other.

It can be tempting to regard the social contract as unwritten and psychological, and the economic contract as written and tangible. Yet the two can be productively dovetailed, with elements of the economic contract directly tied to the social contract. In an intriguing example, Chrysler in the late 1980s deliberately restructured both the letter and spirit of its contracts with suppliers to save its business.[19] The carmaker faced mounting losses, a projected $1 billion overrun on its newly launched LH program, a $4.5 billion unfunded pension liability, and a record loss of $664 million in the fourth quarter of 1989. To stop the bleeding, Chrysler set out to revolutionize its supplier relationships, which had traditionally harnessed the power of brutal competition among as many qualified suppliers as possible through bidding. From the old "lowest qualified bidder" model, the new intended social contract could be described as an "integrated long-term partnership" in which the partner was expected not only to improve its own performance, but also to enhance *Chrysler's* operations beyond the supply relationship. A number of provisions of the new economic contract explicitly supported the new social contract. For example:

- *Selection.* From its long-time approach of choosing the "lowest price of qualified bidders meeting specs," Chrysler moved to prequalify a subset of suppliers (cutting from 2,500 suppliers to 1,140) based on advanced engineering, manufacturing capabilities, and past performance. Within this pool, suppliers were chosen based on their past design and manufacturing performance and their record of on-time delivery, as well as price.

- *Scope of contract.* By working with a smaller set of players, Chrysler shifted from a system in which multiple suppliers competed over separate design, prototype, and production contracts to one in which a single supplier held primary responsibility for the combined design, prototype, and production of a component or system.

- *Contract duration and renewal.* Under the old system, there were no renewal expectations, and supplier contracts averaged 2.1 years. The new approach saw average contract life increase to 4.4 years, with Chrysler giving oral guarantees to more than 90 percent of its suppliers that the current business would remain with them—at least for the life of the relevant model—if performance targets were met.

- *Price.* In the old system, the lowest qualified bid won, regardless of implications for supplier profits. Under the new social contract, Chrysler sought to ensure a fair profit for both supplier and buyer. Instead of relying on commodity pricing to squeeze its suppliers, Chrysler adopted a target costing approach that worked backward from total cost to end user in order to calculate allowable costs for systems, subsystems, and components.

- *Accountability and performance evaluation.* Under the old system, suppliers were accountable for timing, quality, and other elements of arm's-length contract performance. Under the new system, evaluation reached well beyond the economic contract and supplier organizational boundaries to innovation, coordination, relationship-specific investment, and value-chain improvements. In fact, Chrysler formally expected its suppliers to find cost savings for Chrysler equal to at least 5 percent of contract value, but that cost savings could come from the supplier itself or from suggestions that would enable Chrysler to cut its overall costs. Fully half of which would be shared with the suppliers, although they could choose to credit their shared savings toward increasing their market share with Chrysler. Such savings could be very large indeed. Magna International, for example, submitted proposals for savings that generated in excess of $75 million one year.

With a new social contract emphasizing a longer-term, integrated partnership, consciously defined and reinforced by an amended economic contract, Chrysler reduced the time needed to develop a new vehicle to 160 weeks, down from an average of 234 weeks during the 1980s. The cost of developing a new vehicle plunged between 20 and 40 percent during the 1990s, while profit per vehicle jumped from $250 to a record of $2,110 in 1994. These results were significantly driven by the new social contract, which was deeply intertwined and reflected in the new economic one.[20]

We're not saying that this particular social/economic contract combination is right for every company. The downsides of forging tight partnerships with a much smaller supplier base include the difficulty of further rationalizing the base, as well as the risk of being "held up" by a critical supplier without real competition, especially in a tough economy. The crucial point, however, is that many of the expectations of the underlying and ongoing social contracts are not purely psychological; they can and should be embedded in and complemented by the formal economic contract.

Common Misperceptions About the Social Contract

We have witnessed dozens of deals fall well short of their potential—or even unravel—because the participants failed to achieve a meeting of the minds on the spirit of the deal. To avoid that fate, make sure you don't fall prey to the following misperceptions.

- *Misperception #1: The social contract is primarily about the working relationship.* As we've shown, the social contract defines not just how the relationship will proceed but the real nature of the relationship. So while the *ongoing* social contract includes elements of the working relationship—such as expectations about communication, consultation, decision making, dispute resolution, and opportunities for renegotiation—the *underlying* social contract outlines expectations about the fundamental purpose, extent, and duration of the deal.

- *Misperception #2: The term "social contract" implies a relationship that is cooperative, democratic, and participatory.* It's true that the social contract *can* embody those ideals, but it doesn't have to. Indeed, a productive social contract could reflect an autocratic relationship, or an "eat what you kill" culture, or any one of a myriad of other possibilities. What's key is that both parties share expectations about the deal.

- *Misperception #3: The term "social contract" implies a shared view.* In practice, different parties can hold wildly divergent expectations about the deal, even when they've signed the same piece of paper. A healthy social contract, mutually understood, is a *goal*, not a given.

- *Misperception #4: The social contract must be primarily psychological or soft—not something that can be spelled out in a written agreement.* As we've shown, the provisions of the social contract—such as expectations about the nature and duration of the relationship—can often be made explicit in the economic contract. Negotiating complementary economic and social contracts greatly improves the odds that the deal will deliver the benefits it promises on paper.

- The social contract has two levels: (1) The underlying social contract answers the question "what are our expectations about the real nature, scope, and duration of our deal?" (2) The ongoing social contract answers the question "how do we expect to make decisions, handle unforeseen events, communicate, and resolve disputes?"

- Inconsistent perceptions of the social contract can lead to impasse, conflict, and value destruction during both the negotiation process and the postdeal relationship.

- Be especially alert to possible divergences in views of the social contract when the parties are from different organizational, professional, or national cultures. Watch for discrepancies in the principals' views of the social contract when third-party deal makers drive the process. Ensure a meeting of the right minds on the spirit of the deal—among the full set of those who must make the deal work.

- Consider explicit and periodic "audits" of all sides' perceptions both of the underlying and ongoing social contract.

- Strive for a good fit between the social and economic contracts.

- In particular, resist the temptation to treat the social contract as unwritten and purely subjective, with the economic contract written and objective. Properly dovetailed, many of the expectations of the underlying and ongoing social contract can and should be embodied in mutually reinforcing economic agreements.

- Be careful of other common misperceptions about the social contract: that it is primarily about the working relationship; that it must be cooperative, democratic, and participatory; and that much of it can't be captured in writing.

Part Four

Stress Problem-Solving Tactics

"At the Table"

Chapter Twelve

Shape Perceptions
to Claim Value

U P TO THIS POINT, we've emphasized setting up the right negotiation (our third dimension, "away from the table") and designing value-creating deals (our second dimension, "on the drawing board"). While plenty of table tactics have found their way into our discussion so far (such as probing behind positions for interests), we're now at the table itself. In this and the next chapter, we focus on the tactical and face-to-face aspects (our first dimension, "at the table").

The headline for the discussion of our first dimension is "Stress Problem-Solving Tactics." In this chapter, we start with advice on a critical—but narrow—tactical "problem." Specifically, how do you "claim value" at the table? What do you do when more of what I want for me necessarily means less of what you want for you? How can you get the best possible price in a negotiation to buy a car, specialty chemicals in bulk, or a company? A 3-D Negotiator certainly knows how to get a great price, but the price-focused value-claiming tactics we'll develop apply much more broadly. For example, you may be negotiating space allocation for your product line in a department store (you want left aisle, they want right; you want more square feet, they want to give you less), head count (more versus less), or the timing of an event (sooner versus later), and so on. As long as a move in favor of one side entails a loss for the other, some version of the tactics described in this chapter applies.

We certainly don't want to lose sight of value-creating as well as value-claiming moves, which, together, are the subject of the next tactical chapter. We won't forget our earlier point that many seemingly pure price deals conceal significant value-creating potential. But it's important to remember that eventually, virtually *all* negotiations involve claiming value. One last caveat: the vast range of personalities, settings, and contexts out there work against any general theory of tactics. Instead, we focus on a set of at-the-table moves that we've found to be of cross-cutting importance. You might even call this chapter "the art and science of haggling."

How to Prepare for a Price Deal

Let's return to a variant of an example first introduced in chapter 6, this time filling in some more details in a way that makes this a "pure price deal." Imagine that you are looking to sell your ski condo in, say, Telluride, Colorado. You are hoping to get as much money as you can so you can retire to a beach-front getaway in the Caribbean. An investor made you an unsolicited offer of $700,000 a year ago, with conditions that would have cost you about $20,000, but you turned it down. The market has appreciated roughly 10 percent since that time. You haven't hired a real estate agent, but you've looked at a number of comparable condos, and you have a good sense of the market.

Lena, an acquaintance of your next-door neighbor in the condominium complex, has heard about your likely interest in selling. Lena would be interested in buying it as an investment, rather than to live in it. The investor whose offer you rejected a year ago might still be interested. If you can sell to Lena or the other investor, you may not have to pay a 6 percent commission to a real estate agent.

First: Is It Really a Price Deal?

Let's clarify your respective interests. You want to get top dollar for your property. You're moving out of town, so you're not worried about your future relationships in Telluride or with the buyer. You are indifferent about when you close, and your property's in excellent shape, so you're not worried about a home inspection. You're looking for a cash sale. You have already agreed to sell the furniture to someone else.

For her part, Lena wants the condo as an investment. She wants a good return on that investment, which means paying as little as possible. She plans to pay cash. She will insist on a home inspection, but only to ensure that there aren't major structural problems. She doesn't care about moving the closing date earlier to the beginning of ski season, and in fact is indifferent about when you close.

Before entering into any negotiation, you should look for opportunities to create value. (Don't be too quick to decide they're not there!) If they're *not* there—and you won't be dealing with this person again or care about how this negotiation might affect your reputation—you're in a price deal, pure and simple. What do all these details about your condo sale add up to? There is little to no room for value-creation. This negotiation is truly about value-claiming.

Second: Address the Twin Tasks

Once you're certain that you're in a value-claiming situation, you need to address what we call the *Twin Tasks*:

- Learn about the true ZOPA.

- Shape your counterpart's ZOPA perceptions to your advantage.

You'll recall our discussion in chapter 6 of the ZOPA—the zone of possible agreement—that is the set of agreements that is better for both sides than their no-deal options. Obviously, *learning* about the true ZOPA is key, because if you can figure out the other side's true bottom line, you can get them to agree to an offer that lets you claim the most value.

Second, you need to influence your counterparts' perceptions of what is just barely acceptable to you; ideally, they'll end up seeing a price very close to their maximum as just within your range. (Or their minimum, if they're selling and you're buying.) For a picture, look at figure 12-1. When we say "shape perceptions to claim value," this is the specific tactical "problem" we have in mind.

FIGURE 12-1

The ZOPA and how you (as seller) would like it to be perceived

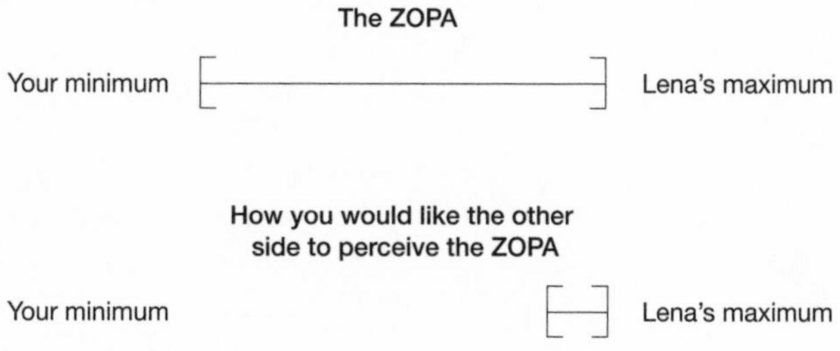

The ZOPA

Your minimum ⌐——————————————⌐ Lena's maximum

How you would like the other
side to perceive the ZOPA

Your minimum ⌐⌐ Lena's maximum

Learn About the True ZOPA

So how do you accurately learn about the ZOPA in this case? Lena's no-deal alternatives are comparable condos on the market. Let's say that there are none that are directly comparable, but there are some similar condos with slightly different features: an extra bedroom, less spectacular views, better trail access, and so on. But since we know that Lena is buying for investment purposes, she is likely to be guided solely by what she perceives to be the market price for each unit.

So let's work on figuring out how she might come to a decision about the most she'd be willing to pay for your condo. One fairly comparable unit with an extra bedroom recently sold for $840,000; another like it is listed at $900,000. A unit with a lesser view sold for $750,000. A unit in a building that isn't really ski-in/ski-out is listed at $725,000. Lena will compare your unit to these and others on the market and will have some price at which she'd prefer to buy another one. Based on these comparables, your sense of the market value of your unit is $825,000, but a reasonable range for her maximum, based on her best no-deal option seems $775,000 to $850,000.

Surprisingly, analyzing your own best no-deal option can be trickier. You received an offer a year ago of $700,000. If the market has appreciated 10 percent, that would be equivalent to $770,000 today, although that offer came with conditions attached that would likely cost $20,000. As noted, you rejected that offer, but that investor is still in the market and probably would likely be a buyer at $750,000.[1] This analysis implies a rough minimum and maximum: The ZOPA goes from $750,000 (your best no-deal option) to somewhere, you think, in the range of $775,000 to $850,000 (see figure 12-2).

Again, your goals are to (1) learn as much as possible about the true ZOPA, and (2) favorably shape Lena's perceptions of it. If you *knew* that the most she would be willing to pay for this unit was $825,000, you'd like her to think that you have another offer at somewhere just above $820,000 and that she'd have to come in just below $825,000 to get the unit (see figure 12-3).

FIGURE 12-2

The ZOPA as you perceive it

NEGOTIATING THE SALE OF A SKI CONDOMINIUM

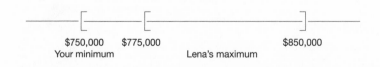

$750,000	$775,000	$850,000
Your minimum	Lena's maximum	

FIGURE 12-3

The ZOPA as you would like the other side to perceive it

NEGOTIATING THE SALE OF A SKI CONDOMINIUM

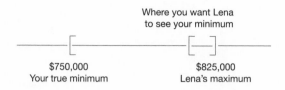

Where you want Lena
to see your minimum

$750,000
Your true minimum

$825,000
Lena's maximum

This simple condo example hints at a broader point: the critical role of superior information about the subject of the negotiation—the product, the market, the buyers and sellers, the changing economic conditions. Leo Hindery Jr., formerly CEO of TCI and chairman of the YES regional sports network (it carries New York Yankees games), was involved in over 250 corporate transactions. Looking back on those transactions, he offers a list of "ten commandments," the first of which is, "Do more homework than the other guy." He elaborates: "No matter which side of the negotiating table you happen to be on, you'll always do better if you're better informed than the other guy."[2]

A procurement manager in the aerospace industry whom we once interviewed demonstrated just how seriously an expert negotiator takes this responsibility. He showed us extraordinarily detailed analyses of the economics of each of his subcontractors. He demonstrated elaborate engineering/economic models of his subcontractors' manufacturing costs. He appeared to know almost exactly his subcontractors' costs for producing one hundred engines and the cost for producing yet one more engine. By understanding in detail the marginal costs of his suppliers, he was usually able to counter the other side's arguments about how it would be losing money if it accepted his price. While it is a cliché that "information is power," some clichés are true—for claiming value (as well as creating it).

Focus on the Opportunity, Rather Than the Downside

An interesting series of experimental studies suggests that negotiators who focus prior to the negotiation on what they hope to *achieve* do better in price negotiations than those who focus on what they hope to *avoid*.[3] Those who wrote a brief paragraph on what they hoped to achieve did much better than those who wrote down the mistakes they hoped to avoid. This suggests that you would do best to approach the negotiation consciously targeting the opportunity at hand. One aspect of doing this involves understanding the best deal the other side could offer you, given its no-deal options.

Set an Ambitious Target Price

We advise negotiators to explicitly set a target price—a price that would represent a very good outcome for them. Why? For a number of good reasons, including:

- You can't hit a target you haven't set.

- Without a target, a natural point of reference is the value of your best no-deal option. Setting a target lets you focus on doing well, not merely doing better than your minimum requirements. We sometimes divide negotiators into two groups: non–target setters who ask "what can I live with?" versus ambitious target setters who ask "how much can I get?" Guess who does better (as long as their targets can pass the giggle test; more below)?

- This isn't just instinct: empirical studies consistently show that setting more aggressive target prices (within reason) leads to better results for at least two reasons.[4] First, higher targets lead you to make higher demands, which we'll soon show tend to generate better outcomes. Second, trying to hit a higher target—a "stretch goal"—generally calls forth more effort from you in all aspects of your negotiation.

So how do you set a target price? It should be (well) above your minimum requirements. It should take into account your analysis of the other side's best no-deal option. And how firm your target is should depend on how well-informed you are about the elements of the negotiation. In this case, as noted, you think Lena's best no-deal option is somewhere between $775,000 and $850,000. So you might set your target at the upper end of this range—say, $850,000. An ambitious target is not an offer or demand. Rather, it serves as a beacon, guiding the rest of your strategy and tactics—especially offers and counters—toward the best possible outcome.

Should You Make the First Offer and, If So, at What Price?

Whether you should make the first offer and, if so, where, depends upon what you know about the ZOPA. If you are pretty confident about your counterparts' end of the ZOPA—that is, you have a good sense of the price that is equivalent in their eyes to their best no-deal option—you might want to make an offer just above the most they'd be willing to pay. Then, you'd likely make a concession or two to get inside the ZOPA and then hold firm.

But what if, as is often the case, you are fairly uncertain about their true walk-away price? Many executives we have worked with espouse the conventional wisdom: they would prefer to let the *other* person make the first offer because (1) they are afraid that, given their uncertainty, their first offer won't be aggressive enough, and they'll leave money on the table; or (2) their first offer will be too aggressive, and they'll damage their credibility or derail the negotiations.

One of Thomas Edison's experiences appears to validate this view:

> *Thomas Edison invented the "Universal" stock ticker, a device used for many years by brokerage houses. When Edison first offered this device for sale, he added up the time and effort he had put into inventing it and concluded he was entitled to $5,000 for it. That's what he decided to ask for it. Ultimately, though, he figured he would accept $3,000. When General Lefferts, the president of the Gold & Stock Telegraph Company, came to negotiate, Edison was going to name his price. But he couldn't, Edison said, because he "hadn't the nerve to name such a large sum." Instead Edison asked General Lefferts to make him an offer. Lefferts offered $40,000. Edison said he thought that was "fair." Edison would have lost $35,000 just by making the first offer.*[5]

Edison's experience notwithstanding, we'd like to offer some contrarian advice here: *In cases when you are not hopelessly uninformed, seriously consider going first.* When you are uncertain about the price that the other side would see as equivalent to its no-deal option, consider making a "but flexible" offer or—perhaps even better—what we call a "high non-offer offer."

To explain this departure from conventional wisdom, let's step sideways into the realm of cognitive psychology and look at the potent phenomenon of anchoring.

The Anchoring Effect

Human beings are notoriously bad processors of uncertainty. Numerous studies have shown that extraneous information—such as that conveyed in a first offer intended to shape the other side's ZOPA perceptions—can profoundly influence judgments in the face of uncertainty.

In an experiment we sometimes conduct with senior executives, we run a scenario whereby a supplier gets a one-time rush order of high-tech motorcycle headlamps from a potential buyer—a Japanese manufacturer—and is asked to provide a price. The scenario notes that the Japanese translator has been very difficult to understand and has made numerous mistakes. Our executives play the role of the supplier. They all get nearly identical sales scenarios: the same product, company, industry, financial, and production data, and so on.

But the scenarios differ in one detail. In the scenario received by half the executives, the translator appears to ask for an offer in the $12 per unit range, but when asked to clarify, he denies that he gave any prices. In the second scenario, the translator appears to ask for an offer in the $32 per unit range, but also denies giving any prices. In both scenarios, the executives are clearly and strongly instructed that, given the difficulty in understanding the translator, they should see the $12 (or $32) suggestion as completely and genuinely meaningless. We then ask each group to make an offer, which they can base on identical product, company, and industry information.

In a typical run, the average offer among executives who heard the meaningless $12 offer was $19.80 per unit. The average offer among those who heard the meaningless $32 offer, meanwhile, was $30.10. In other words, the irrelevant numbers $12 and $32 served as *anchors*, pulling offers in their direction, with the negotiators unaware of the large effect the meaningless offer had on their price proposal.

Even negotiators with deep industry knowledge find their assessments anchored by irrelevant data. In one study, experienced real estate agents received all of the information they might need to assess the value of a house: a detailed description of a house including ten pages of information about its features, its square footage, the prices of comparable houses in the area, and so forth.[6] They also had an actual tour of the house.

Half the agents were told that the asking price—by a nonexpert would-be seller—for the house was one figure, while the other half were given an asking price that was 25 percent higher. After being given as much time as they wished to study the information, the subjects were then asked to assess, among other things, the appraisal value of the house and the lowest price they would accept for the house if they were the seller—neither of which, of course, should be affected by the seller's asking price for the house.

Given the quantity and quality of the information received, and the real estate expertise of the experimental subjects—all actual real estate agents in the area—one might guess that hearing an uninformed seller's asking price would not change either their appraisal of the house or the lowest price they would be willing to accept if they were the seller. Yet, both of the assessed quantities were 11 to 14 percent higher in the group that heard the higher asking price. An irrelevant anchor altered these experts' judgment of the house's value despite their market knowledge.

There are many more such studies that document the potent effects of anchoring in negotiation and other related settings. For example, in auction setting, higher anchors—in the form of minimum bid prices—tend to increase the valuation bidders place on the object being auctioned.[7]

Both experience and these studies suggest that, when an anchor is introduced into a negotiation, it can shift perceptions of the ZOPA in its direction, thereby increasing the odds that any final agreement will drift toward the anchor. The result? A final agreement that's favorable to whomever "dropped" the first anchor.

More specifically, an anchor can change your counterparts' perceptions of their no-deal options. Return to the condo example. If you demonstrate that the market for Telluride condos has risen in the last few months and state that the closest comparable condos would be valued at $850,000, the buyer may conclude that price equivalent to her best no-deal option is closer to $850,000 than to something lower, and you may be able to settle at the upper end of the range. The anchor may also change the other party's perceptions of your no-deal options. If you, the condo seller, can show that the value of holding on to the condo is $800,000—given reasonable assumptions about interest rates, the rental market, and likely appreciation for the condo—you may persuade Lena that she will have to pay more than $800,000 just to make it worth your while to sell.

In line with this reasoning, some researchers argue that you should put the first offer on the table, and make that first offer as aggressive as you can. Because anchors shift negotiators' perceptions of the bargaining range, more aggressive offers tend to be more influential than less aggressive ones.[8] And because anchors are more influential under conditions of greater uncertainty, the first offer can have a much larger anchoring effect than subsequent ones.

Henry Kissinger, for one, would most likely side with these researchers: "If agreement is usually found between two starting points, there is no point in making moderate offers. Good bargaining technique would suggest a point of departure far more extreme than what one is willing to accept. The more outrageous the initial proposition, the better is the prospect that what one 'really' wants will be considered a compromise."[9]

Referring back to an earlier point, laboratory studies suggest that those who take an "opportunity focus" and concentrate on what they hope to achieve in the negotiation tend to set more aggressive targets, and begin with more aggressive first offers that serve as anchors. As a consequence, they tend to get better results in price deals than negotiators who focus on preventing undesirable outcomes and behaviors.[10]

Justify Your Proposal

In light of these studies and analogies, one might be tempted to agree with Kissinger's suggestion that the higher your initial offer, the better. But common sense, backed by lab studies, suggests that Kissinger's conclusion is valid only up to a point. When the other party sees your offer as unrealistic, the offer is not effective as an anchor.[11] And it can be counterproductive; you can lose credibility and look unreasonable. Even if you're prepared to move, the other side may conclude no deal is possible and simply walk prematurely.

The obvious implication: you need to be prepared to justify the price you are asking. People are more likely to accede to your request if you give a plausible reason rather than just tossing out a wish-number; indeed the "because" that follows your number plays an unexpectedly strong psychological role. Merely having some reason—any reason—helps. In a widely cited study, psychologist Ellen Langer had a person approach people at the front of a long line at a library copy machine and ask to cut in front and make a copy. When that person asked, "Excuse me, I have five pages. May I use the Xerox machine?" 60 percent of those asked complied. When the asker gave a reason ("Excuse me, I have five pages. May I use the Xerox machine because I am in a rush?"), compliance with the request was 94 percent. Even more remarkable, when the asker merely gave the form of giving a reason without actually giving a reason ("Excuse me, I have five pages. May I use the Xerox machine because I have to make some copies?"), compliance remained nearly as high, at 93 percent.[12] Surely you can give better reasons than this!

Of course, as you get past simple experimental situations, plausible arguments tend to work much better than implausible ones—but both work better than just throwing an aggressive number onto the table. One of your goals is to help your counterpart explain to himself, his boss, his peers, and his spouse why the price he accepted was fair and reasonable under the circumstances, relative to his alternatives. Offering reasons why the agreement you propose is fair makes this task easier. In general, people are more likely to accept even take-it-or-leave-it offers when justified by reference to forces or principles outside the will of the two parties.[13]

In our condo example, you'd most likely look at comparable sales to justify your price. You'd probably look at the price appreciation that has taken place in the real estate market since you bought the condo, and apply it to the price you paid (plus improvements you put in). What are rental rates for comparable units? How well would the likely rental income cover payments under a standard mortgage, based on your target price? You'd probably examine any changes in the number of days that units stay on the market. Are condos selling faster this year than last, or is it the other way around? If the market is slowing, or if vacancy rates are going up, you're likely to hear these arguments. How do you plan to respond? But this is getting ahead of ourselves.

We don't believe that one always needs to make an extreme first offer, however well-justified, with its risks to credibility and process, to get the benefits of anchoring. Below are several softer methods of anchoring that can achieve the same effect with lower risk.

Use Flexible but Extreme Offers and "Non-Offer Offers" to Anchor

Now let's look at the "extreme but flexible" concept mentioned earlier. Anchoring by this technique can give you a lower-risk approach to favorably shaping your counterpart's perceptions of the ZOPA. Instead of saying, "We'll pay you $11 million for your company" (a very low offer), an extreme but flexible offer would be something on the order of, "We understand from what you've described in our conversations that there is substantial hidden value in the company. We haven't yet been able to evaluate your arguments about the company's value. So, we'll offer you $11 million based on what we know today, but are open to modifying that offer if we're persuaded about the additional value you've described." While the offer is low, the flexibility decreases the loss of credibility and reduces the chances the seller will walk.

Sometime the most effective anchors reduce the risk of appearing extreme because they are not offers, but merely introduce relevant numbers. A job applicant may state his belief that people with his qualifications tend to have annual compensation between $85,000 and $95,000, or that his former colleague just received an offer of $92,000. You can also anchor by citing apparently comparable agreements as precedent. Consider the case of a money manager preparing to negotiate her annual bonus. "While bonuses last year were 50 percent of salary," she might tell her boss, "I recognize that this year will not be as good as last year." Such statements can have an anchoring effect, without requiring her to make an extreme offer that could jeopardize talks.

If you're the prospective buyer of a company, you could anchor without making an offer by saying something like, "We'd obviously need to do our due diligence on your company to determine our valuation. Our general sense is that private companies of this size in this industry tend to sell at twelve times earnings, which is how we're currently thinking."

Let's say this strikes the seller as on the extreme side of low—she was thinking of something like twice that amount. Because you've been flexible, the seller does not have to reject your foolish offer out of hand—in fact there is no offer—but can take the opportunity to try to educate you. The negotiation, if it proceeds, will likely move *up* from twelve times earnings, rather than *down* from what the seller would have asked if she went first. Such an offer also gives you the opportunity to try to learn from the seller's reactions; when you mention the "twelve times earnings," you should watch like a hawk, especially if she seems OK with it. Remember the Twin Tasks here: you are trying to *learn* about the real ZOPA as well as *shape the other side's perceptions* favorably.

A non-offer offer that is viewed as unrealistic may have greater effect as an anchoring device, because it doesn't directly undermine the negotiator's credibility or expertise. For example, the statement that "purchasing is undoubtedly going to demand price cuts of 15 percent or more," just to get the conversation started, may have a strong anchoring effect, even if both the buyer and salesperson know that the 15 percent figure is unrealistic. In contrast, an opening offer of a 15 percent reduction that is clearly unrealistic in current industry conditions might be significantly less effective as an anchor.

Dropping the first "soft anchor" in the form of a non-offer offer can help inoculate you against the other side's anchoring efforts. How? You should certainly do as much prior research as possible to reduce your uncertainty about the ZOPA—and thus your vulnerability to being unfavorably anchored. Yet you will typically need to learn more during the negotiation itself This may open you to their anchoring efforts. Not only can your soft anchor shape their perceptions (offensively), it may focus your own attention favorably away from any anchors they may drop (defensively).

Recognize and Use the Norm of Reciprocity

When someone does something to benefit us, we naturally want to reciprocate. In fact, reciprocity is one of the most powerful norms in human interaction.[14] It is not only highly rational in many circumstances, but it probably reflects some impulse from our genetic code, dating back to our hunter-gatherer forebears.[15] Bargainers sometimes actively appeal to this built-in impulse.

The upscale rug merchant who offers you tea while you are looking at rugs, for example, hopes that you will reciprocate either by buying a rug from him, or by being less tough on price than you would otherwise have been.

If the rug merchant begins by anchoring with an extreme but flexible offer, and then makes a concession, he may tap into your unconscious reciprocity norm. His movement, even though from an unreasonable starting point, often triggers an impulse in the other party to move as well, rather than standing pat. "Influence" guru Robert Cialdini calls this the rejection-then-retreat approach, and documents its effectiveness.[16]

Couple Anchoring with the Use of the "Contrast Principle"

Everything is relative—or at least that is how we humans experience things. To experience this firsthand, put your right hand in hot water and your left in cold water and then put each in lukewarm water. Your right hand will feel cold, and your left hand will feel hot, because your perception is not absolute but is relative to what has come before.

If you want to sell a $100 tie and an $800 suit to a customer, should you start with the "easy" (less expensive) tie, then move up? Not at all. A man who is shown a $100 tie is much more likely to buy if he has *just* purchased an $800 suit. On its own, or first, the $100 tie may seem overpriced relative to the price of the suit. However, for someone who's just dropped $800, the $100 tie seems an easy add-on. Think about overpriced options offered to car buyers. Would you ordinarily consider a $2,000 GPS? But a $54,000 Lexus with a GPS doesn't seem so bad relative to a $52,000 Lexus without. When you make an aggressive offer (or non-offer anchor) and follow this with a less aggressive offer, your counterpart will perceive your second offer as less extreme than he or she would have if you had not started with the more extreme offer.[17]

Recognize and Use Key Steps of the Negotiation Dance

Now let's look at some of the key steps in a typical negotiation, and see how you can influence them to your advantage. These include responding to a first offer and, later, working toward closure.

How Should I Respond to Their Offer?

Maybe you've decided to let the other side make the first offer. Maybe your counterparts sent in a price proposal on the morning of your first meeting. Or maybe it's customary for the seller to open with a price. In any case, you must respond.

THE MIDPOINT RULE. The first thing to remember is the "midpoint rule." As common sense suggests and our experimental studies strikingly bear out, the midpoint between the first offer and the first counteroffer is a very good predictor of the ultimate outcome of the negotiation—if the midpoint is in the ZOPA. If you've done your preparation, you've figured out a target price. Choose your counteroffer so that the midpoint equals your target price.

RESPONDING TO AN EXTREME DEMAND OR OFFER. Hard bargainers may well start with an extreme demand or offer ("I expect all my suppliers to agree before we start negotiations that they will cut prices 10 percent every year if they want to keep our business"). The aims may be both to anchor and rattle you. In such cases, following the midpoint rule could cause you to have to respond with a relatively absurd price. If you are trying to buy a company and your target price is $10 per share and they ask for $30 per share, mechanically following the midpoint rule would require that you counter with a proposal that they pay you $10 per share to take the company off of their hands—not likely to be a winning strategy.

To avoid the anchoring effects of the extreme demand, we suggest two steps. First, rule extreme offers out of consideration firmly and clearly. If you are not clear about the unacceptability of an unacceptable offer, there is a significant risk that the other side will interpret your ambiguous response as an indication that such an offer may be acceptable to you or nearly so. We have seen bright cooperative, problem-solving types record a clearly unacceptable demand in their notes without responding or showing any emotion. The other side quite understandably reads their lack of response as an indication that the offer was in or close to the ZOPA, resets its expectations, and becomes emboldened to ask for more.

Your first step, therefore, should be to politely and clearly communicate that you are ruling the offer out of consideration. Exactly how you do this depends upon your reading of the other side. Humor and nonverbal cues can be effective when you are letting your counterparts know that their offer is completely unacceptable, but humor does not always work well across significant cultural boundaries. Sometimes, you may respond by making an equally absurd counteroffer. Sometimes, you will want to consider walking away. In any case, you must leave no doubt that the extreme offer is not close to acceptable.

Second, you should shift the metric to avoid being anchored by an extreme offer. Even if you have ruled the other side's offer out of bounds, you likely still have been anchored. We'd advise shifting the focus of the negotiation elsewhere; do not let it dwell on that offer, which can serve to strengthen its anchoring effect. Our suggestion is to change the metric under discussion so that the impact of the anchoring is diminished.

Here's an example of what we mean. In an early negotiation on which we served as an adviser, our client was an entrepreneur who had built a software services consulting firm. He had decided to sell his firm if he got an attractive enough price, and was in discussion with several potential buyers before he called us. The most attractive buyer was a company in a related software service sector, and was represented by an investment bank with significant industry expertise. The entrepreneur was quite uncertain as to the most that the buyer would be willing to pay. In a fairly bullish market, he was hoping for a price of about $40 million or above.

But the opposing investment bankers opened with a clear statement: "We've made nineteen acquisitions of software services firms this year, and have never paid more than ten to twelve times earnings, less a private-company discount." Although they did not name a price, it implied a price range of $15–$18 million, below the entrepreneur's walk-away price of $20 million and far from his $40 million target. Through this move by the bankers, the entrepreneur's perceptions of the ZOPA had been influenced, and indeed, the perceived ZOPA had shrunk in his mind. The best he thought he could aspire to get was now closer to $25 million. It was at that point that the entrepreneur, already effectively anchored, called us.

Our suggestion was to let us discuss the valuation issue on his behalf. We presented ourselves as reasonably sophisticated financially—with Wall Street and other investment experience—but not knowledgeable about the software services business. As such, rather than compound the already-set anchor by focusing on price/earnings multiples of comparable transactions (as their investment bank had done, and which requires some industry expertise), we prepared a discounted cash flow (DCF) analysis, which presented a valuation of the company as a whole. We presented the valuation to the seller and investment banker by saying that we had performed a valuation based on a number of assumptions and that we were open to persuasion. In fact, we had made assumptions that seemed (to us) fairly aggressive, and implied a valuation roughly double what the acquirer had proposed, although we consciously never discussed price-to-earnings multiples. We began discussing our assumptions and offered to revise them when we were persuaded by their arguments.

What happened here? The metric had changed from price/earnings multiples to company valuation using DCF analysis. In other words, the bankers were anchored in our new metric, and during the remainder of the negotiation, we were negotiating *down* from a high price, rather than *up* from a low price. The transaction closed at a much higher price/earnings multiple than any in the industry in the previous two years. From a tactical standpoint, we were not attempting to change the valuation method because it necessarily implied a higher valuation, though we used it to do so. Instead, we switched to a new method in order to change the metric, unfreeze the previously established anchor, and set a new, more favorable anchor in the new metric.

How Do I Move Toward Closure?

Negotiators typically close price deals with a series of reciprocal concessions. The negotiation typically ends when:

- One side is convinced that the other side is not going to move further,

- One side or the other is not comfortable using tactics that would induce the other side to make further concessions, or

- Both sides agree on a principle of fairness that implies an outcome in the ZOPA.

Let's look first at the issue of concessions. Remember that each of these steps provides you with an opportunity to learn about *their* end of the ZOPA and to shape their perceptions of *your* end of the ZOPA.

USE CONVERGING CONCESSIONS CREATIVELY. One can use patterns of concessions to shape the other party's perceptions of where one's end of the ZOPA is located. For example, we recently advised a company in the settlement of a series of related lawsuits. The company's no-deal option was to defend itself in court. Our analysis suggested that the expected cost of going to court was in excess of $50 million, based solely on the merits of this case in isolation. But a more thorough analysis also had to factor in the negative precedent on other suits that would be associated either with (1) losing the case or (2) being forced to divulge information, either during discovery or trial, that would likely affect other cases. Beginning settlement negotiations at $20 million, we moved with our first concession to $28 million, then to $32 million, then to $34 million, and so on. Each concession we made decreased by roughly half, designed to imply to the plaintiff that our maximum was at the limit of this series of concessions. The settlement was made at $36 million, which was a desirable outcome for the company.

USE THE RECIPROCITY PRINCIPLE IN THE CONCESSION PROCESS. Keep in mind the powerful norm of reciprocity, discussed earlier. When your counterpart makes a concession, you are likely to feel an urge to reciprocate. This partly explains why, when the midpoint between the opening offer and counteroffer falls in the ZOPA, it is a good predictor of the ultimate outcome.

If you want to avoid the subconscious pull of the midpoint, you may need to indicate an unwillingness to make symmetric concessions. In the legal settlements described above, we argued that our concessions were real money from shareholders' pockets, while their concessions were from speculative damage theories. Therefore, we argued, they had to make much bigger concessions to achieve meaningful parity.

At closing, the norm of reciprocity often pushes both sides to "split the difference." As a way of concluding the process, this makes good sense in some circumstances, especially if the two offers are already close and both are in an acceptable range. However, if you suggest splitting the difference—and the other side's negotiators want to play hardball—your expressed willingness tells them that the midpoint between the last two offers is acceptable to you and hence in the ZOPA. They may simply thank you for your concession to the midpoint, pocket it, and then make a tiny counteroffer. So, split the difference sometimes, but carefully.

AVOID UNSUPPORTED COMMITMENTS; CONSIDER MAKING SUPPORTED COMMITMENTS. In a stripped-down price negotiation, it's often difficult to persuade the other party that you can't move a little bit further. Your final, "take-it-or-leave-it" offer leads to your "final, final" offer, and then your "final, final, final offer." Ideally your conviction, demeanor, and reputation will make this assertion credible. But outside factors can be even more persuasive.

For example, when her customer demands a significant discount, the seller—Rhoda—might explain that she has signed several contracts with other customers, who provide her with higher annual sales than you are proposing, and yet pay a higher price than the one you're hoping to get. Several of Rhoda's key contracts contain a "Most Favored Nation" (MFN) clause, guaranteeing those other customers the best price Rhoda grants to anyone else. For Rhoda to sign an agreement for a lower price would require her to make sufficient compensating payments to other customers that it would make the deal with the current customer immediately unprofitable. We call this a *supported commitment*, because it is not just Rhoda's bald assertion that she won't make further price cuts, but it is supported by something *outside* the will of the parties (the MFN clause).

Laboratory studies suggest that attempts at unsupported commitments at prices within the ZOPA—and thus better than the other side's best no-deal option—are significantly more likely to be rejected by the other side than supported commitments, even if the offer is otherwise acceptable.[18] Giving in to the other party—with a loss of face—may be vastly harder than giving in to an outside force.

RESPONDING TO COMMITMENTS. Like the boss who says she'd like to give you a bigger budget but can't because of the precedent it would set, a purchaser might seek to commit by saying, "I can sign contracts up to $500,000, but above that would require submitting this request to a committee, whose purpose is to look critically at consulting contracts in an effort to keep our costs down. The committee hasn't approved any such requests yet. If you can do this work for $500,000, I'm prepared to engage your firm."

The purchaser has stated an interest that (she thinks) you cannot meet and thus, if it has been credibly conveyed, she need not move further. Such commitments create a negotiation challenge. It becomes your job to understand (1) if such a committee exists and (2) if so, how it functions. Could the contract be split into two parts, one for $350,000 that addresses strategic issues, and another for $275,000 that focuses on organizational design issues that would facilitate implementation? How different would the engagements have to be in order to avoid the sense that your counterpart was just trying to circumvent the committee? Are there any categories of contracts that would avoid the committee? What if a very high-ranking executive felt she needed this contract approved quickly?

Sometimes the best way to deal with a commitment expressed by your counterparts is to help them climb down from it gracefully, by treating it as an aspiration and refusing to hear it as a binding commitment. ("I can understand why you would want to pay only $50,000.") They might make a commitment to a certain clause in a contract by saying, "As a matter of corporate policy, we never sign contracts with vendors who don't indemnify us against all infringements of third-party intellectual property." You might treat the commitment based on corporate policy as an aspiration: "I understand why you'd love to have someone else take all of the risk."

Again, clarification will be the order of the day: "What aspects of IP infringement risk most concern you? Have you ever had a problem with one of your consultants infringing a third party's intellectual property? What was the nature of the infringement?" Frequently by identifying their concern, you can reduce the scope of their demands to an area in which you feel comfortable, and thereby undo or reduce the scope of their commitment.

Meta-Anchoring: Framing the Whole Negotiation

Having dissected the pieces of the common negotiation dance, we'd like to step back and explore how your tactics can advantageously shape the broader context for these steps. Many negotiators successfully anchor a negotiation not by focusing on numbers (such as a price or financial terms), but on the *nature* of the problem that the talks are meant to resolve. Such *meta-anchoring* moves can shape the parties' expectations of the ZOPA at a higher level of abstraction than any specific number could. Because it forms the other side's conceptualization of the problem, meta-anchoring can dramatically influence both the other side's perceptions of the ZOPA, and the ultimate negotiated outcome. (In our discussion above of the sale of the software services firm, we could be said to have "meta-anchored" with an advantageous (DCF) valuation method, not simply "anchored" with a specific price figure.)

Let's take a look at the key steps in preparing to meta-anchor effectively.

Brainstorm Possible Meta-Anchors

To meta-anchor effectively, look creatively at various ways to characterize the negotiation problem. Some characterizations have clear implications for the appropriate kind of resolution, or at least the most appropriate process and personnel needed to get there. For example, framing a negotiation as "a routine extension of an existing deal" may receive far less scrutiny than approaching it as "new contract," even when the substantive issues are identical.

Here's a real case that shows how this first step might play out: a small research-intensive company we'll call R&DCo developed a very innovative piece of technology. Soon after, Acquirer, a much larger firm in a related industry, approached R&DCo to discuss buying out the company. Rather than the dismissing the offer, as it had with previous would-be buyers, R&DCo took Acquirer's suggestion seriously. R&DCo felt that its sales were hampered by its small size and capitalization, by the need to embed its technologies into larger systems such as Acquirer's products, and by its relatively weak distribution channels. Ownership by a strategic buyer such as Acquirer could improve this situation.

In preparation for negotiations with Acquirer, R&DCo identified two likely competing meta-anchors. The first viewed the transaction as the purchase of R&DCo on a *stand-alone* basis. The second viewed the deal as an attempt to create *synergy* by combining R&DCo's technological expertise with Acquirer's sales, marketing, and distribution; by using R&DCo's technologies in other markets; and by using the buyer's greater size to win new sales for R&DCo. In this way, it would be possible to divide that synergy between the two companies.

Evaluate the Implications of Different Meta-Anchors

After identifying ways of conceptualizing the problem, evaluate their implications. Which meta-anchors could lead to more favorable agreements? Which might lead the process off a cliff? For example, non-U.S. international trade negotiators have described the extreme care with which they approach their U.S. counterparts on the subject of regulating transborder data flows. If the meta-anchor becomes "data as information," or worse, "data as written speech," U.S. negotiators are all too likely to focus on First Amendment/free-speech concerns, immensely complicating negotiations. If the metaphor in such negotiations becomes "data as commodity," however, talks can proceed as ordinary trade deals, since regulation of commodities is widely accepted by most countries.

Returning to our ongoing example, the real negotiation between R&DCo and Acquirer over price is likely to be shaped substantially by which meta-anchor they come to accept. Will this be a financial transaction, in which R&DCo is valued on a stand-alone basis based on its current financials? Or will the negotiation be about estimating and dividing the synergy created by the deal? Valuing R&DCo on a current stand-alone basis would favor the buyer, because R&DCo's value would increase greatly in Acquirer's hands. In contrast, meta-anchoring the sale as a problem of dividing future synergy would boost the per share sale price by focusing on the value to be created by combining R&DCo's technologies with Acquirer's products, marketing, and distribution above and beyond its stand-alone value. Clearly, R&DCo should substantially prefer the latter meta-anchor to the former.

Anticipate the Other Side's Point of View

Next, put yourself in the your counterparts' shoes, anticipating both their reactions to your chosen meta-anchor as well as the kinds of meta-anchors they may propose. You will need a plan for dealing with the other side's meta-anchoring attempts, including the possibility of meta-anchoring preemptively. A well-prepared negotiator often can offer an advantageous meta-anchor that the other side almost unconsciously adopts without objection, in the early stages of negotiation. At the same time, a proactive negotiator will take special care to anticipate and prepare a response to the meta-anchors he or she expects the other side to drop.

R&DCo, for example, expected Acquirer to open talks by stating that it buys businesses based solely upon their stand-alone value. To preempt this, and to meta-anchor the talks on its terms, R&DCo's CEO stated politely (and truthfully) very early in the conversation: "Almost monthly, we turn down an approach from potential acquirers who want to value us on a stand-alone basis. We're interested in talking to you because of the significant potential synergy between our two companies. If you want to discuss how we value and divide the joint gains from combining our companies, we're very interested in talking with you. However, if you only want to consider our stand-alone financials, you'll be wasting your valuable time, as well as ours. Do you think it makes sense to proceed?"

R&DCo successfully meta-anchored the negotiation, by making its stand-alone valuation the floor above which estimated synergy could be split between the two parties.

Back to Creating *and* Claiming Value

This chapter has focused solely on tactics for claiming value. Throughout, we've analyzed tactics in terms of the Twin Tasks: (1) learn about the true ZOPA, and (2) favorably shape the other side's ZOPA perceptions.

But as we've stressed in earlier chapters, most negotiations offer the opportunity both to create *and* claim value. The tactics outlined in this chapter, a guide to the art and science of haggling, have applications far beyond the pure price deals that we've focused on here. Our next at-the-table focus moves from the narrow problem of shaping ZOPA perceptions to the joint problem solving required to create and claim value.

- Remember the Twin Tasks of haggling: learn about the true zone of possible agreement (ZOPA), and favorably shape perceptions of it.

- Learn about the ZOPA by using prior research, analyzing your best no-deal option as well as the other side's, and continuously mining the other side's moves for real ZOPA-related information. Update your ZOPA assessment frequently.

- Focus on the opportunity, rather than the downside; as part of your preparation consider writing a short paragraph on what you hope to accomplish, not what you want to avoid.

- Set a fairly aggressive target.

- Shape perceptions of the ZOPA by:

  > Meta-anchoring—implicitly shaping the definition of the problem the negotiation will solve. Brainstorm possible meta-anchors, assess their implications, and take the initiative to meta-anchor the negotiation favorably and head off unfavorable meta-anchors.

  > Anchoring directly with favorable offers, numbers or data, and "non-offer offers" and "extreme but flexible offers." Don't forget to justify your proposals.

- Strongly consider making the first offer—an extreme but flexible or non-offer offer—to gain the benefits of anchoring.

- Use the midpoint rule to respond to their offer; counteroffer so the midpoint between the two offers is your target.

- Avoid being anchored by an extreme offer—clearly communicate that the offer is unacceptable, and shift the metric to unfreeze the anchor and drop your own more favorable counter-anchoring.

- Use patterns of concession converging to a supposed limit, and be aware that your counterpart may use this tactic.

- Use and be alert for the norm of reciprocity—your concession may induce one from them, and vice versa.

- Use the contrast principle—the offer that follows an extreme offer may look more generous than it would have if it didn't follow the extreme offer.

- Be wary of splitting the difference and consider it only when when last offers are close and both acceptable.

- Persuade your counterparts that saying yes to your price is better than their alternatives, that accepting a price that you like is a good (and fair) choice for them, and that the constraints upon you make it hard for you to move.

  - Prepare fairness arguments and prepare to respond to fairness arguments.

  - Avoid unsupported commitments. Consider making supported commitments.

  - Treat unsupported commitments as aspirations. When they support their attempted commitments with a clear rationale that certain interests would be damaged if they moved, undo their commitments by finding other ways to meet those interests.

Chapter Thirteen

Solve Joint Problems to Create and Claim Value

To solve your individual value-claiming "problem," your tactics must help you to learn accurately about the true zone of possible agreement (ZOPA) and to shape the other side's perceptions of the ZOPA in a manner favorable to you. Yet most negotiations are not purely about value claiming. Our four-chapter discussion on designing value-creating deals offered general principles and advice for "moving northeast" (for example, think of our advice to dovetail differences and to maximize the total net pie) and provided many examples of seeming price deals that in fact masked considerable cooperative potential.

Armed with these deal-design principles and an understanding of pure claiming tactics derived from the last chapter, we now move to the table in search of tactics that *both* create and claim value, ideally on a long-term basis. At the end of the day, you want to create all possible value jointly, claim a full share of it, and prevent yourself from being exploited by a value-claimer. This can be a challenge, especially when the other side is playing a hardball, claiming game. Perhaps this stance is purely tactical or perhaps your counterparts simply don't see the potential for joint gains. Either way, this chapter offers a number of suggestions to push the negotiation in a productive direction.

Here's the essence of the joint problem that our tactics must solve. Creating value requires cooperation to elicit information—about interests, views, capabilities, and so on—and use that information to generate mutually beneficial options. This takes communication, trust, openness, and creativity. Yet those very qualities can open you up to exploitation by a determined value claimer. If you put all your cards on the table, while others play theirs close to the vest, you're likely to get nailed. And yet if everyone hides his or her cards, revealing little, and searching for openings to exploit, it becomes nearly impossible to come up with joint gains. You and your counterparts are likely to have a battle royal over a small pie.

Put otherwise, information in negotiation is a two-edged sword: essential to solve the joint problem and to create value, but also a source of vulnerability to a value-claimer on the other side. You can't easily separate the creating and claiming processes. It turns out that the way you create value affects how it gets divided. And the battle over dividing the pie often affects how much, if at all, it gets expanded. Managing this creating-claiming tension productively is the essence of successful negotiation. Problem-solving tactics, undertaken with a full understanding of the value-claiming aspect of negotiation, offer the best route to great outcomes.

Constructive negotiation processes, in which value is created as well as claimed, nevertheless tend to emphasize the joint nature of the problem to be solved. They stress:

- Reconciling the parties' real interests, rather than battling over their positions

- The future and mutual possibilities, rather than the past and who was right, wrong, and to blame for what happened before

- Factual discussions, rather broad generalizations

- Joint problem solving, rather than adversarial posturing

As was the case with the claiming tactics used in our first dimension—the subject of the previous chapter—we can't hope to compress all of what's known about creating and claiming value at the table into a single chapter. But we will combine our own experience and the prescriptions of others to suggest some tactical guidelines that will make you more effective in wide range of situations where there is the opportunity both to create and claim value.[1]

Our tactical advice falls into four basic areas, which serve as the main sections of this chapter:

1. Ask, listen, and learn.

2. Divulge information strategically.

3. Foster an appealing and productive negotiation process.

4. Adopt a persuasive style.

Each class of tactics needs to be approached with a keen sense of productively managing both the creating and claiming aspects.

Ask, Listen, and Learn

At the table, you learn by listening and observing. You rarely learn much when you are talking!

Sales experts say that most salespeople talk 80 percent of the time and listen 20 percent of the time—but that the most *effective* salespeople listen 80 percent of the time and talk 20 percent of the time. One of the toughest things about negotiation is that it is hard to listen while you are talking. Even when the other side is talking, you tend to focus on what you are going to say next. So, actually listening to the other party, and processing what they're saying, requires extra effort. A few tactical suggestions follow.

TRY ACTIVE LISTENING. Active listening, in which you play back to the other party what you just heard her say, helps you slow down and focus your attention on what she is saying. For example: "Let me just make sure that I understood you. You are concerned that if your bonus formula is tied to the projects you work on, and if the company decides to allocate more work to others, your compensation would go down even if allocating the work to others makes the company more profitable. If I understood you correctly, you'd like to have your bonus guaranteed at the level you received last year. Could you say a bit more about that?"

Even repeating back what you've heard without paraphrasing, followed by a pause, often prompts your counterpart to expand upon the point, and share more of his or her motivations in ways that may be helpful. It also may allow your counterpart to clarify her statement in a way that gracefully backs down from some aspects of the position or assertion. And, critically, when you keep testing your understanding, they *know* that you are listening.

AVOID QUESTIONS THAT ASK FOR A YES OR NO ANSWER. Questions that elicit flat yes or no answers can be damaging. For example: "Do you mean you won't do a deal if it doesn't provide full indemnification for you and your team?" The answerer either has to undercut himself (unlikely) by saying "no," or by saying "yes" invest personal and perhaps organizational credibility in not backing down from the statement (in which case you're worse off having asked this yes-or-no question).

ASK OPEN-ENDED QUESTIONS. In many cases, the most effective questions are open-ended. For example:

- "Why?" "Why not?"—as in, "You've said that your contracts people don't want to reimburse us for expenses that you have historically reimbursed us for. Can you say a little more about why this has become an issue at this point?" Or, "You say you can't agree to any price increases for two years. Could you tell us more about your situation and what's behind your thinking?"

- "What if we did it this way?"—as in, "What if we were to give you a bigger piece of our business? How would that affect your cost and sales situation? How much could you reduce the per unit price?"

- "How would that work from your perspective?"—as in, "How would it work from your standpoint if we were to raise fees on the following services, in the following circumstances?"

- "What kinds of problems would that create for you?"—as in, "If we were to reach agreement to provide the capital to fund the cash calls that the partnership agreement requires you to make in return for a significant share of the returns you would get, what kind of pluses and minuses would that involve for you?"

And after you ask, *really listen*. When you start making proposals, listen to their objections. These objections may spotlight interests that they had not disclosed previously, and which as a result are not reflected in your proposals. Objections can enable you to shape new packages that better meet *your* interests, as well as theirs.

BRING A DESIGNATED LISTENER. When you bring a team to negotiate, it is helpful to include on the team a designated listener—someone whose role is not to talk, but carefully listen and take notes.

Divulge Information Strategically

Of course, you will be expected to do more than listen at the table; you will be expected to talk about your own needs and expectations. Here are some battle-tested ideas for revealing information in ways that also elicit information from the other side.

Begin with the End

A successful executive we know in the outsourcing industry begins his major negotiations by sitting down with his customer to write the positive press release that the two sides hope will result from the conclusion of a successful negotiation. By hashing out the joint ideal up front, he learns about key interests of his counterpart and also shares important interests. Both focus away from the barriers and on the opportunity, the "pot of gold" that could result from effective cooperation. At the same time, both sides may be gaining some psychological commitment to making a deal. When the negotiation hits a tough patch, the executive pulls out the release to reorient the effort.

Use the Norm of Reciprocity to Build Trust and Share/Gain Information

In the last chapter, we introduced the concept of the "norm of reciprocity," which leads us to want to reciprocate when someone does something that's helpful to us. It is a powerful psychological force, which you can tap into to gain information.[2]

Share some low-cost information, and encourage the other side to share some information, as well. If your opposite numbers fail to reciprocate—or if, based on your prior research, they appear to be trying to mislead you—consider having an explicit discussion about what you have been trying to do: that is, to give and get enough information to enable you to jointly design a mutually beneficial deal. Sharing that information makes each of you vulnerable but is safer if both of you do it.

If they *do* reciprocate, provide additional information, and request more.[3] In many negotiations, you can tap the power of the reciprocity norm to build trust over time. You may perform a personal favor, take your counterpart out for drinks or coffee, provide some helpful information outside of the negotiation, or in some other way do something positive. All of these moves are designed to build trust. The trust, in turn, will enable you and your counterpart to share information that will enable you both to create value.

Present Multiple Equivalent Offers

To learn more about your counterpart's interests and trade-offs, you can present her with a choice of two packages of equal value to you, and—without asking her to accept or reject either—ask her which package is better for her. If you have designed your packages carefully, you will learn something about her side's trade-offs, and move in a value-creating direction while revealing little about your preferences.

Similarly, if you are a buyer of a multifeatured product or service, you can ask the seller to price the product or service both with and without a certain feature. In this way, you can learn about the seller's trade-offs without revealing yours.[4]

Sequence Issues Carefully and Negotiate Packages

In chapter 7, we focused on sequencing the parties and stages of the negotiation itself; now we turn to how sequencing the issues properly helps to create and claim value. Of course, to sequence issues properly, you need to understand your full set of interests associated with that issue and its relationship to other issues. For example, if you are negotiating the form of a transaction—merger, acquisition, or equity joint venture, for example—there are powerful implications for the rest of the negotiation of how you settle that initial issue.

The most common advice about issue order is to settle the "easy issues first." On the positive side, this approach can help build trust, rapport, a sense that progress is possible, and momentum as you tackle harder issues. Getting easy issues out of the way can simplify the remaining negotiation.

Yet if you do settle the easy issues first, the only ones left at the end may require tough, value-claiming battles. This issue-by-issue approach may inadvertently transform a potentially cooperative deal into a highly competitive one, with real deadlock risks near the close. This often happens when everything but price is settled and the parties are far apart on this particular issue. As we discussed in chapter 5, working out an overall, value-creating package for the endgame—in which nothing is settled until everything is settled, and there is mutual gain realized relative to no-deal options—can shift the dynamics in a much more positive direction.

When U.S. President Jimmy Carter was in the final stages of peace treaty negotiations between Egyptian President Sadat and Israeli Prime Minister Begin at Camp David, he confronted just such a situation: "The only serious problem was [Sadat's] desire to delete the entire paragraph on Jerusalem. I knew that the Israelis wanted the same thing, but I confess that I did not tell Sadat. I reserved that concession just in case I needed some bargaining points later on.[5] Earlier in the process, Carter had packaged a classic easy issue—on which both Egyptians and Israelis wanted the identical outcome (to defer the status of Jerusalem)—with other, more contentious items. By doing this,

Carter turned the ultimate package (minus Jerusalem) into more of a plus for each side, rather than setting up a much riskier, win-lose finale.

The negotiating dynamics involving easy issues can become complex. For example, faced with two main issues—one not too important to them and the other vital to them—some negotiators will fight hard on the vital one, then be flexible for the easier one, hoping to make up for any hard feelings. Other negotiators make a point of "giving in" first on the less key issue, hoping to generate some pressure for reciprocity from the other side on the remaining question. However, what is an easy issue for you to concede may in fact be the other side's most critical issue to get, or at least quite important to them. You may or may not realize this at the time you "give" on that issue. If you've already said yes to such an issue or issues, you may have little leverage left for your hardest topics when you later tackle them. This possibility amplifies the general wisdom of developing packages rather than settling issue-by-issue.

A further implication of this issue-sequencing logic affects agenda management. When negotiating large contracts, it is common to have one party's attorney make a list of unresolved issues and have the group work down the list one issue at a time, attempting to get closure on each before moving on to the next. While this method of agenda setting can help the parties to organize the remaining questions, it is almost guaranteed to leave unrealized value on the table for all parties. If the parties have opposing interests on each issue, they will typically reach mid-range settlements on each of the issues. Yet doing so fails to heed a basic principle of value creation. Specifically, for each side to do better, the party that places greatest weight on each issue should receive more favorable treatment on that issue in return for "compensation," such as giving the other(s) favorable treatment on the issues most important to them (providing the issues are of roughly similar importance). Thus, the agreement reached by finalizing one issue at a time is likely to be substantially worse for all parties than that reached by a process that is geared to look for differences in interest and thereby to facilitate trades. Although issue-by-issue agenda management is often the default procedure in many complex negotiations, we'd advise a focus on negotiating packages where possible.

Foster an Appealing and Productive Negotiation Process

Process matters.

As we explained in chapter 5, people tend to feel better about an agreement—and value it more highly—if it was reached by a process that they feel was fair.

Conversely, they tend to reject offers, even economically attractive offers, if the process feels coercive.

We have found very useful negotiation process advice in *Getting Past No*, written by our friend and colleague Bill Ury.[6] While it is framed as advice for dealing with difficult people, the book's advice works equally well in less adversarial settings. At its core is the notion that you should try to transform your negotiation process from one that is "face-to-face against each other" to "side by side against the problem." Don't think of the other side as "them," or as your adversaries; seek to align both your efforts against the problem of jointly craft agreements that meet each side's interests on a lasting basis, rather than glare at each other each other across the table.

The physical setup of the negotiations can play a role here. When both sides troop into a meeting room and position themselves on opposite sides of the conference table, this physical setup can almost function like a stage set, unconsciously cuing each side to fall into a well-worn script and adversarial roles. ("Ladies and gentlemen, this afternoon's production will be 'Face-to-Face Against Each Other.'") We have seen negotiators break this unconscious mold by inviting both sides to set up on the same side of the table, together opposite a white board on which the "problem" was summarized. ("Instead, this afternoon's production will be 'Side by Side Against the Problem.'") Would it surprise you that encounters of the second tend to be more productive?

In line with Ury's advice, we suggest that you relentlessly reframe your negotiation process in the following four directions.

Move from Positional to Interest-Based Conversations

Even when the discussion may seem to be narrowly focused, the interests that motivate the other side are often much richer than their bargaining positions; remember our elaboration of such interests in chapter 5.

Many tough negotiators are quick to stake out firm positions: "You have to cut your price by 5 percent per year if you want to keep our business." Our first advice is *not* to encourage this by, for example, starting or responding with "Here's my position. What's yours?" Although your counterpart may not be eager to engage in a collaborative process, consciously reframing away from bargaining positions to broader interests can help engage the other side in a more productive discussion. "I take it that you are trying to decrease your overall costs of manufacturing by 5 percent. What is the overall plan for doing this? What if we could figure out how to cut your manufacturing costs by

5 percent of what you pay us?" Often the kinds of questions we outlined above will help move past positions to interests.

The hard positional bargainer will likely require a lot of effort before engaging in a value-oriented discussion. But consciously focusing the discussion on how you can help the other side make more money—without cutting your prices!—can help engage a positional bargainer.

Move from Blaming and Past Actions to Problem-Solving and the Future

When there have been problems in a relationship, they can infect the negotiations and turn the at-the-table interactions into a blame game. "You guys just can't perform. You set deadlines and don't meet them. You've introduced new features that don't work they way you said they would." And so on.

There's usually little advantage in arguing about who is to blame for what hasn't worked in the past, especially where the complaints have some validity. Your goal should be to learn from the past and push the focus to the future, by asking, "Let me get this straight. Which new features were you planning to use? How were you planning to use them? We need to make sure that the development group really understands what you are trying to accomplish." Instead of arguing about who's right and who's wrong, aggressively reframe to focus on to a joint quest to make the product do what they want. "I don't think the features you are using were meant to do what you intend, but I'm pretty confident that with a few modifications, we can enable the system to deliver what you want."

When there is a strong emotional content to your counterpart's presentation, you may need to acknowledge that emotion in a productive way, and then move toward problem solving—a subject that we'll return to below.

Move from High-Level Assertions to Fact-Based Statements

Negotiations can founder when they focus on high-level generalizations and assertions.[7] This is especially true when the discussion degenerates into a "did not"/"did so" interchange. For example, in a negotiation to renew a large outsourcing contract, a customer was convinced—and repeatedly asserted—that an outsourcer was overcharging them by significant amounts relative to their competitors in a highly competitive industry. The outsourcer protested strongly. The negative generalization cast a shadow over all of the substantive negotiations on the renewal of the contract: "How can we trust them on this issue if they've been screwing us for the last few years?"

We played a mediating role in this negotiation. To move from generalizations and assertions to facts, the parties agreed to our suggestion that we look on a confidential basis at how much the customer would have paid, given its usage, if it had been subject to the contracts of each of the comparable competitors also served by the outsourcer. Our analysis showed the customer actually enjoyed *better* contracts than all but one company. The outsourcer readily agreed to retroactively adjust the customer's contract so that it received the benefits of the one superior contract. The customer felt less aggrieved and greatly appreciated the outsourcer's gesture. By moving from assertions and counterassertions at high levels of generality to a more specific fact-based discussion, the two parties got their renewal negotiations back on track; in fact, signed a several-hundred-million-dollar contract several months later.

Move from Price Haggling to Joint Problem-Solving

Among the pitfalls of standard tactical negotiation is a relentless tug toward the kind of pure price negotiation that we dissected in the last chapter. To maintain a productive climate, you may need to relentlessly reframe the negotiations away from that pure price focus, in favor of a fuller package of interests. For example: "I understand that you want to reduce costs of operation, and that the prices we charge you are important. We will respond to you on pricing. As we've discussed, price is only one part of what gives you a competitive advantage relative to your competitors, and we believe that we should focus not on price alone but on how we can help you maintain and strengthen your overall competitive position." If you've done a good job of understanding the other side's interests and situation—both from a business standpoint and from the personal standpoint of the individuals with whom you are negotiating—you can probably steer the conversation toward proposals that solve broader problems for your counterpart, rather than just reducing prices.

What if you can't? Then it's time to look for a way to appeal to the other side's stated interests, while still meeting your own. One of our clients—an engineering-oriented company, whose products include all the bells and whistles that its engineers could pack in—was losing ground to several Chinese firms that had begun offering a stripped-down version of the product for a fraction of our client's price. In negotiations with its customers, our client tried to explain that, as the customer grew, it would need to buy many more of the Chinese products. Because of the extra features, the customer would have to buy far fewer of our client's products to get the same functionality. This would mean lower total overall costs. The Procurement VP, who was clearly rewarded on minimizing total current outlay and not on lowering total lifetime outlay, continually demanded that our client match that low Chinese price and didn't want to budge from that position. In response, we advised our client to deactivate all the advanced features in their product, and sell it as a "stripped-down model" at very low margin that would be cost-competitive with the Chinese models. When the customer grew and needed to expand its network, it would then have to purchase those advanced features—and would have to negotiate to get access to them at more attractive margins. But, at that point, purchasing these additional features even at high margins would be better than its no-deal option of purchasing another slew of the Chinese products.

In other words, our client turned the Procurement VP's price-focused tactics *against* him by meeting his customer's interests of minimizing current cash outlays—while securing a higher-margin growth path for the long term. Our client followed this strategy with a number of customers, simultaneously increasing margins while becoming the market share leader in its product category.

Adopt a Persuasive Style

To work with your counterpart to create value—and at the same time to claim sufficient value for yourself—you should adopt a persuasive style. A persuasive negotiator:

- Understands the other side's story

- Is open to persuasion

- Is both empathetic and assertive

- Uses reciprocity to build trust

- Matches appeals to the other side's circumstances

- Recognizes how people process information

Let's look briefly at each of these points.

UNDERSTAND THEIR STORY. Different people interpret the same information or event differently. What set of facts, assumptions, and world view causes the other side to interpret things the way that they do? What are you missing?

BE OPEN TO PERSUASION. If you are not (or do not appear to be) open to persuasion, your counterparts very likely will sense that and adopt a similar stance. *Being open to persuasion is persuasive.*[8]

BE BOTH EMPATHETIC AND ASSERTIVE. Robert Mnookin has identified two key dimensions of negotiation behavior: empathy and assertiveness.[9] You are empathetic when you try to understand the interests and desires and motivations of the other side. You are assertive when you make your interests and demands clearly known to the other side. Many people feel that they must choose between being assertive and being empathetic—being "hard" or being "soft." But that's a false choice. Showing empathy about your counterpart's interests, perceptions, and constraints may make him or her more open to providing you with useful information. The more empathetically you understand your counterpart, the more effectively you can design value-creating deals and the better positioned you are to claim a full share of that value.

FRAME PROPOSALS IN TERMS OF WHAT THEY CARE ABOUT. You are always more persuasive when you frame your proposals in terms of the values, beliefs, goals, and incentives of the recipient—and you deliver them in language used by the recipient.[10] An associate of Rupert Murdoch remarked that, as a buyer, Murdoch "understands the seller—and, whatever the guy's trying to do, he crafts his offer that way."[11]

For example, Paul Levy, CEO of Beth Israel Deaconess Medical Center in Boston, wanted his institution to be named the Official Hospital of Boston's immensely popular baseball team, the Red Sox. Before Levy had even heard about the opportunity, several other distinguished local hospitals had already made proposals to the Red Sox for this designation. Levy listened carefully to the new Red Sox management as it expressed a strong interest in being a good steward of a great franchise and actively participating in the life of the community. Accepting the baseline proposal for financial contributions by hospitals, Levy's team developed a detailed plan and presentation. Not only did this plan involve a financial relationship, but it also explained Beth Israel's own mission of community service and Levy's own role as a steward for an institution with a distinguished history. Against this backdrop, the presentation outlined several concrete steps through which Beth Israel and the Red Sox could jointly perform meaningful, visible service to their communities. Levy's suggestions included (1) a September 11th blood drive at Fenway Park (the team's stadium); (2) an Organ Donor Awareness Night at the stadium introduced by two players whose friend's wife survived as a result of a liver transplant; and

(3) funding and managing a Red Sox Scholars Program, which annually established college scholarships for twenty-five academically talented but financially challenged middle school students who would be mentored by Beth Israel doctors, and who would shadow key people in the club offices and at the hospital on "career days." The Red Sox were persuaded by this approach, adopting these and other initiatives within eighteen months.[12]

SEEK AGREEMENTS THAT FEEL FAIR TO BOTH SIDES. At the end of the day, as noted earlier, most of us want to believe that the agreement we reached was both fair and reached by a fair process. So your preparations for negotiations should include: (1) developing compelling, fact-based arguments supporting your position; (2) identifying fairness rationales likely to be advanced your counterpart; and (3) formulating counterarguments disputing the fairness of the counterpart's rationales. If the people on your side find it difficult to put themselves in your counterpart's shoes, consider bringing in someone who is not directly involved in the negotiation to try to think like the other side.[13] Being seen as genuinely caring about fairness as well as making proposals that seem fair can both enhance your persuasiveness.

PERSUADE WITH STORIES, AS WELL AS ANALYSIS. Many businesspeople try to hammer away at those they're trying to persuade with compelling facts, logic, and analysis. But this may not be the most effective way to get people to act. In fact, psychologists have monitored subjects' brain activity during various kinds of persuasive appeals and have noted that many people's brains tend to "go dark" (i.e., show little brain activity) when presented with fact/logic-based appeals. In contrast, when people hear vivid stories or analogies, their brains light up, or become more active, and they tend to have much higher retention of the implications of what they've heard.[14] In the last chapter, after our discussion of whether to make the first offer, were you more likely to recall (1) the general arguments pro and con, or (2) what happened when Thomas Edison's fumbling efforts to ask General Lefferts to pay an "aggressive" $5,000 for the rights to Edison's novel stock ticker were preempted by the General's first offer of $40,000—a $35,000 reward to Edison for keeping his mouth shut! (We do hope, though, that our anchoring stories cause you to consider going first in other settings.)

INOCULATE AGAINST POTENTIALLY DISADVANTAGEOUS ARGUMENTS. If you can anticipate the counterarguments to your proposal that are likely to occur to your counterparts, you should acknowledge and deal with these counterarguments as part of your own approach.[15] If you fail to raise the obvious counterarguments, they may reverberate inside the heads of the other side and weaken the persuasiveness of your overall appeal.

From a psychological standpoint, it doesn't much matter whether you address the counterarguments at the end or intersperse them throughout in your appeal.[16] However, there are tactical considerations. For example, if you are presenting your argument in a context where you are likely to be interrupted and unable to complete the full argument, start with a clear presentation of your own complete argument before dealing with the counter-arguments.

BUILD BOTH SUBSTANTIVE AND RELATIONSHIP CREDIBIL-
ITY. Building credibility along two dimensions—your knowledge and your relationships—can enhance your persuasiveness.[17] You will be more persuasive on subjects in which you are perceived to have expertise. Thus, either be or bring a subject-matter expert. On the *relationship* level, establishing and continually strengthening your relationships with the other side will also go a long way toward making you more persuasive. If you don't have a strong relationship with your counterparts, look to bring in people who already have one. For example, a new key account manager might want to enlist the aid of her predecessor, if that predecessor had a good relationship with the executive on the other side. Where possible, *plan ahead*. Build relationships with the people on the other side *before* the negotiations get started.

MATCH YOUR APPEAL TO WHERE THE OTHER SIDE IS. Our colleagues Doug Stone, Bruce Patton, and Sheila Heen argue that conversations take place on multiple levels: the rational, the emotional, and the "identity" level.[18] The rational conversation is all about facts: What happened, and what should happen? Who said what, and who did what?[19] Many negotiators try to operate only on the rational level and are uncomfortable about acknowledging feelings in the context of a professional negotiation. But the fact is, many meaningful negotiations raise *feelings,* and some raise strong feelings. Rather than denying that fact, acknowledge it, and tailor your approach to take account of emotional issues. And pay attention as well to identity issues—the most fundamental issues of self-image and who we are: good/bad, competent/incompetent, and so on.

RESPOND TO THE EMOTION WHEN YOUR COUNTERPART
DISPLAYS EMOTION. A counterpart who is angry, tense, or hurt is unlikely to react constructively to or even be able to hear a rational appeal.

While you normally want to *move* to the rational level in the negotiation, you often have a *choice* about whether to respond to the substance or respond to the emotion. It is usually better to respond first to the emotion and its underlying basis: "It sounds like you are pretty unhappy. I imagine I would be unhappy too if I understood the situation as you did." But being empathetic does not mean that you have to accept responsibility for the other person's feelings or allow these feelings to serve as a basis for action. Remember: be both empathetic *and* assertive. Once your counterpart's feelings are better understood and acknowledged, he or she may be able to engage more effectively in substantive discussion.

Let's raise one important caveat here. There are negotiators who use anger and intimidation as bargaining tactics. We know a successful investment banker who, at critical moments on conference calls, sometimes reaches into his pocket for his "angry man pills." It often works; the recipients try to buy their way back into his good graces with concessions. In such cases, the attacker may pull back as soon as he is convinced that these tactics won't work. In some cases, blustering back may be exactly what is needed; in others, ignoring the outburst can be most effective.[20] A great deal depends on the specific person. Learning about their history and style is vital to avoid a "blind" response.

Sometimes, however, you need to step back and negotiate explicitly about the process of negotiation: "We have to tell you that we are offended by what felt to us like accusations and insults. We don't think discourse of this kind is going to help us resolve the problems we jointly need to resolve. We are not interested in continuing this kind of discussion. Would you prefer to take a break for half an hour so that we can refocus, or would you prefer to reschedule at a later date?"

DEAL WITH YOUR FEELINGS, TOO. You have feelings, too, and these are likely to be engaged by a difficult negotiations. You will be more effective if your feelings don't seep out in the form of barbed comments, sarcastic questions, or the inability to listen. You need to find an effective way to express your feelings without asking the other side to take responsibility for your feelings.

One way to do this is to make "I" statements rather than "you" statements. Rather than saying, "You are untrustworthy," try, "When you make me a verbal offer and then follow up with a letter of intent that doesn't seem to match it, it becomes hard for me to trust you."

It's also important to disentangle the *impact* of your counterparts' actions from their *intent*. The fact that their actions had a negative impact on you does not mean that the impact was intended.[21] After you have delved into their intent, it can make sense to explain how you experienced the impact of these actions.

MAKE YOUR APPEAL WORK THROUGH THEIR CULTURAL FILTERS. Culture matters in negotiation.[22] You and your counterparts may have very different cultural perspectives on the purpose of the negotiation, on communication, and on appropriate and constructive behavior. Is a long silence awkward, a sign of respectful consideration, or a tactic to get the other side to blurt out something of use? When your negotiation crosses national borders—or straddles other kinds of divides—a conscious focus on culture can be helpful to effectively create and claim value.

Bookstores are full of books focusing on cross-cultural negotiation, mostly with an emphasis on surface behavior and etiquette—to get to "yes," should you "kiss, bow, or shake hands"?[23] Some of this advice is useful. But if you are not sure about how to avoid unintentionally offensive acts or gestures, we suggest any number of handbooks that go deeper than surface behavior or, better, getting local advice.[24] The point is to avoid falling prey to national cultural stereotypes, most of which contain at least a grain of truth, but many of which can be dramatically off base. For example, in its approach to decision making, Sony is less like a traditional, consensus-driven Japanese firm and more like a Western company. Similarly, when negotiating with U.S. counterparts, it matters a great deal whether you are on Wall Street or in Kansas.

And culture is not merely geographically based. For example, we sometimes find greater similarities among engineering-oriented firms from different countries than we do among, say, between marketing- and engineering-oriented companies from the same country.

Culture (whether national, corporate, or professional) is embodied in *expectations* of more than surface behavior. Indeed, while surface behavior is the tip of the iceberg, deeper culturally based issues are like the invisible mass under the surface, far more likely to cause a deadly crash. Table 13-1 highlights a number of such negotiation-related expectations that are strongly influenced by culture. Think of it as a kind of checklist as you move into less familiar territory. If you aren't confident in a given category, seek advice.

If you are negotiating in a culture in which agreements follow from relationships, as is often the case, for example, in South America, you're generally well advised to begin by developing relationships, rather than jumping into the details of the deal. If the other side expects agreement to follow from the

TABLE 13-1

Cultural expectations in negotiation

DEEPER EXPECTATIONS

Negotiation objective	Is the ultimate goal of negotiation more a signed contract or a relationship between the two sides?
Fundamental view of negotiation process	Is negotiation a process through which both sides can gain, or through which one side gains and the other loses?
Social unit	Is it an individualistic or group-oriented culture?
Power/decision making	Does the other side make decisions in an authoritarian fashion, with one key person? Is it a small group process? Is there a formal or informal hierarchy involved? Is consensus required?
Implementation	How likely and expected is literal implementation of the agreement? Or is the deal merely a starting point for further negotiation?

SURFACE AND PROCESS EXPECTATIONS

Team organization and representation	What level, type, and number of team members are expected?
Etiquette	Introductions, business cards, gifts, and socializing before substance of negotiation; expected deference, etc.
Formality level	How formally does a negotiator talk to others, use titles, dress, speak, and interact with other people?
Communication	Do negotiators place emphasis on direct and simple methods of communication, or do they rely on indirect and complex methods? Is persuasion, for example, fact-based and technical in nature, driven by deductive logic, argued from precedent, or a function of the status of the would-be persuader?
Emotional expression	Do negotiators show or hide their feelings; that is, do they exhibit a high or low degree of emotionalism?
Risk and uncertainty tolerance	Do participants have a high or low propensity to take risks and handle uncertainty while negotiating? In deals?
Sensitivity to time	How important is it to minimize the time spent negotiating? Do negotiators exhibit a high or low degree of impatience and urgency? Many or few interruptions? Long or short time horizon?
Building an agreement	Does an agreement begin from general principles and proceed to specific items, or does it begin with agreement on specifics and build "up" to an overall deal?
Form of agreement	Do negotiators prefer detailed contracts or agreement on general principles?

development of general principles—as might be the case in France, for example—don't come into the first meeting with a detailed term sheet. Instead, be prepared to introduce general principles and work out the *conception* of the deal first.

We have found that negotiators tend to overattribute problems in negotiations to cultural differences. A U.K. CEO, for example, persisted in attributing his French counterpart's actions to French "arrogance," although upon further investigation, we found that the French negotiators were following an entirely rational, and almost obvious, strategy. That said, getting the right cultural filters in place—national or otherwise—is an important input to our method. How the other side sees its interests (both in substance and in the process of negotiation) and understands the game you are jointly playing— and what its expectations are of that game—should be key inputs into your tactical choices.

Can You Write Their Victory Speech?

Can you write the thirty-second, three-minute, and ten-minute versions of the your counterparts' "victory speech"—the speech they would give to their peers, bosses, and spouses about why the agreement they made with you is smart, fair, reasonable, and better than the alternatives? The point is not altruism; if you can't convincingly write such a speech, your proposal may not be persuasive and you probably need to learn more about the other party's situation, interests, and no-deal alternatives. Beyond serving as a rough diagnostic, the victory-speech exercise may also help you in framing proposals to the other side that "let them have your way" (for their reasons, not yours).

Finally, keep in mind that the potential to create value does not mean that claiming tactics go away or are somehow irrelevant. Many of the tactics we describe in this chapter are designed to help you create value, claim a full share of that value, and defend yourself against exploitation.

We'll end the chapter by returning to research we discussed on the importance of focusing on the opportunity and not the downside, even to the extent of committing a brief paragraph to paper on your positive aspirations for the deal. Negotiators who emphasize the outcomes and behaviors they want to promote, as opposed to those they want to avoid, tend to do better in the kinds of situations we've been discussing. Focusing on the opportunity— the possibilities of creating value and claiming a full share, on a long-term basis—is likely to cause you to reach and sustain attractive agreements in your negotiations.

- Effective tactics must productively manage the tension between the cooperative moves necessary to create value jointly and the competitive moves to claim it individually. This means eliciting enough information to generate good options while managing your vulnerability.

- Ask, listen, and learn:

  ➤ Listen actively.

  ➤ Ask open-ended questions rather than yes/no questions: "What if? Why? Why not? How would that work for you?"

  ➤ Bring a designated listener.

- Divulge information strategically:

  ➤ Begin with the end: at the beginning, jointly envision the pot of gold at the end of the rainbow, perhaps by writing a press release in advance on the hoped-for outcome that meets everyone's core interests.

  ➤ Use the norm of reciprocity to build trust and share/gain information: start by offering low-risk information and ratchet up.

  ➤ Present multiple equivalent offers.

  ➤ Sequence issues carefully and negotiate in packages.

- Foster an appealing, productive negotiation process by establishing a positive atmosphere:

  ➤ Psychologically place the parties side by side against the problem rather than face-to-face against each other.

  ➤ Focus on advancing interests rather than arguing positions.

  ➤ Focus on the future instead of the past and on problem solving instead of blaming.

  ➤ Focus on disaggregated fact-based communications rather than high-level assertions.

- Adopt a persuasive style.

  ➤ Be open to persuasion.

  ➤ Be both empathetic *and* assertive.

➤ Tell stories as well as using facts and logic.

➤ Inoculate against potentially disadvantageous arguments.

➤ Match your appeal to where your counterparts are and how they process information.

➤ Make your appeal work through their cultural filters.

- For the deal that "lets them have your way," write your counterparts' victory speech, showing their key audiences why accepting your proposal was a wise decision.

Part Five

3-D Strategies
in Practice

"Let Them Have Your Way"

Chapter Fourteen

Map Backward to Craft a 3-D Strategy

W HERE ARE YOU, and where do your negotiations stand? You've mapped all the parties, their interests, and no-deal options. You've assessed the sequence and basic process choices, as well as the deal design and tactics. Your 3-D barriers audit is complete. Now you must craft a 3-D strategy to overcome the barriers you've identified in order to realize the potential for agreement.

By a *3-D strategy*, we mean an aligned combination of moves at the table, on the drawing board, and away from the table. Setup moves will help you put the most favorable situation in place. Deal-design moves will help you design value-creating agreements. Given the right provisional setup and deal design, you'll be able to choose the right problem-solving tactics to create and claim value on a sustainable basis. Chosen well, these moves will reinforce each other's effectiveness, and directly overcome the barriers you've diagnosed. As the negotiation unfolds and you learn more, you'll update your assessments and revise your 3-D approach to be even *more* effective.

While combining your actions into an overall 3-D strategy is as much art as science, this brief chapter will elaborate a key organizing idea—*backward mapping*—to help pull the elements of your approach together.[1] We've seen this concept before in chapter 7, as part of figuring out the most promising sequence. In the chapter 15 we will apply it to the broader challenge of crafting a 3-D strategy. Now we need to to show you how backward mapping fits into our overall approach, and how it works in practice. To do this, and as a good place to start our review and synthesis, we turn to a remarkable negotiation from the pages of the history books—one that reminds us of our path so far, and hints at where we are going.

Back to 1912: The Roosevelt Campaign and Moffett Studios

In 1912, Theodore Roosevelt was nearing the end of a hard-fought presidential election campaign.[2] Critical to his success was a final whistle-stop journey through the American heartland. At each stop, Roosevelt planned to inspire his audiences with his powerful oratorical skills, and give everyone in attendance a small pamphlet, some three million of which had been printed and packed away in boxcars. On the cover of the pamphlet was a stern, "presidential" portrait; inside was the transcript of a stirring speech called "Confession of Faith." With luck, this strategy would clinch the critical votes.

The barnstorming campaign was about to begin when a campaign worker discovered a small line on each photograph that read, "Moffett Studios, Chicago." Since Moffett held the copyright, the unauthorized use of each photo could each cost the campaign one dollar. The potential $3 million cost of distributing all the pamphlets would greatly exceed the campaign's available resources. The campaign workers were near panic. What should they do? What *could* they do?

All the options looked bad. Not using the pamphlets might sink Roosevelt's chances at the polls. But if the campaign used the pamphlets without Moffett's permission and got caught, all kinds of bad things might result: they could be sued for copyright infringement, a scandal might break out very close to the election, and the campaign might be liable for an unaffordable amount.

Quickly, the campaign workers reached a consensus: they would have to negotiate something with Moffett. At the same time, they realized that they had no idea how to approach this negotiation. Research by their Chicago operatives turned up discouraging news. While Moffett had been a photographer for years, with both artistic and commercial aspirations, he had achieved little critical success, and virtually no financial success. He was now approaching retirement, reportedly bitter and cynical, with a single-minded focus on money.

It's not hard to put yourself in the shoes of those campaign workers as they tried to plot their negotiating strategy, or to imagine the queasy feelings in their stomachs. It must have seemed a hopelessly weak position: approaching a photographic studio whose owner had a keen interest in money, facing a pressing time deadline, thinking of three million pamphlets already packed in boxcars with no time to redo them, contemplating a potential $3 million price tag—or possibly worse, in the case of a lawsuit—and having nothing like the resources that they appeared to need.

If we were to translate their predicament into the language we've been developing in the preceding chapters, the campaign workers assessed their no-deal options in negotiations with Moffett as exceedingly weak. As they saw the situation, if Moffett were to say "no" to any affordable price proposal, the campaign would either (1) face an unaffordably large financial exposure if it went ahead and used the photos, or (2) risk losing any shot at the presidency if it did not use the pictures. By contrast, Moffett seemed to enjoy a commanding option in the event of no deal. Given this assessment, the only deals that might induce a "yes" from Moffett would involve impossibly large payments. In brief, the campaign faced a potent barrier: an exceedingly adverse deal/no-deal balance. Again: what on earth could they do, and should they do?

Dispirited, the campaign workers approached George Perkins, noted financier, partner of J. P. Morgan, California railroad builder, and Roosevelt's campaign manager. Perkins lost no time summoning his stenographer to dispatch the following cable to Moffett Studios in Chicago: "We are planning to distribute millions of pamphlets with Roosevelt's picture on the cover. It will be great publicity for the studio whose photograph we use. How much will you pay us to use yours? Respond immediately." Virtually by return telegraph, he received the following reply from Moffett: "We've never done this before, but under the circumstances we'd be pleased to offer you $250." Reportedly, Perkins accepted the offer—without trying to get even more from Moffett.

One might well object to the misleading tactics at the core of Perkins's negotiating strategy. They plainly don't represent a model process for crafting sustainable agreements that enhance working relationships. (We'll return to this question shortly.) Yet the episode memorably underscores several key elements of pulling together a 3-D approach to negotiation.

Six Lessons/Reminders from the Moffett Studios Saga

Let's reconsider the Moffett saga in terms of six lessons that also serve as reminders of the 3-D approach we've developed so far.

First, while the parties to the deal were clear—though not initially including George Perkins as a key "internal" player—the campaign workers missed the full set of Moffett's *interests*. They focused almost exclusively on price and overlooked the photographer's potential interest in widespread publicity. The lesson: *think beyond price to map the full set of interests potentially at stake.*

Second, by focusing on price, the campaign workers limited their thinking about potential deals to a simple Battle Line over the price to be paid. Reflexively, they saw their best no-deal option as awful: risking Roosevelt's presidential election prospects, and/or incurring a huge financial liability. They implicitly judged Moffett's best no-deal option to be robust: a credible lawsuit threat on very strong legal grounds. As such, the campaign workers readily assumed that the zone of possible agreement (ZOPA) in this case—the deals between each side's best no-deal options—ran from the campaign paying nothing all the way up to its paying $3 million, or at least its total resources.

That the ZOPA could also include *Moffett's* paying something to the campaign—a logical possibility that in reality became the actual result—did not occur to them. (When we tell this story, it rarely occurs to our listeners either.) Yet there is absolutely nothing in the situation, *save the limits of our own frequently unwarranted assumptions,* that prevents the ZOPA from including a scenario in which Moffett pays an amount of money to the campaign. (And, by the way, had the campaign acted on the basis of such an incorrect assumption—for example, had the workers started the negotiation by offering to pay Moffett something—they could have created the very outcomes that they assumed to be inevitable. Bad assumptions can be self-fulfilling.)

But back to the ZOPA assessment: the value to Moffett of this wide public exposure and potential association with a president probably exceeded $250 by a substantial amount. Arguably, Moffett got a very good deal, relative to the outcome in which the photograph went unused. When we rely on unexamined assumptions, we have a powerful tendency to see the ZOPA far too narrowly. The lesson: *in assessing the deal/no-deal balance, beware of unspoken and unwarranted assumptions.* (This caution extends as well to unexamined assumptions about parties, interests, sequence, and process choices!) Check and recheck your assumptions about the deal/no-deal balance, especially with trusted friends or advisers who are not too close to the situation.

Third, we are intrigued at the reasons *why* the campaign workers found this negotiation to be so difficult. Clearly there were delicate tactical aspects, yet their inability to see what Perkins immediately perceived has to do with the fact that they were focused virtually entirely on negative aspects of *their own side's deal/no-deal balance.* Yes, the campaign workers had already made a serious mistake by printing so many unauthorized copies. More missteps in the negotiation could lead to disastrous political and financial consequences. This risk loomed very large in their thinking. Yet they should have paused for a moment to ask how Moffett saw the deal/no-deal balance from *his* perspective, given what he actually knew (which was *nothing,* at that point!). Had they done so, they could immediately have realized that Moffett didn't even know he had an unusual opportunity with strong potential leverage.

Perkins's entire approach was calculated to shape Moffett's perceptions of the deal/no-deal balance (and hence the ZOPA). Because of their understandable—and completely common—obsession with their *own* situation, the campaign workers entirely missed the existence of an obvious solution, at least in purely economic, short-run terms. The lesson: *don't become a prisoner of your own problem and perceptions.* Just as we have earlier counseled you to assess your counterparts' interests as *they* see them, discipline yourself to assess the deal/no-deal balance from their perspective as carefully as you do from your own viewpoint. To let them have your way, you need to start with a clear understanding of how *they* now see the situation. Then you can shape their deal/no-deal choice so that what they choose—in their interest, as they see it—solves your problem.

Fourth, having diagnosed a seemingly adverse deal/no-deal balance as the major barrier to a good agreement, Perkins could have taken actions to set up the negotiation in very different ways.

- **Setup option #1 (hypothetical).** "Let's just meet and work this thing out." Someone whose view of negotiation was mainly about tactics "at the table" might simply have arranged a face-to-face, open-ended meeting between an interpersonally skilled campaign staff member and Moffett. After the usual pleasantries, the campaign representative might have tried to get the two sides to brainstorm a solution to the "joint problem" of three million already-printed pamphlets, the campaign's desperate need to use them, high copyright fees, and Moffett's intense interest in money. (Our assessment: "Good luck with this set up! The campaign will really need it!")

- **Setup option #2 (actual).** "Let's *not* 'just meet.'" Perkins's approach to Moffett was by telegram, with a tight deadline, no opportunity to meet and probe, and the implication that the campaign had a good no-deal option. Deal-design reasoning suggested crafting an agreement driven by the lure and value of publicity to Moffett, rather than drawing attention to potential legal action or holding presidential aspirations hostage. (Our assessment: "Good luck will still be needed. But at least there is a decent shot.")

Ironically, Perkins's advantageous framing of Moffett's choice—coupled with a tight deadline—exploited Moffett's tendency toward the same cognitive myopia displayed by the campaign workers. (In fairness, we can imagine less risky possibilities associated with a "just meet" setup than asking how much Moffett would pay the campaign. For example, a campaign representative might have innocently inquired: "Relative to other small studios, how much do you normally charge to reprint a candidate's photo?") The broader point is simple: with the barriers to the deal that you want clearly in the front of your mind, think creatively about how an overall 3-D strategy might surmount them. The lesson: *Don't limit your thinking to tactics "at the table"; be sure to weigh of a range of setup possibilities "away from the table" aligned with attractive deal designs "on the drawing board."*

Fifth, within his chosen setup, Perkins very carefully shaped perceptions of the deal/no-deal balance. If no agreement could be reached with Moffett, the campaign would be in a terrible bind—yet Perkins worded the cable carefully to *imply* no problems if there were no deal. The clear inference to be made was that the campaign would merely use another photo. Further, Perkins's deliberate omissions and approach masked *Moffett's* likely no-deal option and seemed to permit little time for Moffett to investigate them. The studio was left with the impression that, without a deal, life would continue as usual—not the fact that if the campaign went ahead and used the already printed photos, Moffett could certainly win a huge settlement in court. Moffett's mere awareness of either party's alternative to agreement could have dramatically improved his position in dealing with the campaign.

More broadly, Perkins could have sought to frame how Moffett saw his deal versus no-deal choice in two very distinct ways. He might have framed Moffett's choice in the form that terrified the campaign workers: how much could a greedy Moffett squeeze the desperate Roosevelt camp, threatened with losing the election? Instead, Perkins framed Moffett's choice altogether differently: "How much would you be willing to pay for something (publicity) of great potential value to your studio? And you must act fast on this rapidly fading opportunity." By taking the second route, Perkins sought to shape *Moffett's* perception of the deal/no-deal balance such that the solution Moffett chose was in the campaign's interest. Perkins implicitly defined a "target" deal/no-deal balance that would induce Moffett to opt for Perkins's preferred choice. *The lesson: Framing both elements of the deal/no-deal balance advantageously can be a key element of "the art of letting them have your way."*

Finally, let's go back to a broader view of "interests." In our view, this story should leave us with a feeling of ethical discomfort about deceptive or manipulative tactics. Perkins's deal depended on Moffett's unawareness of a highly material fact. Perkins's tactics intimated—though they did not explicitly assert—that the campaign had a good no-deal option.

The actual and perceived ethics of your actions can matter both as *intrinsic* interests, in and of themselves, and also *instrumentally*, since unethical behavior tends to be counterproductive over time. But before one sides too strongly with Moffett, hornswoggled by a sophisticated tycoon, remember that it was a simple oversight that the campaign did not seek Moffett's original permission to use the photos. Had Moffett sought to extract an excessive price earlier on, the campaign simply would have found another photograph. Did the oversight "entitle" Moffett to a windfall? If not, did that justify Perkins's tactics? The lesson: *Ethical considerations should be a consistent part of your interests, and that interest should be reflected in all three dimensions of your negotiations.* Remember, though, that reaching ethical judgments is often a complex process.

"Begin with the End": Backward Mapping to Develop a 3-D Strategy

While the Roosevelt episode reminds us of many key lessons we have discussed earlier, what was the source of its crucial tactical insight? In our view, that moment occurred when George Perkins put himself in Moffett's shoes—attempting to understand how Moffett would see his studio's deal/no-deal choice—to visualize different possible approaches by the campaign. Having pinpointed the key barrier to success—that the wrong approach by the campaign would highlight Moffett's superior no-deal option and the campaign's extreme vulnerability—Perkins could think through how he wanted Moffett's choice to look in order to induce the "yes" that the campaign sought. Instinctively mapping backward from this "target choice" to the present, Perkins could craft an approach that would shape Moffett's perceptions accordingly. Doing so faced Moffett with a perceived deal/no-deal balance that "let him have the Perkins's way": Moffett offered to pay $250 rather than forgo what he saw as an opportunity for valuable publicity.

To do this effectively in your own negotiations, you must have (1) a clear sense of your target deal, and (2) a clear understanding how the other side sees the deal/no-deal balance. According to our colleague Bill Ury, "If you want to change someone's mind, you should first learn where that person's mind is." Then, together, you can try to build what he calls a "golden bridge," working backward to span the gulf between where your counterpart's mind is now and your desired end point.[3]

Suppose that you've sized up the negotiation and you now have a target deal in mind. With respect to that agreement, *you* clearly favor a "yes." Yet why will *they* go along? Your assessment of how *they* would ideally see the *deal/ no-deal* balance, given the deal you have in mind, should guide your strategy. While much more than this balance affects the outcome of a negotiation, it is a useful backbone around which to organize the elements of a strategy.

At a minimum, the proposed agreement should look more attractive to the other side than its best no-deal option. If not, your negotiating approach should reshape your counterparts' currently perceived deal/no-deal balance. You want to transform their current choice into the target balance that will lead them to choose the deal you prefer. This transformation can be a matter of changing the actual situation, their perceptions, or both. These are the necessary ingredients for implementing Daniele Vare's (modified) advice that negotiation is the art of letting them have your way (in 3-D).

The idea of mapping backward is simple: in order to figure out what to do *next*, start by figuring out what you ideally want to have happen *last* (that they say "yes" to your preferred deal). Then work back from this endpoint—across the barriers to the agreement you want—to where you are now.

Take a look at figure 14-1. Begin with the endpoint: your target deal (on the right side of the figure). "Map backward" from this deal to the target deal/no-deal balance (the middle "column") that the other side would have to face to find your target deal attractive relative to its best no-deal option, and, therefore, to say "yes." Determine what it would take to transform its *currently perceived* deal/no-deal balance (on the left side of the figure) into this desired choice. Now cycle among moves in each of our three dimensions until you can

FIGURE 14-1

Map backward from your target deal (right to left)

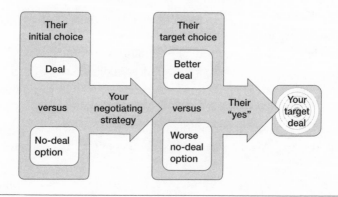

see your way clear, over the barriers, and to an overall 3-D Negotiation strategy that accomplishes this transformation.

Building from their interests to your interests in this manner is much more effective than trying to shove them from their position to yours. An eighteenth-century pope once assessed the remarkable diplomatic skills of Cardinal de Polignac as follows: "This young man always seems to be of my opinion and at the end of the conversation I find that I am of his."[4] How this works in practice, in a full 3-D context, is the subject of our final chapter.

- An effective 3-D strategy is an aligned and mutually reinforcing combination of setup, deal-design, and tactical moves chosen to overcome barriers to agreement.

- To help organize the elements of your strategy, map backward from your target deal to the deal/no-deal balance that will most likely induce them to make this choice, and then make your way back to the current situation. This enables you to determine the actions you must now take to face them with the right deal/no-deal balance.

Chapter Fifteen

Think Strategically,
Act Opportunistically

A s a 3-D Negotiator, you have a clear, guiding objective: to *create and claim value for the long term*. Accomplishing this requires you to do a *3-D barriers audit* to determine what stands between you and the deal you want. Doing that audit takes several steps:

- Assess setup barriers:
  - Map all the parties, full set of their interests, and their best no-deal options.
  - Check the sequence and basic process choices.
- Assess deal-design barriers.
- Assess tactical and interpersonal barriers.

To overcome these barriers, you map backward from the deal you want in order to *craft a 3-D strategy*. This means an aligned combination of moves away from the table, on the drawing board, and at the table in which you:

- Set up the right negotiation
- Design value-creating deals
- Stress problem-solving tactics

Over the course of this book we have explored these moves in detail. Throughout, we emphasized that a barrier encountered in one dimension can often push you into other dimensions for a solution. In this concluding chapter, we will give you a more granular sense of 3-D Negotiation in practice, presenting three examples in which the protagonists overcame daunting barriers by changing the game to their advantage through their moves in multiple dimensions. In each instance, we'll highlight aspects of the 3-D strategy that can enhance *your* effectiveness in the negotiations that *you* face.

AOL, Microsoft, and Netscape: Negotiating the Browser Wars

Sometimes, you are simply outclassed on the central competitive aspects of a deal. For example, the customers of America Online (AOL) in 1996 were clamoring for an Internet browser. Despite its huge commercial success, AOL was developing an image as the "Internet for dummies." Top management was concerned that this perception would spread, damage its franchise, and blunt future growth prospects. In short, AOL had a pressing need for a cutting-edge browser to improve its image and to allow its customers easy access to the Web that lay beyond AOL's proprietary confines. In a brutally competitive process, Netscape and Microsoft negotiated with AOL over which browser it would adopt.[1] Netscape's technically superior Navigator, with a 75 to 85 percent market share, contended with Microsoft's much buggier Explorer, then stuck at 3 to 4 percent and struggling for a market foothold, but a critical strategic priority for Bill Gates.

A confident, even arrogant, Netscape held out for a high per-copy fee from AOL, in effect defining a technically based "browser-for-dollars" deal. From the perspective of Steve Case, AOL's CEO, "They [Netscape] were very aggressive about selling the browser, but they wanted a very high per-copy fee. The attitude was, 'We're so hot, we'll license to everyone, so you better take it.'"[2] And Netscape was playing a very strong hand vis-à-vis both its direct negotiating counterpart (AOL) and competitor (Microsoft). As AOL's senior vice president Jean Villanueva later observed, "The deal was Netscape's to lose. They were dominant. We needed to get what the market wanted. Most importantly, we saw ourselves as smaller companies fighting the same foe—Microsoft."[3]

So how did Microsoft prevail in this negotiation and, ultimately, win the browser wars? What kind of choice would lead AOL chief Steve Case to opt for Microsoft? In part, the answer can be found in the deal terms. When the deal was done, Microsoft's Explorer would be provided to AOL for free, in contrast with the fee-based Navigator arrangement, with Microsoft also promising AOL a series of technical adaptations in a multiyear context.

Most remarkably to outside observers, Microsoft agreed that AOL client software would be bundled with the new Windows operating system. Even as a direct competitor to AOL, Microsoft would position the AOL icon on the Windows desktop right next to the icon for the Microsoft Network (MSN)—the online service created in direct response to AOL's success. This positioning on "the most valuable desktop real estate in the world" would permit AOL to reach an additional 50 million people per year at effectively zero cost, compared to the $40 to $80 per-customer acquisition cost it currently incurred by "carpet bombing" the country with AOL disks. The value to AOL of having its icon on the Windows desktop was immense for marketing, distribution, and competitive reasons, in effect, blunting the threat posed by MSN. In effect, Bill Gates sacrificed the medium-term position of MSN to his larger goal of winning the browser wars.

Microsoft's technically inferior browser meant that its prospects of winning on that battleground were poor regardless of its negotiating skills and tactics at the table. Yet while Netscape was confidently playing a waiting game to bring AOL around, Microsoft undertook a 3-D effort to favorably shift the negotiating ground from Netscape's technical "browser-for-dollars" deal toward wider business issues that keenly interested AOL and on which Microsoft held a decisive edge. Moreover, rather than focus on the technologists, Microsoft concentrated on AOL's more business-oriented executives. As AOL's lead negotiator and business development head David Colburn stated, "The willingness of Microsoft to bundle AOL . . . with the Windows operating system was a critically important competitive factor that was impossible for Netscape to match."[4] Rather than trying to play a poor tech hand well, Microsoft changed the negotiating setup to a business arena in which it had the edge.

This episode has important game-changing lessons: Are you in a weak position on issues A and B? Can you change the setup to emphasize issues D and E, on which you are strong? Moreover, are you dealing with person X, whose interests do not match your strengths? In tandem with your revised issues focus, can you shift the emphasis to person Y, who will be more receptive?

Microsoft did not simply prevail by changing the issue setup. Perhaps unexpectedly, given the heavy-handed reputation Microsoft has in many quarters, Netscape's arrogant actions at the table put it at a major disadvantage. As Alex Edelstein, Netscape senior product manager, put it, "We were too arrogant . . . Netscape thought its stuff was so good, it was enough to just put it out there." On the receiving end, AOL CEO Steve Case observed, "[Netscape had] no desire to treat us as a partner; they only wanted to treat us like a customer." In contrast, Microsoft deployed its massive resources toward meeting a much richer set of AOL's interests than Netscape even appeared to acknowledge with its stubborn "browsers-for-dollars" hardball price proposal. This reminds us that tactics—in tandem with the setup and deal design—can carry, or lose, the day.[5]

Realistically, though, how could Netscape (David) have had a prayer against (Microsoft) Goliath? Wasn't Microsoft's victory inevitable, given its vast resources and powerful strategic interest in winning the browser wars? In our view, Netscape could indeed have carried the day. In January 1996, three months before the finale, AOL chief Steve Case flew out to California to have dinner at Jim Barksdale's home while discussing potential AOL links to Netscape. Case proposed that Netscape produce a special Navigator version for AOL that would serve as the principal browser for AOL's 5 million subscribers. He also proposed that AOL run Netscape's extremely popular but woefully underexploited Web site, which was receiving millions of hits daily. AOL certainly had the capacity to leverage the commercial potential of such massive traffic (it may also have wanted to control a potential competitor to its own site). Finally, Case suggested that Netscape and AOL actively cross-promote each other and that Netscape include an AOL seat on its board in order to cement the partnership. All Netscape had to do to shut out Microsoft was be more flexible on its price demands and "say yes!" to Case (while asking for a bulletproof exclusive).

Barksdale discussed this proposal with managers and engineers at Netscape. They opposed the move, citing the effort that would be required to create an AOL-specific Navigator, one that would be "componentized" to fit with AOL's look and feel. Blocked by the failure of his internal negotiations, Barksdale ended up telling Case that the partnership proposal was a nonstarter. He countered by saying that AOL would be a "good distribution channel for Navigator" at a cost to AOL of $10 per downloaded copy.

Incredibly, Netscape failed to do the deal not once, but *twice.* Four months after the Microsoft-AOL agreement, the door to an AOL-Netscape deal re-opened. Ram Shriram, then a vice president of Netscape, recounted what happened next: "AOL came to us again. AOL's stock was tanking and it was getting sued by the attorneys general of various states. They were keen to come back to the table and forge a relationship with us." Barksdale and Shriram met with AOL's Steve Case, but Netscape's engineering team rejected the proposed deal, saying, as Shriram put it, "'Look, we're all busy. We're not really interested. Our focus is not consumers.' We lost out another opportunity to take charge of another 10 to 12 million browsers."[6] Thus Netscape lost another opportunity to make a deal that would keep its control of the browser market.

Given these facts, it's hard to see Microsoft's victory as a foregone conclusion. Had Netscape acted on a clearer analysis of the full set of parties (internal as well as external), their interests (beyond the technical aspects of a browser and price), and no-deal options (for itself, AOL, and Microsoft)—and had it looked for ways to create as well as try to arrogantly claim value with AOL— the outcome of these negotiations could have been far more favorable. But Netscape did not, and its failure to do so gave Microsoft the opening to reset the table, design a value-creating deal behind which to put its massive resources, and ultimately win the browser wars.

Kennecott in Chile: Negotiating Expropriation

What do you do when they want a divorce—but you don't—and they seem to hold all the cards?

A version of this situation faced Utah-based Kennecott Copper during the 1960s. At the time, it was operating the huge El Teniente copper mine in Chile, about a hundred kilometers southeast of the capital city of Santiago. Chile had long been the world's leading copper producer, and—along with Argentina and Peru—controlled 30 percent of the world's known copper reserves. El Teniente commenced operations in the early years of the twentieth century and was developed by the Guggenheim family in the prewar era. In 1917, a year in which copper accounted for 20 percent of Chilean exports, Kennecott bought the property from the Guggenheims.[7] Over the years, El Teniente grew into the largest underground copper mine in the world. With more than 2,000 kilometers of tunnels—about 64 kilometers of new tunnels and galleries are still excavated each year—the mine still produces more than 350,000 tons of copper annually.[8]

Through the early 1960s, Kennecott enjoyed a long-term, low-royalty contract to operate the enormous mine. But the election of Eduardo Frei and the Christian Democrats in 1964 drastically changed Chile's political landscape. Frei's party began pushing for increased Chilean participation in the production, refining, and marketing of copper, as well as for increased output from the mining sector. It targeted both Kennecott and rival Anaconda for renegotiations of all existing contracts. And Chile had what appeared to be a very attractive no-deal alternative if Kennecott refused to bargain: it could change the terms of the deal unilaterally, or even expropriate Kennecott's El Teniente assets outright.

Let's imagine that Kennecott had adopted a negotiating strategy that relied mainly on interpersonal effectiveness at the bargaining table, and other, similar "1-D" tactics. Using that approach, Kennecott's management team would have assessed the personalities of the government officials with whom it would be negotiating, taken steps to become more culturally sensitive, and figured out ways to demonstrate its respect for the Chileans.

In fact, Kennecott *did* take all these tactical steps, and many others as well. But it was clear that such efforts wouldn't do enough to improve Kennecott's bargaining position. The Chilean officials seemed to hold all the cards. They had their own experienced managers, engineers, and miners, so they didn't need Kennecott's expertise. Kennecott obviously couldn't move the mine. Nor did it have a lock on downstream processing or on the marketing of copper. And the days of gunboat diplomacy seemed long past; there was no chance that U.S. troops would arrive to defend Kennecott's property. A 3-D barriers audit would have suggested a deal/no-deal balance that was highly adverse to Kennecott. Indeed, the entire setup appeared bleak from a company perspective.

It was a tough situation, to put it mildly. What should Kennecott do? To answer this question, try to think of a target negotiating setup that would induce the Chileans to say yes to a proposal that Kennecott would prefer to its best no-deal option under that new setup? Then, map backward from that ideal to the present situation. And remember, mapping all the parties—actual and potential—and the full set of their interests often requires a disciplined act of imagination rather than a mechanical list.

In retrospect, it's clear that Kennecott conceived and implemented what we have called a 3-D Negotiation strategy. To overcome these formidable barriers, it took steps to *set up* the impending talks in a way that was most favorable to the company's position. It focused on *deal design* that would create more value for the Chileans—but also capture value for itself. And, as noted, it focused on the kinds of *tactics* that would help close the deal.

Let's look at the six steps that Kennecott's team took to transform the negotiations. First, in a bold move that took the government by surprise, Kennecott offered to sell a majority equity interest in the mine to the Chilean government. Second, in an effort to make the deal still sweeter to Chile, the company proposed to use the proceeds from its sale of equity to Chile—along with additional resources from an Export-Import Bank loan—to finance a large expansion of the mine. Clearly, this particular move tracked with the government's expressed desire to increase output across the mining sector.

Third, it persuaded the Chilean government to guarantee the Export-Import Bank loan, and make the guarantee subject to the laws of the State of New York. Fourth, Kennecott insured as many of its assets as possible under the terms of a U.S. government guarantee against expropriation. Fifth, it arranged for the expanded mine's output to be sold under long-term contracts with North American and European customers. Finally, the collection rights under these contracts were sold to a consortium of European, U.S., and Japanese financial institutions.

The deal was completed in 1968, with Chile buying 51 percent of Kennecott's assets for $81.6 million, and implementing all of the other provisions outlined above.

What happened here? Why was Kennecott's effort successful?

First let's look at the revised *setup*, the third of our 3-D dimensions. By involving a wide array of customers, governments, and creditors, Kennecott broadened the base of institutions that had a vested interest in the course of events in Chile. It's fair to assume that many of those newly recruited constituents had deep concerns—rightly or wrongly—about Chile's ability to run the mine efficiently over time, and had a stake in Kennecott's continued involvement at El Teniente. So instead of facing a simple negotiation with Kennecott on the other side of the table, Chile now faced a multiparty negotiation with players who would have future dealings with the country—not only in the mining sector, but also in the financial, industrial, legal, and public sectors. Chile's original no-deal alternative was to simply throw Kennecott out or brutally renegotiate; now, while Chile still had precisely the same alternatives, thanks to Kennecott's careful setup moves, those alternatives had become a lot less attractive. Hurting Kennecott would put a much wider set of Chile's present and future interests at risk. And finally, the guarantees, insurance, and other contracts vastly improved Kennecott's walk-away option. If agreement were *not* reached, and if Chile expropriated the operation, Kennecott would have a host of powerful allies on its side.

Now let's look at *deal design*, the second of our 3-D dimensions. At the outset, the negotiation looked as if it would be a simply a fight, and probably a tough one, over royalties—a fight that Kennecott could only lose. (Even without a formal expropriation, Chile could unilaterally raise the royalty rates high enough to effectively seize the mining assets.) By proposing a larger mine with Chile as the majority owner, Kennecott was creating value for the host country in two ways: a bigger pie, and a bigger piece of that pie. The proposed change in ownership structure also addressed the mounting political pressure on Chile's leaders to assert control over a valuable national resource. By adding new issues to what had been a value-claiming tug-of-war over royalties, Kennecott *reset the table* in ways that opened the door to a new kind of partnership, offering more *economic* value on more *politically* attractive terms.

We should point out that Kennecott's victory was a temporary one, since Chile ultimately nationalized the mine in the 1970s. But the 3-D strategy that the company brought to a successful conclusion in 1968 gave Kennecott additional years of highly valuable cash flow, and protected its operating position in that time period. But far more interesting and important, for our purposes, was the unlikely turnaround of a truly difficult bargaining situation. As we see it, the Kennecott/Chile example underscores the key message of this book: *a comprehensive 3-D strategy, combining tactics, deal design, and setup, gives you the greatest prospects of negotiating success.*

In many cases, you can't succeed by just playing the negotiating hand that you are dealt, even if you play that hand with great skill. It's unlikely that tactical brilliance at the table could have saved Kennecott from its adverse bargaining position. No amount of blustering and bluffing—or, at the other end of the tactical spectrum, active listening and cultural sensitivity—could have turned the tide, although an approach that was culturally sensitive and was respectful of the skill and training of Chilean nationals was important. Instead, Kennecott reset the original table, designed a partnership-like deal, and stressed problem-solving tactics in a manner that overcame truly formidable barriers. That 3-D strategy created more value for all involved, and enabled Kennecott to claim much of that value for itself.

Concord Pulp and Paper: An Unfolding 3-D Negotiation

In our third case, we consider the experience of Henry Iverson and his partners, who acquired Concord Pulp and Paper Co. (CPP) for $8.5 million in a highly leveraged transaction.[9] After the basic deal was done, they needed additional financing to make a profitable improvement in CPP's production process. Yet even after a few elegant lunches and a persuasive appeal by one of the partners to Holmes Throckmorton, senior VP of Federal Street Bank, they were flatly turned down. Beyond more interpersonal moves at relationship building with the skeptical Throckmorton, as well as (dubious) efforts to brainstorm, decipher his body language, and plead for a "win-win solution," what could be done to obtain a "yes" on the added loan? Even when mild-mannered and polite, some of the most implacable of hard bargainers can found across the desk from you when you are seeking a loan or other financial backing! When you've tried out your most sober suit, spent hours polishing your business plan and proposal, and yet sense your persuasive appeals are just not working, how can you convert that seemingly final "no" to "yes"?

How the Deal Unfolded

First, some background. To acquire the bankrupt CPP from its creditors, Iverson and his partners had put up $700,000 in equity, and obtained $7.8 million in financing from Federal Street Bank (FSB), consisting of a $1.3 million short-term loan against receivables and a $6.5 million loan against assets. Soon after the transaction, the opportunity arose for CPP to add a "recovery boiler," which would increase plant capacity by one hundred tons per day, improve overall quality and margins, and boost yearly net cash flow by $4.1 million. The boiler would cut by 95 percent CPP's emissions in Concord, its host town, where, although it provided welcome jobs, the plant had "perfumed" the air for years. Over a two-year construction period, the boiler project would cost $9 million, of which $6 million would be paid to Bathurst and Felson Engineering (B&F), a national firm, with the balance going to smaller regional and local contractors.

When Iverson had unsuccessfully approached Throckmorton for financing against future cash flows of project, the loan officer reiterated FSB's policies: "We will loan against 50 percent of unencumbered inventory and 80 percent of receivables. CPP has neither, and its capital structure is already 93 percent leveraged. 93 percent! Forget it!" Then things got a bit nasty as Throckmorton folded his hands and sniffed, "FSB does not do junk loans." Not giving up, Iverson pressed, "What would it take?" FSB eventually answered that, if CPP had more equity as a cushion, FSB might at least consider a short-term construction loan—but only if a credible third party was willing to provide guaranteed takeout financing after two years.

Now we will trace Iverson's 3-D path after he had "mapped backward" from his current predicament to put in place the prior agreements (with as-yet-uninvolved parties) that would maximize the chances that Throckmorton would ultimately change his mind. We trace a schematic of Iverson's 3-D approach in figure 15-1 and invite you to follow that diagram as we describe the twists and turns of Iverson's evolving analysis and successive actions.

3-D MOVE #1: INVOLVE UNIFIED INSURANCE CO. (UIC). Iverson approached two insurance companies for takeout financing: Worldwide Insurance, which had higher fees, was completely uninterested in the deal. UIC, which had the most attractive fee structure, also thought that CPP was too leveraged, and, moreover, would lend only against the cash flow of fully completed, actually successful projects. Nevertheless, Iverson coaxed a conditional

FIGURE 15-1

Mapping backward to yes

Figure Key

B&F: Bathurst & Felsen Construction
FSB: Federal State Bank
UIC: Unified Insurance Co.
EDA: Economic Development Administration
LDA: Local Development Administration
Derano: National project management firm (bondable)

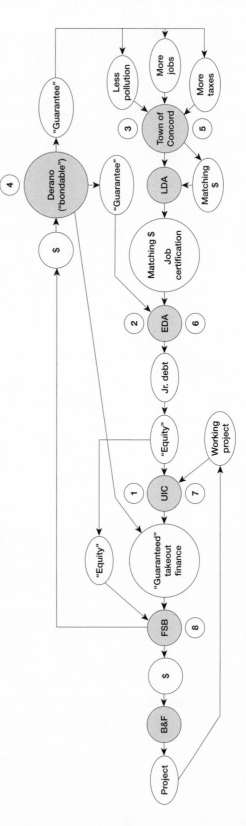

Note: Circled numbers track Iverson's successive 3-D moves; see text for elaboration.

deal from UIC for a commitment fee plus a share of increased profits from the boiler, Unified agreed to lend, but only contingent on the actual, successful completion of the project—and more equity in CPP's capital structure. Note Iversen's tactics: As with FSB, he probed behind the "No" position to learn the conditions under which UIC would provide financing. Pushing even further, he figured out the conditions under which UIC would provide financing if it received an up-front commitment fee and a piece of the project's profits.

3-D MOVE #2: INVOLVE THE EDA. Iverson canvassed his partners and other potential investors for more equity. Each answered with a resounding "no." So he dug further, eventually learning that the U.S. Economic Development Administration (EDA) could make junior (subordinated) loans to firms for certified job-creating projects, with the overall loan limit equal to the number of jobs times $50,000. Since the recovery boiler project would generate at least thirty new full-time jobs, this implied a junior loan of up to $1.5 million. However, the loan had to be 50 percent matched by the Local Development Administration (LDA)—which did not exist in Concord.

INTERIM BARRIERS ASSESSMENT. Iverson took stock of the barriers he so far faced; they amounted to a sea of adverse deal/no-deal balances, all flashing red: B&F wouldn't proceed without money and, in any case, wouldn't guarantee more than the boiler itself—the only thing B&F would itself build—and the rest of the required system would be complex. Local and regional contractors were in no position to guarantee the overall project. The FSB wouldn't approve a construction loan without guaranteed takeout financing and more equity. Unified wouldn't do takeout permanent financing without an actually successful project and more equity. The EDA wouldn't lend without LDA matching funds and a guarantee of a successful, certified, job-creating project. And there was no LDA to certify the jobs or provide matching funds. (Otherwise, no problem.) Even with thus much wider potential scope, each and every potential player—given its best no-deal option—found "no" better than saying "yes" to what Iverson proposed. How could these "reds" turn "green"?

3-D MOVE #3: INVOLVE CONCORD. Undaunted, Iverson approached the Concord Town Council and proposed that it form an LDA, which could raise matching funds, to facilitate the recovery boiler project. He argued that both construction and operation of the project would create new jobs and dramatically cut CPP's odors and pollution levels. And property taxes would increase at least $180,000 per year if the new boiler were built. The council received these arguments favorably but, before committing, wanted assurances that the project would actually work.

3-D MOVE #4: INVOLVE DERANO. In great need of some plausible "guarantee" of project success, Iverson approached Derano, Inc., a large national ("bondable") engineering, design, and project-management firm. Derano expressed serious doubts about managing an already-designed project with B&F and local contractors in place. But, by offering an above-normal fee (15 percent of total cost), Iverson coaxed an agreement from Derano to manage the overall project and to give a nonrecourse "performance guarantee"— all conditional on raising project finance. Here too, Iverson went beyond Derano's initial "no" to understand the conditions under which Derano would provide a pseudo-performance guarantee.

3-D MOVE #5: BACK TO CONCORD WITH DERANO DEAL. Carrying the letter that contained Derano's provisional "guarantee," Iverson revisited Concord's Town Council, which agreed to create an LDA. The LDA would be instructed to issue bonds for $500,000, backed by tax revenue increases and presold to wealthy citizens, local and regional contractors, and other area businesses. Further, as a government entity, LDA would formally certify the expected successful job-creation impact of the recovery boiler project.

3-D MOVE #6: BACK TO EDA WITH DERANO LETTER AND LDA COMMITMENTS. Arm-in-arm with the Concord LDA, which brought matching fund commitments and its formal "job certification" (along with "bondable" Derano's "guarantee") of the boiler project, Iverson next approached the EDA. Now that it had the provisions it had requested, EDA committed to a $1 million junior (subordinated) loan; this loan and the $500,000 matching loan from Concord's LDA, were conditional on Iverson's obtaining construction and long-term financing.

3-D MOVE #7: BACK TO UIC TO MODIFY ITS "MORE EQUITY" PROVISION. Armed with these commitments, Iverson successfully negotiated with UIC to modify the "more equity" term of its commitment letter to include the EDA-LDA junior debt. In simple terms, UIC wanted more cash invested in the form of equity so that if the project were to do poorly, the equity investors would lose their money before UIC's loan would be at risk. But because the EDA-LDA junior loan would be subordinated to UIC's loan, UIC's real interest in a greater financial cushion was still met. This represents a classic case of moving behind incompatible *positions* to ferret out compatible *interests*.

3-D MOVE #8: BACK TO THROCKMORTON WITH DERANO, LDA, AND EDA COMMITMENTS AND UIC MODIFICATION. Returning to FSB's Throckmorton, Iverson argued that junior EDA-LDA loans would provide the functional equivalent of FSB's requirement for more equity; in making the case, he tactfully noted that UIC, a "notoriously demanding creditor," was willing to treat these loans as equity to financially cushion UIC's "permanent" takeout financing. Surely that would be adequate to protect FSB's much briefer (two-year) exposure. With this condition met and given Derano's performance "guarantee" and LDA's "certification," Throckmorton agreed that UIC's commitment letter met FSB's interest in guaranteed takeout financing. FSB's new construction loan commitment then unlocked the EDA-LDA money, which started funds flowing to Derano and B&F. Project launched! (You can trace Iverson's involved negotiating path on figure 15-1 if you are interested.)

How 3-D Moves Shaped the Deal

Several implications from this example serve to reinforce, pull together, and unify much of our advice on 3-D moves to affect a deal's scope, sequence, and basic process choices:

- **Make key moves away from the table.** Moves at the table are only part of the negotiating game. Treating this negotiation as a matter of further interpersonal skill with Throckmorton at the FSB table would have been pointless; only creative, persistent, and entrepreneurial moves to reset that table and change the game itself could offer a more promising scope and sequence.

- **Scan widely.** Widen your scope to determine which potential parties might be usefully involved and for what roles in the target deal, how these parties might see their interests, what potential relationships might exist among them, and on what basis they could best be approached. Notice that this scanning process sets the stage for determining the most favorable scope of the negotiation. Getting the parties right requires disciplined imagination, not merely a mechanical exercise in making lists.

- **Map backward.** Iverson began with his ultimate FSB "target" to determine which prior deals to put in place that would maximize the chances of an ultimate FSB "yes." Keep mapping backward until you have figured out the most promising *sequence* of players to involve in your desired setup.

- **Manage the information flow and design your proposed deals carefully.** At each stage of this negotiation, Iverson maximized the deal's attractiveness in terms of that party's interests and obtained from it what would be most useful to him in later stages of the process. For example, Derano wanted a fee and was willing to give a form of "guarantee." Concord valued more jobs, higher taxes, and less pollution; it could create a job-certifying LDA with a mandate to issue bonds. The EDA wanted "certified" job creation and could give junior debt. Ultimately, Iverson made it easier for the bureaucratic, risk-averse Throckmorton to OK the loan by pointing to the "backing" of Derano, UIC, EDA, and LDA.

Notice how complementary "differences" of interest and priority drove the separate stages of this deal by creating value relative to each party's best no-deal option. In the separate "bilateral" components of this entire multiparty exercise, each player's no-deal option was to ignore this highly leveraged project. To overcome this possibility, Iverson listened hard and probed into what was needed to meet each party's interests so that that player could be locked in, making a "yes" from the subsequent players even more likely. In every bilateral negotiation, Iverson's actions created significant value and ensured that his counterpart claimed a full share of that *bilaterally created* value. (For example, Derano got a 15 percent above-normal fee; Throckmorton got the financial cushion and the political cover in case the loan actually failed to perform; etc.) Yet, when Iverson had negotiated the gauntlet of individual barriers and the overall deal was done, the *aggregate* value created was substantial and Iverson had claimed the lion's share of it. While bilaterally generous, given how each player saw its piece of the puzzle, Iverson was a multilateral winner as he looked at the whole.

Concluding Thoughts

Let us briefly revisit our core 3-D prescriptions in light of the three cases presented in this chapter.

GET THE SETUP RIGHT I: MAP ALL THE PARTIES, THE FULL SET OF THEIR INTERESTS, AND THEIR BEST NO-DEAL OPTIONS. For your most challenging deals, this step is anything but a mechanical process. Think back to the principles that we laid out in part 2 for getting the parties right. Keep in mind the high-value players, as well as those involved in several other categories: internal, external, principals, agents, formal, informal, influential, as well as those who will ratify and implement the deal. Don't forget about *potential* players as well as those already part of the negotiation. Think about how to engage the full set of actual and potential issues—beyond price and bargaining positions; theirs as well as yours—and assess them with an awareness of likely cognitive biases. And think about favorably reshaping the deal/no-deal balance.

Imagine that Microsoft had treated its dealings with AOL as a "browsers-for-dollars" contest rather than dramatically shifting the issues and target parties in AOL. No deal. Say that Kennecott had confined itself to negotiating only with the Chilean government, rather than resetting the table to include a range of other parties with a broad range of nonmining interests, extending into the future. Again, no deal. If Iverson had focused his entire energies on the loan officer at the Federal Street Bank, he would still be pointlessly arguing. and the valuable recovery boiler would be but an empty option for Concord Pulp and Paper. Across these cases, the parties, interests, and no-deal options should hardly be taken as "givens" in analyzing barriers and crafting strategy.

When these setup elements are wrong, you face formidable barriers. In response, 3-D Negotiators entrepreneurially act in accord with our bottom line advice: Get the parties right. Get the interests right. Get the no-deal options right.

GET THE SETUP RIGHT II: CHECK THE SEQUENCE AND BASIC PROCESS CHOICES. The approaches taken by Kennecott and especially Iverson remind us of the vital importance of the sequence and basic process choices. When they are wrong, they present potentially high barriers. Notice the role that these elements play, as critical parts of the right setup, in ensuring the involvement of key players dealing with the right issues in the right manner. Bottom line advice: Get the sequence right. Get basic process choices right.

DESIGN VALUE-CREATING DEALS. Proposed agreements may pose barriers to success if they offer insufficient value and/or fail to accomplish their objectives. From what was initially framed as a narrow "browsers-for-dollars" transaction, Microsoft creatively designed a much higher-value deal to AOL by expanding the set of issues, offering better distribution and blunted competition with MSN. While AOL claimed much of this value, the outcome was far better for Microsoft than losing to Netscape. In the case of Kennecott and Chile, notice the "northeast movement"—relative to a straight royalty transaction and certainly relative to expropriation—offered by a deal design that was the equivalent of a partnership meeting both political and economic interests. And at each "node" of Iverson's dealings, he found a way to dovetail his counterpart's different interests with his prime concern at that stage of his overall approach. In each of these three cases, the initial deal design posed a barrier that a new design surmounted by moving northeast and dovetailing differences, to create greater value. Across these examples, however, the sustainability and spirit of the deal could be faulted. Bottom line: Get the deal design right.

STRESS PROBLEM-SOLVING TACTICS. Without effective tactics to take advantage of a more promising setup and superior deal design, none of these three negotiations would have come to fruition. In Iverson's and Kennecott's negotiations, many of their counterparts had perfectly good no-deal options. Tactics that offended the other side or left that side feeling uncomfortable could easily have led to no deal. Moves at the table to create and claim value called, at a minimum, for avoiding arrogance, showing respect, demonstrating cross-cultural sensitivity, being endlessly persistent, probing and listening for the full set of real interests, and fostering creativity. Microsoft demonstrated persistence when uncovering interests that it could creatively meet. Iverson was relentless in seeking to learn what could work for each of the various parties. At each stage of the process, he framed his proposals in terms to which his counterpart would be most responsive. At the same time, carefully divulging information and credibly hinting at good no-deal options led to his claiming a full share of the value created. Shaping ZOPA perceptions and solving joint problems at the table were the hallmarks of these parties. Bottom line: Stress problem-solving tactics to create and claim value.

3-D STRATEGY AS A MAP, NOT A PATH. Throughout this book, we have presented our ideas in a logical sequence—first you *diagnose* (in the form of a 3-D barriers audit) and then you *act* (by developing a 3-D strategy). This is a natural order for a book exposition. Yet, especially after you have parsed the browser wars, Kennecott, and Concord Pulp and Paper negotiations, it is evident that the reality is more complex. Negotiating effectively is not like following a recipe that is written out before you start: step 1, step 2, . . . then you're done. In 3-D Negotiation, the various elements tend to stay in play and to evolve, often dramatically. You must take actions in many different dimensions, sometimes at the same time, and continually update and adjust your approach.

The idea of a 3-D strategy is not well captured by a blueprint a master plan or detailed path you've figured out in advance to reach your target deal. Those who think of strategy as a preset path, however cleverly constructed, risk finding themselves at a loss if (when!) the inevitable unforeseen event knocks them off track. Indeed, as our colleague, Roger Fisher, has observed, a robust negotiating strategy is more like a map with a provisional route sketched from here to there, than it is like a set path.

With a good grasp of the key elements of our 3-D barriers/strategy framework, you can craft a map whose landscape contains your assessment of these now-familiar critical features: parties, interests, no-deal options, sequencing, basic process choices, potential northeast moves, differences, the letter and spirit of agreements, tactics to create and claim value. Bottom line: This 3-D map will help you to thread a successful path—by coordinated moves away from the table, on the drawing board, and at the table—over the changing barriers landscape and through the complexities and challenges that inevitably arise.

THINK STRATEGICALLY, ACT OPPORTUNISTICALLY. And, when unforeseen events render your original approach invalid, you can reexamine your map to work out a promising new path past the new barriers. Indeed, successful negotiators expect to learn along the way and to be surprised, but to regain their bearings. With such a 3-D map, they are able to embrace the most effective negotiating approach we know. Bottom line: Think strategically, but act opportunistically.

The 3-D Negotiator: Creative Setup Architect, Insightful Deal Designer, Persuasive Tactician

With the negotiating approach we suggest, you will not be hobbled as a 1-D player in a 3-D world, condemned to seeing negotiation mainly as a tactical, face-to-face affair. Rather, you will move away from the table to set up the right negotiation. You will work on the drawing board to design value-creating deals. You will stress problem-solving tactics at the table. You will combine these elements into a 3-D strategy to overcome the barriers you have diagnosed. As you create and claim value for the long term, you will be a confident 3-D negotiator, armed with a complete approach that fits the challenges and potential of a fully dimensional world.

Notes

Chapter 1

1. R. Fisher, W. Ury, and B. Patton, *Getting to Yes: Negotiating Agreement Without Giving In* (New York: Penguin, 1991); W. L. Ury, *Getting Past No* (New York: Bantam, 1991).

2. Here again, Fisher, Ury, and Patton are the trailblazers. *Getting to Yes* has done more to highlight the critical value of "interest-based" negotiations, as opposed to "positional bargaining," than any other work on the subject. The first systematic exploration of the role of differences in deal design can be found in J. K. Sebenius, "Anatomy of Agreement," (PhD diss. Harvard University Economics Department and Harvard Business School, Cambridge, MA, 1980); J. K. Sebenius, *Negotiating the Law of the Sea: Lessons in the Art and Science of Reaching Agreement* (Cambridge, MA: Harvard University Press, 1984); and in chapter 5 of D. A. Lax and J. K. Sebenius, *The Manager as Negotiator: Bargaining for Cooperation and Competitive Gain* (New York: Free Press, 1986).

3. We learned of this episode from Jeffrey L. Cruikshank. This version is taken, in part verbatim, from his book *Shaping the Waves* (Boston: Harvard Business School Press, 2005), 27. We also draw on later communication with William Sahlman that refined our understanding, as did Thomas Stemberg's account in *Staples for Success* (Santa Monica, CA: Knowledge Exchange LLC, 1996), 44–47.

4. Cruikshank, *Shaping the Waves*, 27.

Chapter 2

1. Our Harvard Law School colleague Robert Mnookin was the first to systematize the notion of barriers to negotiated agreement, but his insightful set of barriers—cognitive, strategic, principal-agent, and reactive devaluation—more closely track their underlying academic disciplines such as psychology and game theory than the practice-oriented 3-D barriers schema that we develop here. See the work of Mnookin and his colleagues; K. Arrow et al., eds., *Barriers to Conflict Resolution* (New York: W.W. Norton, 1995).

2. Overwhelming strategic logic ultimately drove the companies back together, but only after nearly two years had passed.

3. H. W. Huizenga, introduction to *Masters of the Universe: Winning Strategies of America's Greatest Deal Makers*, by D. J. Kadlec (New York: Harper Business, 1999), ix.

4. Fisher, Ury, and Patton popularized the importance of best alternative to a negotiated agreement, or BATNA, in *Getting to Yes: Negotiating Agreement Without Giving In* (New York: Penguin, 1991); a history of this venerable concept, as well as some of its wider ramifications, can be found in J. K. Sebenius and D. Lax; "The Power of Alternatives or the Limits to Negotiation," *Negotiation Journal* 1 (1985): 77–95.

That said, we don't usually use the BATNA acronym. As a kind of jargon it can be confusing to our business audiences.

5. See Michael Watkins's insightful "The Gulf Crisis: Building a Coalition for War," Case no. C16-94-1264.0 (Cambridge, MA: Kennedy School of Government, 1994), 53.

Chapter 3

1. Our description of the negotiations between the longshoremen and shippers, along with all the relevant facts and quotes that follow comes from K. L. McGinn and D. Witter, "Showdown on the Waterfront: The 2002 West Coast Port Dispute (A)," Case no. 9-904-045 (Boston: Harvard Business School, 2004); idem, "Showdown on the Waterfront: The 2002 West Coast Port Dispute (B)," Case no. 9-904-067 (Boston: Harvard Business School, 2004).

2. Steven Greenhouse, "The Nation: The $100,000 Longshoreman: A Union Wins the Global Game," *New York Times*, October 6, 2002, sec. 4, 1.

3. David Greenberg, "Ports Seek Swap of Job Security for Automation," *Los Angeles Business Journal*, July 15, 2002, http://www.findarticles.com/p/articles/mi_m5072/is_28_24/ai_91092608.

4. Larry Kanter, "On the Waterfront: Possible Strike by Longshoremen Threatens L.A.'s Economy," *Los Angeles Business Journal*, February 22, 1999, http://www.findarticles.com/p/articles/mi_m5072/is_8_21/ai_54222190.

5. As quoted in W. L. Ury, *Getting Past No* (New York: Bantam, 1991).

6. McGinn and Witter, "Showdown on the Waterfront: The 2002 West Coast Port Dispute (A)," 9.

7. Ibid., 11.

8. Ibid.

9. Ibid., 14.

10. Ibid, 12.

11. "Miniace Resigns PMA Post After Seven Years at Helm; Industry Veteran McKenna to Lead Organization," Pacific Maritime Association Press Release, March 18, 2004, http://www.pmanet.org/docs/index.cfm/id_subcat/35/id_content/2142590158.

12. J. G. Stein, "Structure, Strategies, and Tactics of Mediation: Kissinger and Carter in the Middle East," *Negotiation Journal* 1, no. 3 (1985): 331–334.

13. A. M. Brandenburger and B. J. Nalebuff, *Co-opetition*, (New York: Doubleday, 1996).

Chapter 4

1. In *Co-opetition* (New York: Doubleday, 1996), Adam Brandenburger and Barry Nalebuff have developed a perspective on business strategy that is very much in the spirit of 3-D Negotiation. Their concept of the "value net," which we will later put to use, can be helpful in finding the right parties.

2. Laboratory experiments have found this to be true in "matching" problems, where the challenge is to get the right (high-value) parties to transact, yet people look too narrowly. See A. E. Tenbrunsel et al., "The Negotiation Matching Process: Relationships and Partner Selection," *Organizational Behavior and Human Decision Processes* 80 (1999): 252–283.

3. J. K. Sebenius and H. Riley, "Stone Container in Honduras (A)," Case no. 9-897-172 (Boston: Harvard Business School, 1997).

4. Ibid., 9.

5. This anecdote is from G. Anders, "Top Negotiator Wins Top Pay for Executives," 2003, http://www.carerrjournal.com/salaryhiring/negotiate/20030708-anders.html.

6. N. D. Kristof, "Death by Optimism," *New York Times*, November 5, 2003, 25.

7. For an insightful, broader study of this problem of principals and agents, see J. Pratt and R. Zeckhauser, eds., *Principals and Agents: The Structure of Business* (Boston: Harvard Business School Press, 1985). For extended application to negotiating situations, see R. H. Mnookin, L. E. Susskind, and P. Foster, eds., *Negotiating on Behalf of Others* (Thousand Oaks, CA: Sage Publications, 1999).

8. Bob Mnookin and his colleagues have explored this principal-agent tension as a centerpiece of their analysis in R. H. Mnookin, S. R. Peppet, and A. S. Tulumello, *Beyond Winning: Negotiating to Create Value in Deals and Disputes* (Cambridge, MA: Harvard University Press, 2000).

9. D. J. Kadlec, *Masters of the Universe* (New York: Harper Business, 1999), 85–92.

10. J. Kaplan, *Startup* (Boston: Houghton Mifflin, 1995), 120.

11. B. Wasserstein, *Big Deal: 2000 and Beyond* (New York: Warner Books, 2000), 622–623.

Chapter 5

1. E. Schmitt, "Questions for Charlene Barshefsky: the Negotiator." *New York Times Magazine*, October 1, 2000, 4.

2. M. D. Watkins, "Strategic Deal-making at Millennium Pharmaceuticals," Case no. 899-242 (Boston: Harvard Business School, 1999), 12.

3. L. M. Holson, "The Cisco Whiz Kid: Young Deal Maker Is Force Behind the Company's Growth," *New York Times*, November 19, 1998, C9.

4. L. Brahimi, transcript of remarks at the Great Negotiator Awards (Cambridge, MA: Program on Negotiation at Harvard Law School, 2002).

5. S. Stein and H. Book, *The EQ Edge: Emotional Intelligence and Your Success* (Toronto: Stoddart Publishing, 2000).

6. See C. Camerer and R. Thaler, "Anomolies: Ultimatums, Dictators, and Managers," *Journal of Economic Perspectives* 9, no. 2 (1995): 209–219.

7. H. W. Huizenga, introduction to *Masters of the Universe: Winning Strategies of America's Greatest Deal Makers*, by D. J. Kadlec (New York: Harper Business, 1999), ix.

8. Richard R. Gesteland's book, *Cross-Cultural Business Behavior: Marketing, Negotiating and Managing Across Cultures* (Copenhagen: Handelshøjskolens Forlag, 1996), explains his concept of the cultural "great divide" and informs this paragraph.

9. A classic work establishing the importance of "procedural justice" can be found in J. Thibaut and L. Walker, *Procedural Justice: A Psychological Analysis* (New York: Wiley, 1975). A popular summary of the literature on procedural justice can be found in W. C. Kim and R. Mauborgne, "Fair Process: Managing in the Knowledge Economy," *Harvard Business Review*, July–August 1997, 65–75.

10. For a fuller discussion, see D. A. Lax and J. K. Sebenius, "Three Ethical Issues in Negotiation," *Negotiation Journal* 2, no. 4 (1986): 363–370. *What's Fair: Ethics for Negotiators* (San Francisco: Jossey-Bass, 2004), edited by our colleagues Michael A. Wheeler and Carrie Menkel-Meadow, is by far the best compilation of current thinking on the ethics of negotiation from many perspectives.

11. R. Fisher, W. Ury, and B. Patton, *Getting to Yes: Negotiating Agreement Without Giving In* (New York: Penguin, 1991).

12. See M. H. Bazerman and M. A. Neale, *Negotiating Rationally* (New York: Free Press, 1992); M. A. Neale and M. H. Bazerman, *Cognition and Rationality in Negotiation* (New York: Free Press, 1991); and L. L. Thompson, *The Mind and Heart of the Negotiator*, 2nd ed. (Upper Saddle River, NJ: Prentice Hall, 2001).

13. L. Babcock and G. Lowenstein, "Explaining Bargaining Impasse: The Role of Self-Serving Biases," *Journal of Economic Perspectives* 11, no. 1 (1997): 109–126.

14. For excellent introductions to research findings and negotiating implications of self-serving biases and partisan perceptions see R. J. Robinson, "Errors in Social Judgment: Implications for Negotiation and Conflict Resolution, Part 1," Case no. 9-897-103 (Boston: Harvard Business School, 1997); and "Errors in Social Judgment: Implications for Negotiation and Conflict Resolution, Part 2," Case no. 9-897-104 (Boston: Harvard Business School, 1997).

15. Babcock and Lowenstein, "Explaining Bargaining Impasse."

16. Fisher, Ury, and Patton, *Getting to Yes.*

Chapter 6

1. For these quotes and many other descriptions of Rubin's approach to negotiations, see R. E. Rubin and J. Weisberg, *In an Uncertain World: Tough Choices from Wall Street to Washington* (New York: Random House, 2003), 118, 168.

2. Negotiation experts Roger Fisher, Bill Ury, and Bruce Patton coined a useful acronym to capture this concept: BATNA, short for best alternative to a negotiated agreement. See R. Fisher, W. Ury, and B. Patton, *Getting to Yes: Negotiating Agreement Without Giving In* (New York: Penguin, 1991). We like the term, but have used "best no-deal option" instead simply to avoid jargon. The importance of no-deal options has quite a long intellectual history and many implications for bargaining, which we first detailed in our article "The Power of Alternatives or the Limits to Negotiation" (*Negotiation Journal* 1, no. 2 [1985]: 163–179).

3. For this quote and a fuller discussion of Perlman's approach, see J. K. Sebenius and R. Fortgang, "Steve Perlman and WebTV (B)," Case no. 9-899-271 (Boston: Harvard Business School Publishing, 1999).

4. G. Rivlin, "AOL's Rough Riders" *The Standard*, October 20, 2000, http://www.thestandard.com/article/display/0.1151.19461.00.htm.

5. This quote and an extended discussion of related bargaining implications can be found in G. Subramanian, "The Drivers of Market Efficiency in Revlon Transactions." *Journal of Corporate Law* 28 (2003): 691.

6. See M. D. Watkins, "Strategic Deal-making at Millennium Pharmaceuticals," Case no. 899-242 (Boston: Harvard Business School, 1999), 12.

7. See J. Bulow and P. Klemperer, "Auctions Versus Negotiations," *American Economic Review* 86, no. 1 (1996): 180–194.

8. This example is summarized from information in J. Authers, W. Hall, and R. Wolffe, "Banks Pay a High Price for Putting the Past Behind Them," *Financial Times* (London edition), September 9, 1998, 4.

9. This example is drawn from D. Roberts and R. Waters, "AT&T Battles to Dissolve Loss-making Joint Venture: Lack of Pre-nuptial Deal Hampers Efforts to Divide Concert Assets," *Financial Times*, July 5, 2001, 1; and D. Roberts and R. Waters, "Tale of a Telecoms Heartbreak," *Financial Times*, July 5, 2001, 18.

Chapter 7

1. We introduced this concept in chapter 2; the term "value net" comes from A. M. Brandenburger and B. J. Nalebuff, *Co-opetition* (New York: Doubleday, 1996).

2. For a full story, see J. K. Sebenius and R. Fortgang, "Steve Perlman and WebTV (A)," Case no. 9-899-270 (Boston: Harvard Business School, 1999); and "Steve Perlman and WebTV (B)," Case no. 9-899-271 (Boston: Harvard Business School, 1999).

3. S. Blumenthal, "The Making of a Machine," *The New Yorker*, November 29, 1993, 93.

4. For a much fuller discussion of sequencing in negotiation, see D. A. Lax and J. K. Sebenius, "Thinking Coalitionally: Party Arithmetic, Process Opportunism, and Strategic Sequencing," in *Negotiation Analysis*, ed. H. P. Young (Ann Arbor, MI: University of Michigan Press, 1991), 153–193; and J. K. Sebenius, "Sequencing to Build Coalitions: With Whom Should I Talk First?" in *Wise Decisions*, ed. R. J. Zeckhauser, R. Keeney, and J. K. Sebenius (Boston: Harvard Business School Press, 1996), 324–348.

5. W. Taylor, "The Logic of Global Business: An Interview with ABB's Percy Barnevik," *Harvard Business Review*, March–April 1991, 91–105.

6. For the first use of the "two-level games" metaphor, as well as for the further example of the Bonn Summit, in which internal blockers were thwarted by an external coalition, see R. D. Putnam, "Diplomacy and Domestic Politics: The Logic of Two-Level Games," *International Organization* 42 (1988): 427–460.

7. Mike Moldoveanu related this amusing story to us, for which we are grateful.

8. J. S. Odell, "The Outcomes of International Trade Conflicts: The U.S. and South Korea, 1960–1981," *International Studies Quarterly* 29 (1985): 281–282.

9. In the discussion that follows, analyses of such design issues for the climate change talks, the diplomacy of chlorofluorocarbon control, and the Law of the Sea negotiations can be found in J. K. Sebenius, *Negotiating the Law of the Sea: Lessons in the Art and Science of Reaching Agreement* (Cambridge, MA: Harvard University Press, 1984); J. K. Sebenius, "Designing Negotiations Toward a New Regime—the Case of Global Warming," *International Security* 15, no. 4 (1991): 110–148; J. K. Sebenius, "Dealing with Blocking Coalitions and Related Barriers to Agreement: Lessons from Negotiations on the Oceans, the Ozone, and the Climate," in *Barriers to Conflict Resolution*, ed. K. Arrow et al. (New York: W.W. Norton, 1995): 150–182; and J. K. Sebenius, "Overcoming Obstacles to a Successful Climate Convention," *Shaping National Responses to Global Climate Change: A Post-Rio Guide*, ed. H. Lee. (Washington, DC: Island Press, 1995), 41–79. For a careful look at Mitchell's design choices in the Northern Ireland talks, see D. Curran and J. K. Sebenius, "The Mediator as Coalition-Builder: George Mitchell in Northern Ireland," *Journal of International Negotiation* 8, no.1 (2003): 111–147.

10. A number of accounts detail the special role of mediation in these negotiations; see K. Auletta, *World War 3.0: Microsoft and Its Enemies* (New York: Random House, 2001); E. D. Green and J. B. Marks, "How We Mediated the Microsoft Case," *Boston Globe*, November 15, 2001, A23; J. Heilemann, *Pride Before the Fall: The Trials of Bill Gates and the End of the Microsoft Era* (New York: HarperCollins, 2001).

11. On the role of mediation in personal and business disputes see, for example, J. Folberg and A. Taylor, *Mediation: A Comprehensive Guide to Resolving Conflicts Without Litigation* (San Francisco: Jossey-Bass, 1984); S. B. Goldberg, F. E. A. Sander, and N. Rogers, *Dispute Resolution: Negotiation, Mediation, and Other Processes* (New York: Aspen Publishers, 1999); J. Rubin, *The Dynamics of Third Party Intervention* (New York: Praeger, 1981); D. Kolb, *The Mediators* (Cambridge, MA: MIT Press, 1983); and J. Bercovitch and J. Z. Rubin, eds., *Mediation in International Relations: Multilateral Approaches to Conflict Management* (London: Macmillan, 1992).

12. For a good description of many arbitration and related processes, see "The ABCs of ADR: Private ADR Processes," CPR Institute for Dispute Resolution, 2004, http://www.cpradr.org/.

13. For advice on assigning the right ADR mechanisms, or "matching the forum to the fuss," see F. A. E. Sander and S. Goldberg, "Fitting the Forum to the Fuss," *Negotiation Journal* 10, no. 1 (1994): 49–67.

14. For an analytic discussion of the Texas shootout and other such moves, see H. Raiffa, J. Richardson, and D. Metcalfe, *Negotiation Analysis: The Science and Art of Collaborative Decision Making* (Cambridge, MA: Belknap Press of Harvard University Press, 2002). More technical treatments can be found in S. J. Brams and A. D. Taylor, *Fair Division: From Cake-Cutting to Dispute Resolution* (Cambridge, UK: Cambridge University Press, 1996); and R. P. McAfee, "Amicable Divorce: Dissolving a Partnership with Simple Mechanisms," *Journal of Economic Theory* 56 (1992): 266–293.

15. See W. Ury, J. Brett, and S. Goldberg, *Getting Disputes Resolved: Defining Systems to Cut the Costs of Conflict* (San Francisco: Jossey-Bass, 1988); and C. A. Costantino and C. S. Merchant, *Designing Conflict Management Systems* (San Francisco: Jossey-Bass, 1996).

16. See M. A. Wheeler, "Negotiating NIMBYs: Learning from the Failure of the Massachusetts Siting Law," *Yale Journal on Regulation* 11 (1994): 241–291; M. A. Wheeler, J. Gilbert, and P. Field, "Trading the Poor: Intermunicipal Affordable Housing Negotiation in New Jersey," *Harvard Journal of Law and Negotiation* 2 (1997): 1–33.

17. Though largely beyond the focus of this book, 3-D design principles for global negotiations are an active area of research and practical application. For example, see J. K. Sebenius, "Designing Negotiations toward a New Regime—the Case of Global Warming," *International Security* 15, no. 4 (1991): 110–148; and J. K. Sebenius, "Dealing with Blocking Coalitions and Related Barriers to Agreement: Lessons from Negotiations on the Oceans, the Ozone, and the Climate," in *Barriers to Conflict Resolution*, ed. K. Arrow et al. (New York: W.W. Norton, 1995), 150–182.

18. Larry Susskind is a master at analyzing and offering advice for negotiating public disputes. Along with various colleagues, he has defined and given wide exposure to approaches such as DAD. See L. Susskind and J. Cruikshank, *Breaking the Impasse: Consensual Approaches to Resolving Public Disputes* (New York: Basic Books, 1987); and L. Susskind and P. Field, *Dealing with an Angry Public: The Mutual Gains Approach to Resolving Disputes* (New York: Free Press, 1996).

19. See J. K. Sebenius and H. Riley, "Stone Container in Honduras (A)," Case no. 9-897-172 (Boston: Harvard Business School, 1997); idem, "Stone Container in Honduras (B)," Case no. 9-897-173 (Boston: Harvard Business School, 1997); and idem, "Stone Container in Honduras (C)," Case no. 9-897-174 (Boston: Harvard Business School, 1997).

20. See the case series beginning with M. S. Salter and S. E. A. Hall, "Block 16: Conoco's 'Green' Oil Strategy (A)," Case no. 394001 (Boston: Harvard Business School, 1993).

21. J. K. Sebenius and H. Riley, "Stone Container in Costa Rica (A)," Case no. 9-897-140 (Boston: Harvard Business School, 1997); and idem, "Stone Container in Costa Rica (B)," Case no. 9-897-141 (Boston: Harvard Business School, 1997).

22. B. C. Esty and C. Ferman, "The Chad-Cameroon Petroleum Development and Pipeline Project (A)," Case no. 9-202-010 (Boston: Harvard Business School, 2001); idem, "The Chad-Cameroon Petroleum Development and Pipeline Project (B)," Case no. 9-202-012 (Boston: Harvard Business School, 2001).

23. These and other design issues are discussed at great length in L. Susskind, S. McKearnan, and J. Thomas-Larmer, eds., *The Consensus Building Handbook: A Comprehensive Guide to Reaching Agreement* (Thousand Oaks, CA: Sage, 1999).

24. A popular summary of the literature on procedural justice can be found in W. C. Kim and R. Mauborgne, "Fair Process: Managing in the Knowledge Economy," *Harvard Business Review*, July–August, 1997, 65–75.

Chapter 8

1. As best we can tell, there is no "WORN" broadcasting in the U.S. (There *is* a WEAK, broadcasting out of Athens, Ohio.) Our "WORN" is imaginary but based on real situations we're familiar with.

2. The term "total pie" has some inherent limitations. Up to now, we've talked about "value" in all of its senses: noneconomic as well as economic, subjective and objective, process-related and deal-related, and so on. The term "total pie" implies that you can just add up all of these dissimilar types of value and arrive at an arithmetic total, which both mathematicians and philosophers would say is impossible. But we'll stick with the term, because it keeps negotiators focused on joint gains, past and future.

3. This example comes from a useful book, *Getting Partnering Right* (N. Rackham, L. Friedman, and R. Ruff [New York: McGraw-Hill, 1995]), 47.

4. Ibid., 39–40.

5. We are indebted to Roger Fisher, Bill Ury, and Bruce Patton for these phrases and the concepts behind them; see R. Fisher, W. Ury, and B. Patton, *Getting to Yes: Negotiating Agreement Without Giving In* (New York: Penguin, 1991).

6. Rackham, Friedman, and Ruff, *Getting Partnering Right*, 118–119.

7. This memorable phrase, popularized in Richard Dawkins's *The Selfish Gene* (Oxford: Oxford University Press, 1996), was originally from Alfred, Lord Tennyson's, cantos "In Memoriam A.H.H."

8. This and number of related other studies illustrating this point can be found in L. L. Thompson, *The Mind and Heart of the Negotiator*, 2nd ed. (Upper Saddle River, NJ: Prentice Hall, 2001).

9. Productively managing what we dubbed the *negotiator's dilemma*—the inherent tension between cooperative moves necessary to create value jointly and the competitive moves to claim it individually—is a centerpiece of our earlier book, *The Manager as Negotiator: Bargaining for Cooperation and Competitive Gain* (New York: Free Press, 1986).

Chapter 9

1. Numerous examples can be found in the online version of the "Daily Deal"; for example, see http://www.thedailydeal.com/topstories/A21955-2000May3.html.

2. All sorts of relatively complex analytical issues lie behind this discussion—most obviously, the extent to which differences in probabilistic assessments are a function of differential informational heritage. These issues are considered narrowly in J. K. Sebenius and J. Geanakoplos, "Don't Bet on It: Contingent Agreements with Asymmetric Information," *Journal of the American Statistical Association* 78, no. 382 (1983): 424–426; and much more broadly in the technical sections of J. K. Sebenius, *Negotiating the Law of the Sea: Lessons in the Art and Science of Reaching Agreement* (Cambridge, MA: Harvard University Press, 1984).

Chapter 10

1. To learn more about this example, see M. Y. Yoshino and U. S. Rangan, *Strategic Alliances: An Entrepreneurial Approach to Globalization* (Boston: Harvard Business School Press, 1995), 30–32 and 48–58.

2. See "The Partners," *BusinessWeek*, February 10, 1992, as cited in Yoshino and Rangan, *Strategic Alliances*, 30.

3. Ibid., 32, 48–58, and 108; and communication with our Harvard Business School colleague Ashish Nanda.

4. See G. Witzenburg, "Mazda Man: Mark Fields Hopes to Work His Mazda Magic on Ford's Premier Automotive Group," *Automotive Industries*, November 2000, http://www.ai-online.com/issues/article_detail.asp?id=614.

5. This example, the quotes, and the three stages—philanthropic, transactional, and integrative—later described for the City Year-Timberland social contract come from James E. Austin, *The Collaboration Challenge: How Nonprofits and Businesses Succeed Through Strategic Alliances* (San Francisco, Jossey-Bass, 2000), 19–39.

6. We are grateful to Ashish Nanda for this example.

7. This example was suggested by our Harvard Business School colleague Myra Hart.

8. See J. S. Hammond and G. B. Allan, "Bougainville Copper Ltd. (B)," Case no. 174104 (Boston: Harvard Business School, 1974); idem, "Bougainville Copper Ltd. (C)," Case no. 175071 (Boston: Harvard Business School, 1974); idem, "Bougainville Copper Ltd. (D)," Case no. 175072 (Boston: Harvard Business School, 1975); and idem, "Bougainville Copper Ltd. (E)," Case no. 175204 (Boston: Harvard Business School, 1975).

9. Information about this situation, and sources for the quotes that follow, can be found in T. Reiterman and V. Ellis, "State Reworks Deals With 5 Power Firms," *Los Angeles Times*, April 23, 2002, http://www.caltax.org/LATimes4-23-02.pdf; and B. C. Esty and M. Kane, "Calpine Corp.: The Evolution from Project to Corporate Finance," Case no. 9-201-098 (Boston: Harvard Business School, 2003).

10. See, e.g., D. Gram, "Ben of Ben & Jerry's Bemoans Betting on Big-Business Benevolence," *South Coast Today-Standard Times*, December 3, 2000, http://www.s-t.com/daily/12-00/12-03-00/d01bu111.htm; and "The ice cream industry's most progressive leaders were bought out by Unilever in April, and were discouraged with the recent appointment of a Unilever veteran as CEO, instead of their preferred candidate. The founders say they were duped into believing empty promises from Unilever. 'I am troubled because there were a bunch of commitments made by Unilever which I thought were legally binding, but now I understand they are not,' said co-founder Ben Cohen." (JKM, "Icy Goodbye from Ben and Jerry," MotherJones.com, January 4, 2001, http://www.motherjones.com/news/mustreads/2001/01/010401.html).

11. We've written about the insecure contracts problem in much more detail; see D. A. Lax and J. K. Sebenius, "Insecure Contracts and Resource Development," *Public Policy* 29, no. 4 (1981): 417–436. For a broader treatment of sustainability issues, see D. A. Lax and J. K. Sebenius, *The Manager as Negotiator: Bargaining for Cooperation and Competitive Gain* (New York: Free Press, 1986), 276–289.

12. We are grateful to Ashish Nanda for raising this issue and suggesting creative responses.

Chapter 11

1. We are especially grateful to our colleague, Ron Fortgang, with whom versions of these ideas were worked out and jointly published; see R. S. Fortgang, D. A. Lax, and J. K. Sebenius, "Negotiating the Spirit of the Deal," *Harvard Business Review*, February 2003, 66–75. With permission, this chapter is closely based on that article. Ashish Nanda was an invaluable colleague in working out these ideas.

2. We are not the first to employ these ideas in this way: our colleagues Richard Walton, Joel Cutcher-Gershenfeld, and Robert McKersie explored social and economic contracts negotiated between employers and unions, especially at times of major economic change, in *Strategic Negotiations: A Theory of Change in Labor-Management Relations* (Boston: Harvard Business School Press, 1994). For academic views on "relational" and "implicit" contracts, see S. Macaulay, "Non-Contractual Relations in Business: A Preliminary Study," *American Sociological Review* 28, no. 1

(February 1963): 55–67. On implicit and relational contracts as explored in economics, see, for example, O. Williamson, *Markets and Hierarchies* (New York: Free Press, 1975); and O. Williamson, *The Mechanisms of Governance* (New York: Oxford University Press, 1996); as well as a very nice introduction and evaluation in R. Gibbons, "Why Organizations Are Such a Mess (and What an Economist Might Do About It)," draft chapter for *Organizational Economics* (March 2000), http://web.mit.edu/rgibbons/www/; and G. Baker, K. Murphy, and R. Gibbons, "Relational Contracts and the Theory of the Firm," *Quarterly Journal of Economics,* 117 (2002): 39–83. On behavioral studies dealing with trust, relationships, and psychological contracts see, for example, C. Sabel, "Studied Trust: Building New Forms of Cooperation in a Volatile Economy," chapter 4 in *Explorations in Economic Sociology,* ed. R. Swedberg (New York: Russell Sage Foundation, 1993); B. Uzzi, "Social Structure and Competition in Interfirm Networks," *Administrative Science Quarterly* 42 (1997): 35–67; and D. Rousseau, *Psychological Contracts in Organizations* (Thousand Oaks, CA: Sage, 1995). A comparison and extension of these two sets of views can be found in J. H. Dyer and H. Singh, "The Relational View: Cooperative Strategy and Sources of Interorganizational Competitive Advantage," *Academy of Management Review* (October 1998): 660–679.

3. For more on this episode, see "Torch That Sent a Deal Down in Flames," *Financial Times,* April 12, 2000, 22.

4. For more detail, see, e.g., S. Tully, "Northwest and KLM: The Alliance from Hell," *Fortune,* June 24, 1996, 64–71.

5. Jerry Kaplan, *Startup* (Boston: Houghton-Mifflin, 1995), 120.

6. C. A. Hollaway, "Supplier Management at Sun Microsystems (A)," Stanford University Graduate School of Business Case OIT-16A, March 9, 1996, 9, 12.

7. J. H. Dyer, "Effective Interfirm Collaboration: How Firms Minimize Transaction Costs and Maximize Transaction Value," *Strategic Management Journal* 18 (1997): 553–556, directly quoted from Dyer and Singh, "The Relational View."

8. Dyer and Singh's "The Relational View" provides an excellent survey that cites and evaluates a large number of studies that support the claims made in this paragraph.

9. Sources for the Ford-Mazda example include M. Y. Yoshino and U. S. Rangan, *Strategic Alliances: An Entrepreneurial Approach to Globalization* (Boston: Harvard Business School Press, 1995), 30–32 and 48–58.

10. See N. Rackham, L. Friedman, and R. Ruff, *Getting Partnering Right* (New York: McGraw-Hill, 1995).

11. M-J. Chen, *Inside Chinese Business* (Boston: Harvard Business School Press, 2000), 142–143.

12. Ibid.

13. See J. K. Sebenius, "The Hidden Challenge of Cross-Border Negotiations," *Harvard Business Review,* March 2002, 76–85; J. Salacuse, *Making Global Deals: What Every Executive Should Know About Negotiating Abroad* (New York: Times Business, Random House, 1991); S. E. Weiss, "Negotiating with the Romans, Part I," *Sloan Management Review* 35, no. 2 (Winter 1994): 51–61; idem, "Negotiating with the Romans, Part II," *Sloan Management Review* 35, no. 3 (Winter 1994): 85–99; and Jeanne Brett, *Negotiating Globally* (San Francisco: Jossey-Bass, 2001).

14. The example in this paragraph is taken from D. Rousseau, *Psychological Contracts in Organizations* (Thousand Oaks, CA: Sage, 1995), 12.

15. These insights parallel Rousseau's observations of how employees view breaches of psychological contracts with their employers (*Psychological Contracts in Organizations,* 112–127).

16. This example is taken from A. Nanda and G. Levenson, "Komatsu and Dresser: Putting Two Plus Two Together," Case no. 9-898-269 (Boston: Harvard Business School, 1998).

17. R. Dow, L. Napolitano, and M. Pusateri, "The Trust Imperative: The Competitive Advantage of Trust-based Business Relationship," (Chicago: National Account Management Association, 1998), 96–113.

18. D. C. Mowery, J. E. Oxley, and B. S. Silverman, "Strategic Alliances and Interfirm Knowledge Transfer," *Strategic Management Journal* 17 (1996): 77–91.

19. J. H. Dyer, "How Chrysler Created an American Keiretsu," *Harvard Business Review*, July–August 1996, 42–56.

20. An elaboration of the view that "relational" contracts should be thought of as complements rather than substitutes for legal contracts can be found in L. Poppo and T. Zenger, "Substitutes or Complements: Exploring the Relationship Between Formal Contracts and Relational Governance" (unpublished manuscript, Virginia Tech and Washington University, 2001).

Chapter 12

1. In fact, this analysis is a little simplistic. Since you don't yet have any other buyers, valuing your best no-deal option involves assessing the value the sale price you could get from other potential buyers. You are convinced that the unit would sell quickly for $750,000, and you are pretty confident that it would sell for $775,000 with some wait and perhaps some incremental cost. There is a reasonable chance that another buyer would pay up to $800,000, and a small chance a buyer would pay $850,000. Somewhat sophisticated techniques exist to evaluate best no-deal options (also known as BATNAs), including decision analysis; see H. Raiffa, *Decision Analysis: Introductory Lectures on Choices under Uncertainty* (Reading, MA: Addison-Wesley, 1968). For more specific analysis of searching among possible buyers, see D. Lax, "Optimal Search in Negotiation Analysis," *Journal of Conflict Resolution* 29 (March 1985): 456–472.

2. See L. Hindery Jr. and L. Cauley, *The Biggest Game of All: The Inside Strategies, Tactics, and Temperaments That Make Great Dealmakers Great* (New York: Free Press, 2003), 57.

3. See A. D. Galinksy et al., "Regulatory Focus at the Bargaining Table: Promoting Distributive and Integrative Success," *Personality and Social Psychology* 31 (August 2005): 1087–1098.

4. See V. L. Huber and M. A. Neale, "Effects of Experience and Self and Competitor Goals on Negotiator Performance," *Journal of Applied Psychology* 72 (November 1987): 197–203.

5. M. Latz, *Gain the Edge!: Negotiating to Get What You Want* (New York: St. Martin's Press, 2004), 155, based on a story from Donald Gifford's "Legal Negotiation."

6. M. A. Neale and G. B. Northcraft, "Experts, Amateurs, and Refrigerators: A Comparison of Expert and Amateur Negotiators in a Novel Task," *Organizational Behavior and Human Decision Processes* 38(1986): 305–317.

7. G. Ku, A. D. Galinsky, and J. K. Murnighan, "Starting High But Ending Low," *Journal of Personality and Social Psychology* (in press).

8. See A. D. Galinsky, "Should You Make the First Offer?" *Negotiation* 7 (2004): 1–4.

9. See H. A. Kissinger, *The Necessity of Choice* (New York, Harper and Row, 1961): 205.

10. Galinsky, "Should You Make the First Offer?"

11. Ibid.

12. See E. J. Langer, "Minding Matters," in *Advances in Experimental Social Psychology*, vol. 22, ed. L. Berkowitz (New York: Academic Press, 1989), 137–173.

13. J. T. Tedeschi, R. B. Schlenker, and T. V. Bonoma, *Conflict, Power, and Games: The Experimental Study of Interpersonal Relation* (Chicago: Aldine, 1973).

14. For an excellent discussion of reciprocity, see R. Cialdini, *Influence: The Psychology of Persuasion* (New York: William Morrow, 1984), 17–36.

15. See, for example, T. Burnham and J. Phelan, *Mean Genes* (Cambridge, MA: Perseus Publishing, 2000).

16. See Cialdini, *Influence*, 38.

17. Ibid., 11–16.

18. See S. B. Bacharach and E. J. Lawler, *Bargaining: Power, Tactics and Outcomes* (San Francisco: Jossey-Bass, 1981).

Chapter 13

1. Books that have important contributions: R. Fisher, W. Ury, and B. Patton, *Getting to Yes: Negotiating Agreement Without Giving In* (New York: Penguin, 1991); W. L. Ury, *Getting Past No* (New York: Bantam, 1991); D. Kolb and J. Williams, *Everyday Negotiation: Navigating the Hidden Agendas in Bargaining* (San Francisco: Jossey-Bass, 2003); R. Cialdini, *Influence: The Psychology of Persuasion* (New York: William Morrow, 1984); J. Conger, *Winning 'em Over: A New Model for Management in the Age of Persuasion* (New York: Simon & Schuster, 1998); R. H. Mnookin, S. Peppet, and A. Tulumello, *Beyond Winning: Negotiating to Create Value in Deals and Disputes* (Cambridge, MA: Harvard University Press, 2000); D. Stone, B. Patton, and S. Heen, *Difficult Conversations: How to Discuss What Matters Most,* (New York: Penguin Books, 1999); and R. Levine, *The Power of Persuasion: How We're Bought and Sold* (Hoboken, NJ: Wiley, 2003).

2. See Cialdini, *Influence*, 17–56.

3. This section summarizes a much more extensive discussion in D. A. Lax and J. K. Sebenius, *The Manager as Negotiator* (New York: Free Press, 1986), 158–166; and draws heavily on R. Axelrod, *The Evolution of Cooperation* (New York: Basic Books, 1984).

4. Negotiators have been using this tactic for many years. We proposed its use in *The Manager as Negotiator*, and it was previously suggested in H. Raiffa, *The Art and Science of Negotiation* (Cambridge, MA: Harvard University Press, 1982); see also V. Medvec and A. D. Galinsky, "Putting More on the Table: How Making Multiple Offers Can Increase the Final Value of the Deal," *Negotiation* (2005): 1–4; and V. Medvec et al., *Navigating Competition and Cooperation: Multiple Equivalent Offers in Deal-Making* (Toronto: University of Toronto, Rotman School of Management, 2005).

5. J. Carter, *Keeping Faith: Memoirs of a President* (New York: Bantam, 1982), 397.

6. Ury, *Getting Past No*. Some of Ury's advice derives from Fisher, Ury, and Patton, *Getting to Yes*.

7. Argyris and Schön focused on the implications of problems that arose by focusing on high-level assertions. See C. Argyris and D. Schön, *Theory in Practice* (San Francisco: Jossey-Bass, 1974). Roger Fisher has championed this wise point in R. Fisher, "Negotiating Power: Getting and Using Influence," in *Negotiation Theory and Practice*, ed. J. W. Breslin and J. Z Rubin (Cambridge, MA: The Program on Negotiation at Harvard Law School, 1991).

8. J. Conger, *Winning 'em Over,* 79.

9. See R. H. Mnookin, S. Peppet, and A. Tulumello, "The Tension Between Empathy and Assertiveness," *Negotiation Journal* 217 (1996): 217–230.

10. Ibid.

11. C. Bruck, "The Big Hitter," *The New Yorker*, December 8, 1997, 86–93.

12. From Red Sox press releases, May 8, 2003; June 9, 2003; August 8, 2003; and September 20, 2004; available on http://boston.redsox.mlb.com/NASApp/mlb/news/search_archive.jsp? c_id=bos&category=pr.

13. See G. A. Hauser, *Introduction to Rhetorical Theory* (New York: Harper and Row, 1986), 73–75.

14. See D. J. O'Keefe, *Persuasion: Theory and Research* (Thousand Oaks, CA: Sage Publications, 2002), 221.

15. Ibid.

16. Ibid.

17. Conger, *Winning 'em Over*, highlights these two key dimensions of credibility.

18. See Stone, Patton, and Heen, *Difficult Conversations*.

19. Ibid., 7

20. For a lovely example of the effectiveness of blustering back in dealing with the bullying personality of Robert Moses. See R. A. Caro, *The Power Broker: Robert Moses and the Fall of New York* (New York: Vintage Books, 1975), 474–475.

21. See Stone, Patton, and Heen, *Difficult Conversations*, 44–57.

22. This section draws heavily on J. K. Sebenius, "The Hidden Challenge of Cross-Border Negotiations," *Harvard Business Review,* March 2002, 76–85.

23. T. Morrison, W. A. Conaway, and G. A. Borden, PhD, *Kiss, Bow, or Shake Hands: How to Do Business in Sixty Countries* (Holbrook, MA: Adams Media Corporation, 1994).

24. A number of good sources are profiled in Sebenius, "The Hidden Challenge of Cross-Border Negotiations."

Chapter 14

1. We learned this phrase from Mark Moore of Harvard's Kennedy School. Its deep analytic roots derive from the theory of dynamic programming; see R. Bellman, *Dynamic Programming* (Princeton, NJ: Princeton University Press, 1957); and S. E. Dreyfus, *Dynamic Programming and the Calculus of Variations* (New York: Academic Press, 1965).

2. This is an embellished version of an example from our book, *The Manager as Negotiator: Bargaining for Cooperation and Competitive Gain* (New York: Free Press, 1986), 117–118, which we originally based on the account in L. Bacow and M. Wheeler, *Environmental Dispute Resolution* (New York: Plenum Press, 1984), 73–74. In the interest of a memorable, educational anecdote, we have manufactured details, though we've sought to stay faithful to the spirit of the original negotiation.

3. W. Ury, *Getting Past No* (New York: Bantam, 1991).

4. Cited in I. W. Zartman, *The 50% Solution* (New York: Anchorage Doubleday, 1976), 57.

Chapter 15

1. The account of the AOL-Netscape-Microsoft negotiations that follows is adapted from a much fuller analysis in J. K. Sebenius, "Negotiating Lessons from the Browser Wars," *Sloan Management Review* 43, no. 4 (Summer 2002): 43–50.

2. K. Swisher, *AOL.com: How Steve Case Beat Bill Gates, Nailed the Netheads, and Made Millions in the War for the Web* (New York: Times Business, 1998), 114.

3. Ibid., 135.

4. See David Colburn's deposition in "United States of America v. Microsoft Corporation" (1998), http://www.usdoj.gov/atr/cases/ms_index.htm.

5. Swisher, *AOL.com*, 136.

6. These quotes are taken from M. Cusumano and D. Yoffie, *Competing on Internet Time: Lessons from Netscape and Its Battle with Microsoft* (New York: Free Press, 1998), 116–118.

7. See S. Pawlett, "Report on the Chilean Copper Industry," http://archives.econ.utah.edu/archives/pen-1/1999m09.c/msg00068.htm.

8. Statistics from Allan Taylor's account of a tour of El Teniente, www.bootsnall.com/travel/stories/sa/dec02elten.shtml.

9. Names and locations are disguised in this otherwise accurate case.

Authors' Note

1. R. Fisher, W. Ury, and B. Patton, *Getting to Yes: Negotiating Agreement Without Giving In* (New York: Penguin, 1991).

2. 3-D Negotiation™ is a registered trademark of Lax Sebenius LLC.

3. A. M. Brandenburger and B. J. Nalebuff, *Co-opetition* (New York: Currency Doubleday, 1996).

Authors' Note

W E SEE *3-D NEGOTIATION* as a milestone on a professional journey that has spanned more than twenty-five years. In the early 1980s, we cofounded Harvard's Negotiation Roundtable where, along with colleagues from many disciplines, we probed hundreds of deals and disputes for their most important lessons. At that early stage in our careers, we tried to advance much of the scholarly and practical work on negotiation in two main directions. First, we argued that the battle then raging between the (good, new) "win-win" and the (bad, old) "win-lose" approaches to negotiation was simply off the mark. In reality, all negotiations involve joint, cooperative moves to "create" value that are entwined with individual, competitive moves to "claim" value. We showed how value-claiming moves often drive out value-creating ones, resulting in poor deals, deadlocks, and conflict. Rather than endlessly debating whether "win-win" was better than "win-lose," or vice versa, we developed a concept, the Negotiator's Dilemma, which led us to many practical strategies and tactics for productively managing this creating-claiming tension.

If recognizing the Negotiator's Dilemma and working out its implications was our first milestone, the second grew from the Roundtable's focus on negotiations *inside* organizations. Case after case, together with our growing advisory practice, highlighted the substantial time and energy that managers spend wrestling with internal negotiations. As well as exercising authority, they are constantly dealing with others who, as a practical matter, may not want to fully cooperate and often do not have to do so. Not only do managers informally negotiate with peers and those outside the chain of command, but also with subordinates and even superiors to elicit productive cooperation.

As a consequence, we came to argue that negotiation—both internal and external, formal and informal—should be honed as a core skill for virtually all managers, not just those in deal-intensive functions such as labor relations, business development, large sales, or procurement. Partly building on this work, the faculty of the Harvard Business School voted in the mid-1990s to become the first major business school to require a full negotiation course in its core MBA curriculum, along with traditional subjects like finance and marketing.

Twenty years have passed since we published *The Manager as Negotiator*, a book that helped lay the groundwork for those two early milestones. In the intervening time, we both left academia, Jim for several years and David permanently. In our nonacademic careers, both before and after leaving Harvard, we played various roles in investment banking, private equity, hedge fund management, public policy, and diplomacy, where we applied and tested our knowledge, advised on deals, and negotiated them directly. In the process, we had the opportunity to work with and observe many great (and not-so-great!) negotiators. Among the very best from whom we learned a great deal early in our careers—and to whom we owe much—are Tommy Koh of Singapore, the late Elliot Richardson, Pete Peterson and Steve Schwarzman at the Blackstone Group, and Robi Blumenstein.

We have spent much of the last fifteen years as negotiation advisers to companies and governments on mergers, acquisitions, divestitures, joint ventures, startups, private equity investments, commercial contracts, distribution contracts, value chain restructuring, large sales and purchasing transactions, intellectual property and class action lawsuits, oil and mineral agreements, pipeline and power plant projects, and internal organizational change initiatives, as well as the content and application of regulation and regulators' rulings.

As advisers, we've tried to work with diverse clients in very challenging circumstances to develop and implement the most promising approaches. As students of negotiation, we have drawn on this rich vein of direct experience. And as faculty teaching negotiation to some of the world's most able MBA students and experienced executives, we enjoy a constant back-and-forth interplay around our evolving prescriptive views.

As authors of a continuing stream of case studies and articles on negotiations large and small, with a variety of protagonists, in diverse settings, and facing a daunting range of barriers to agreement, we are constantly able to test our approach and refine our thinking. In particular, Jim has taken the lead role in the annual Great Negotiator Award series, sponsored by an interuniversity consortium of Harvard, MIT, and Tufts through the Program on Negotiation at Harvard Law School. Honorees have included such figures as George Mitchell, Charlene Barshefsky, Richard Holbrooke, Lakdhar Brahimi, Stuart

Eizenstadt, and Sadako Ogata. We've written detailed cases on the most challenging negotiations faced by these remarkable men and women—whether ending the war in Bosnia, creating an interim government in Afghanistan, or crafting a U.S.-Chinese trade deal over intellectual property, or getting Protestants and Catholics in Northern Ireland to come to terms. By spending intensive time with these Great Negotiators and relentlessly probing their thought processes and approaches to some of the world's most difficult negotiations, we are able to add even more valuable source material to our intellectual and practical treasury.

So how does all this relate to *3-D Negotiation*, which we characterized above as the most recent milestone on our negotiation journey? When we read the great bulk of academic writing and how-to guides on negotiation, we see that most treat the parties and subjects of negotiation as fixed. As social scientists, most academics carefully analyze how people actually do or should behave in well-specified situations. Apart from good advice to get other offers or develop what the authors of *Getting to Yes* call your "Best Alternative to Negotiated Agreement," the practical guides mainly tell you how to be effective once you're *at the table*.[1]

Interpersonal and tactical skill at the table is certainly vital. But remarkably often, the great negotiators whom we've worked with and studied *do not take the negotiation as fixed*; they do much more than cleverly play their cards at the table in well-specified situations. Looking back at really effective negotiators, both inside and among organizations, we see a powerful pattern in how they create and claim value for the long term. Time and again, we've seen them size up a potential negotiation. If it does not seem like fertile ground for the kind of agreement they seek, they relentlessly act *away from the table* to set up the situation most advantageously or reset it more favorably. They attain superior results by scanning widely and imaginatively, working on which parties will be involved, and in what sequence, taking coalition-building or -breaking initiatives, influencing the agenda and what interests will be engaged at what stages of the process, setting expectations, and orchestrating the away-from-the-table consequences for the parties if there is no agreement. Then they go to work at the table.

Yet this intensive work away from the table to set up and often reset the table to advantage is what often gives these negotiators their edge, especially in tough situations. And it turns out that creative moves away from the table can make all the difference in routine business (and even personal) negotiations as well as in higher-profile deal-making challenges. Increasing recognition of this often hidden, away-from-the table dimension, ultimately prompted us to write this book. Crystallizing and developing this insight in tandem with the more familiar dimensions of negotiation formed the basis for our 3-D Negotiation method.[2]

You might find it almost startling that what sets the many effective negotiators apart has not been a central focus of many scholars or those writing how-to books. Of course, many people have noted important away-from-the-table aspects of the process and there are a few explicit precursors to the present work, including a chapter that we wrote twenty years ago in *The Manager as Negotiator*. In related fields, like corporate strategy, authors such as Adam Brandenburger and Barry Nalebuff have developed analogous ideas.[3] Yet, in over two decades of deal-making experience and study, we've been struck at how often skillful negotiators change the game they're playing to their advantage—while less skillful players suffer for failing to do so. We've also been struck at how little attention has been paid to such moves. Systematically combining these observations with important scholarly findings from many sources has led us to craft *3-D Negotiation*. We believe that this method—time-tested and yet almost brand-new in its focus—offers you a powerful, practical method to prepare for and carry out your negotiations. We have every hope that it will change the way you think about negotiation, change the way you negotiate, and help guide you to better results in your most important negotiations. If these hopes pan out, *3-D Negotiation* will in fact constitute a milestone.

Acknowldegments

We were fortunate to begin our work on negotiation in the late 1970s when an academic field that had been fairly dormant for at least a decade awoke with a vengeance. The Program on Negotiation (PON) based at Harvard Law School was created at that time, spurred in part by the passion and intellectual focus of Howard Raiffa, Roger Fisher, Tom Schelling, Larry Susskind, Frank Sander, the late Jeff Rubin, and soon thereafter, Robert Mnookin. We are grateful to this generation of PON founders and leaders for their simultaneous pursuit of analytical depth and practical power as well as for their encouragement and support.

We owe much to this group as a whole and as individuals. In particular, Howard Raiffa has been a mentor to us both, always probing for the "analytical essence" of complex problems and setting a sterling example as a human being. Over his long and creative career tackling some of world's hardest problems, Roger Fisher has shown an almost uncanny ability to zero in on critical elements of negotiation and to find remarkably clear and compelling ways to communicate his insights to those on the front lines. Tom Schelling's extraordinary depth, clarity, and expression have always served as an unattainable aspiration. In writing *3-D Negotiation,* we hope to have found a fitting way to honor this very special threesome.

It is our further pleasure to acknowledge some distinctive debts. Bill Ury has been a friend to us and to our work from the beginning; his own focus on the truly important, his genuine originality, his intellectual and personal courage, and his gifts as a communicator are an inspiration. Mike Wheeler has been an innovative analyst and an incisive critic, as well as a great colleague and friend. We have especially drawn on the work and insights of Graham Allison and the late Richard Neustadt, both of whom have unfailingly supported our enterprise in many ways for which we are deeply appreciative. In chapter 11, "Negotiate the Spirit of the Deal," we've drawn heavily on an article that we wrote with Ron Fortgang, whom we thank for his contributions there and in many other facets of our work.

Beyond these exemplars and supporters, we're the fortunate beneficiaries of many scholars, colleagues, and friends. For vital insights, comments on drafts, ongoing encouragement, and other contributions we variously thank Hannah Riley Bowles, Terry Burnham, Ben Esty, Susan Hackley, Myra Hart, Phil Heymann, Rosabeth Kanter, Paul Levy, Brian Mandell, Jan Martinez, Ken Mildwaters, Mike Moldoveanu, Mark Moore, Ashish Nanda, Phebe Farrow Port, Mal Salter, Ben Shapiro, Howard Stevenson, Guhan Subramanian, Lauren Walters, Michael Watkins, Andy Wasynczuk, and Lou Wells.

On the writing and production front, our editor, Jeff Kehoe, together with his Harvard Business School Press colleagues, offered good judgment and enthusiastic faith in the 3-D enterprise down what has proved a very long road to publication. An anonymous reviewer of our first manuscript gently remarked that, despite our earnest efforts at an informal style, we had produced a book that needed to be "studied, not read." Ouch. We are, therefore, particularly indebted to Jeff Kehoe for introducing us to Jeff Cruikshank, whose fine editorial hand helped us simplify our message, strike a clearer tone, and jettison many cherished but nonessential examples and distinctions. Nancy Buck provided Jim with a discerning sounding board, reacting to numerous flawed drafts with suggestions that greatly improved the final version. Ilana Manolson offered continuing guidance to David on how the writing style, graphics, and title could best connect with our target audience. John Hammond has been a constructive presence throughout our writing careers, always prodding us to think hard about our readers' real needs and to pinpoint exactly what we want "to be ringing in their ears"; it is to John that readers owe the end-of-chapter boxed summaries. Pragati Thakkar worked many late nights helping us with cases, notes, sources, and more. Rich Swartz was a wizard with graphics. Susan Gorr helped make sure that the various other business aspects of life were organized enough to provide us time to write. We are grateful to the Division of Research at the Harvard Business School for its generous support of this and other projects over the years.

Of course, given busy personal and professional lives, much of the time to think and write comes out of hours that would otherwise be spent with family. We offer our greatest thanks to our wives, Ilana Manolson and Nancy Buck, and to our children, Eric and Lena Lax and Zander, Alyza, and Isaac Sebenius, for their love and understanding during the interminable stretches while we wrote (or stayed home) during vacations, and otherwise slaved over hot computers. Without their support and consistent efforts to help us create and protect writing time where none reasonably existed, this book would still be an aspiration.

So it is to those associated with the real milestones in our lives, our families—Ilana Manolson, Eric and Lena Lax; Nancy Buck, Zander, Alyza, and Isaac Sebenius—that we dedicate this book with unbounded love and highest hopes.

David Lax and Jim Sebenius
May 2006

Index

About the Authors

DAVID A. LAX and JAMES K. SEBENIUS have spent decades as advisers and direct participants in high-level corporate, financial, public sector, and diplomatic negotiations. Informed by this experience, their writing has had a major impact on negotiation theory and practice. Early in their careers, they cofounded the Harvard Negotiation Roundtable, an ongoing research group that examined hundreds of deals and disputes in order to extract the most important lessons. This led them to coauthor *The Manager as Negotiator*, a foundational negotiation text used by many leading graduate and professional schools. They have written many articles in academic journals as well as business publications such as the *Financial Times*, the *Wall Street Journal*, and the *Harvard Business Review*. They developed Harvard Business School's flagship negotiation program for top executives, "Strategic Negotiation: Dealmaking for the Long Term." Lax Sebenius LLC, the negotiation strategy firm they founded, now advises dozens of the world's leading companies and several national governments on a wide range of their most challenging negotiations. The firm also helps organizations develop their capacity to negotiate more effectively. Information about Lax Sebenius LLC can be found at www.negotiate.com.

JAMES K. SEBENIUS holds the first Gordon Donaldson Professorship at Harvard Business School, serves as Vice Chair of the Program on Negotiation at Harvard Law School, and was formerly on the faculty of Harvard's John F. Kennedy School of Government. He played the lead role in Harvard Business School's decision, unique among major business schools, to require a full negotiation course in its core MBA program. Sebenius left Harvard in the mid-1980s to work full-time for investment banker Peter G. Peterson, co-founder with Stephen Schwarzman of the New York–based Blackstone Group, now one of the world's leading merchant banking and private equity firms. For several years following Blackstone's launch, Sebenius worked closely with Peterson and Schwarzman, initially as vice president and later as special adviser to the firm after returning to Harvard. Early in his career, he was an assistant to U.S. Secretary of Commerce Elliot Richardson, served on the U.S. State Department Delegation to the Law of the Sea negotiations, and was elected a term member of the Council on Foreign Relations. Educated at Vanderbilt, Stanford, and Harvard, Sebenius holds a doctorate from Harvard in business economics. He wrote *Negotiating the Law of the Sea*, coedited *Wise Decisions*, and has authored numerous classic case studies on negotiation, as well as papers in academic journals and mainstream publications. He can be reached at jsebenius@hbs.edu.

DAVID A. LAX is Managing Principal of Lax Sebenius LLC. *Forbes* described him as a "new negotiation theorist" on the cutting edge of his field. He served for several years on the Harvard Business School faculty. He later was an investment banker representing labor unions and a merchant banker at First City Capital Corporation, where he was involved in transactions such as venture capital, acquisitions, leveraged buyouts, joint ventures, privatizations, and financings. He also served as vice president of ICF Kaiser Engineers in its American Venture Investments subsidiary. Lax has started two investment management companies, sits on the board of a privately held health care company, and is chairman of the board of a privately held oil and gas company. Educated at Princeton, Stanford, and Harvard, Lax holds a doctorate from Harvard in statistics and has written many articles on negotiation. He can be reached at lax@negotiate.com.